The Voice
of a People

The Voice
of a People

Speeches from Black America

MINT EDITIONS

The Voice of a People: Speeches from Black America contains speeches first given between 1787 and 1923.

This edition published by Mint Editions 2021.

ISBN 9781513297033 | E-ISBN 9781513298535

Published by Mint Editions®

MINT
EDITIONS

minteditionbooks.com

Publishing Director: Jennifer Newens
Design & Production: Rachel Lopez Metzger
Project Manager: Micaela Clark
Typesetting: Westchester Publishing Services

Note from the Publisher

The idea for this book was conceived at a particularly difficult time in our country's history. Wherein accountability does not always feel like justice and a system continues to show the ugliness of its prejudice—unhidden and unashamed—to the rest of the world.

The speeches contained in this collection speak to the voice of a people who built a nation—their struggles and adversities, but also their hopes for a better future, generations down the line.

M. Clark
Mint Editions
Berkeley, CA

Lift every voice and sing
Till earth and heaven ring
Ring with the harmonies of Liberty
Let our rejoicing rise
High as the listening skies
Let it resound loud as the rolling sea

Sing a song full of the faith that the dark past has taught us
Sing a song full of the hope that the present has brought us
Facing the rising sun of our new day begun
Let us march on till victory is won

Stony the road we trod
Bitter the chastening rod
Felt in the days when hope unborn had died
Yet with a steady beat
Have not our weary feet
Come to the place for which our fathers sighed?

We have come over a way that with tears has been watered
We have come, treading our path through the blood of the slaughtered
Out from the gloomy past
Till now we stand at last
Where the white gleam of our bright star is cast

God of our weary years
God of our silent tears
Thou who has brought us thus far on the way
Thou who has by Thy might Led us into the light
Keep us forever in the path, we pray
Lest our feet stray from the places, our God, where we met Thee

Lest, our hearts drunk with the wine of the world, we forget Thee
Shadowed beneath Thy hand
May we forever stand
True to our God
True to our native land
Our native land

Contents

An Address to the Negroes
in the State of New York

To the Members of the African Society in the city of New York

Gentlemen

I take the liberty to dedicate an address to my poor brethren to you. If you think it is likely to do good among them, I do not doubt but you will take it under your care. You have discovered so much kindness and good will to those you thought were oppressed, and had no helper, that I am sure you will not despise what I have wrote, if you judge it will be of any service to them. I have nothing to add, but only to wish that "the blessing of many ready to perish, may come upon you."

I am Gentlemen, Your Servant,

Jupiter Hammon

To the Public

When I am writing to you with a design to say something to you for your good, and with a view to promote your happiness, I can with truth and sincerity join with the apostle Paul, when speaking of his own nation the Jews, and say, "That I have great heaviness and continual sorrow in my heart for my brethren, my kinsmen according to the flesh." Yes my dear brethren, when I think of you, which is very often, and of the poor, despised and miserable state you are in, as to the things of this world, and when I think of your ignorance and stupidity, and the great wickedness of the most of you, I am pained to the heart. It is at times, almost too much for human nature to bear, and I am obliged to turn my thoughts from the subject or endeavour to still my mind, by considering that it is permitted thus to be, by that God who governs all things, who seteth up one and pulleth down another. While I have been thinking on this subject, I have frequently had great struggles in my own mind, and have been at a loss to know what to do. I have wanted exceedingly to say something to you, to call upon you with the tenderness of a father and friend, and to give you the last, and I may say, dying advice, of an old man, who wishes our best good in this world, and in the world to come. But while I have had such desires, a sense of my own ignorance, and unfitness to teach others, has frequently discouraged me from attempting to say anything to you; yet when I thought of your situation, I could not rest easy. When I was at Hartford in Connecticut, where I lived during the war, I published several pieces which were well received, not only by those of my own colour, but by a number of the white people, who thought they might do good among their servants. This is one consideration, among others, that emboldens me now to publish what I have written to you. Another is, I think you will be more likely to listen to what is said, when you know it comes from a negro, one your own nation and colour, and therefore can have no interest in deceiving you, or in saying anything to you, but what he really thinks is your interest and duty to comply with. My age, I think, gives me some right to speak to you, and reason to expect you will hearken to my advice. I am now upwards of seventy years old, and cannot expect, though I am well, and able to do almost any kind of business, to live much longer. I have passed the common bounds set for man, and must soon go the way of all the earth. I have had more experience in the world than the most of you, and I have seen a great deal of the vanity, and wickedness of it. I have great reason to be thankful that my lot has been so much better than most slaves have had. I suppose I have had more advantages and privileges than most of you, who are slaves have ever known, and I believe more than many white people have enjoyed, for which I desire to bless God, and pray that he may bless those who have given them to me. I do not, my dear friends, say these things about myself to make you think that I am wiser or better than others; but that you might hearken, without prejudice, to what I have to say to you on the following particulars.

1st. Respecting obedience to masters. Now whether it is right, and lawful, in the Sight of God, for them to make slaves of us or not, I am certain that while we are slaves, it is our duty to obey our masters, in all their lawful commands, and mind them unless we are bid to do that which we know to be sin, or forbidden in God's word. The apostle Paul says, "Servants be obedient to them that are your masters according to the flesh, with fear and trembling in singleness in your heart as unto Christ: Not with eye service, as men pleasers, but as the servants of Christ doing the will of God from the heart: With good will doing service to the Lord, and not to men: Knowing that whatever thing a man doeth the same shall he receive of the Lord, whether he be bond or free."—Here is a plain command of God for us to obey our masters. It may seem hard for us, if we think our masters wrong in holding us slaves, to obey in all things, but who of us dare dispute with

God! He has commanded us to obey, and we ought to do it cheerfully, and freely. This should be done by us, not only because God commands, but because our own peace and comfort depend upon it. As we depend upon our masters, for what we eat and drink and wear, and for all our comfortable things in this world, we cannot be happy, unless we please them. This we cannot do without obeying tem freely, without muttering or finding fault. If a servant strives to please his master and studies and takes pains to do it, I believe there are but few masters who would use such a servant cruelly. Good servants frequently make good masters. If your master is really hard, unreasonable and cruel, there is no way so likely for you to convince him of it, as always to obey his commands, and try to serve him, and take care of his interest, and try to promote it all in your power. If you are proud and stubborn and always finding fault, your master will think the fault lies wholly on your side, but if you are humble, and meek, and bear all things patiently, your master may think he is wrong, if he does not, his neighbors will be apt to see it, and will befriend you, and try to alter his conduct. If this does not do, you must cry to him, who has the hearts of all men in his hands, and turneth them as the rivers of waters are turned.

2d: The particular I would mention is honesty and faithfulness, You must suffer me now to deal plainly with you, my dear brethren, for I do not mean to flatter, or omit speaking the truth, whether it is for you or against you. How many of you are there who allow yourselves in stealing from your masters. It is very wicked for you not to take care of your masters goods, but how much worse is it to pilfer and steal from them, whenever you think you shall not be found out. This you must know is very wicked and provoking to God. There are none of you so ignorant, but that you must know that this is wrong. Though you may try to excuse yourselves, by saying that your masters are unjust to you, and though you may try to quiet your consciences in this way, yet if you are honest in owning the truth you must think it is as wicked, and on some accounts more wicked to steal from your masters, than from others.

We cannot certainly, have any excuse either for taking anything that belongs to our masters without their leave, or for being unfaithful in their business. It is our duty to be faithful, not with eye service as men please. We have no right to stay when we are sent on errands, any longer than to do the business we were sent upon. All the time spent idly, is spent wickedly, and is unfaithfulness to our masters. In these things I must say, that I think many of you are guilty. I know that many of you endeavor to excuse yourselves, and say that you have nothing that you can call your own, and that you are under great temptations to be unfaithful and take from your masters. But this will not do, God will certainly punish you for stealing and for being unfaithful. All that we have to mind is our own duty. If God has put us in bad circumstances that is not our fault and he will not punish us for it. If any are wicked in keeping us so, we cannot help it, they must answer to God for it. Nothing will serve as an excuse to us for not doing our duty. The same God will judge both them and us. Pray then my dear friends, fear to offend in this way, but be faithful to God, to your masters, and to your own souls.

The next thing I would mention, and warn you against, is profaneness. This you know is forbidden by God. Christ tells us, "swear not at all," and again it is said "thou shalt not take the name of the Lord thy God in vain, for the Lord will not hold him guiltless, that taketh his name in vain." Now though the great God has forbidden it, yet how dreadfully profane are many, and I don't know but I may say the most of you? How common is it to hear you take the terrible and awful name of the great God in vain?—To swear by it, and by Jesus Christ, his Son—How common is it to hear yon wish damnation to your companions, and to your own souls and to sport with in the name of Heaven and Hell, as if there were no such places for you to hope for, or to fear, Oh my friends, be warned to forsake this dreadful sin of profaneness. Pray my dear friends, believe and realize, that there is a God—that he is great and terrible beyond what you can think—that he keeps you in life every moment—and that he can send you to that awful Hell, that you laugh at, in an instant, and confine you there for ever, and that he will certainly do it, if you do not repent. You certainly do not believe, that there is a God, or that there is a Heaven or Hell, or you would never trifle with them. It would make you shudder, if you heard others do it, if you believe them as much, as you believe anything you see with your bodily eyes.

I have heard some learned and good men say, that the heathen, and all that worshiped false Gods, never spoke lightly or irreverently of their Gods, they never took their names in vain, or jested with those things which they held sacred. Now why should the true God, who made all things, be treated worse in this respect, than those false Gods, that were made of wood and stone, I believe it is because Satan tempts men to do it, He tried to make them love their false Gods, and to speak well of them, but he wishes to have men think lightly of the true God, to take his holy name in vain, and to scoff at, and make a jest of all things that are really good. You may think that Satan has not power to do so much, and have so great influence on the minds of men: But the scripture says, "he goeth about like a roaring Lion, seeking whom he may devour— That he is the prince of the power of the air—and that he rules in the hearts of the children of disobedience,—and that wicked men are led captive by him, to do his will." All those of you who are profane, are serving the Devil. You are doing what he tempts and desires you to do. If you could see him with your bodily eyes, would you like to make an agreement with him, to serve him, and do as he bid you. I believe most of you would be shocked at this, but you may be certain that all of you who allow yourselves in this sin, are as really serving him, and to just as good purpose, as if you met him, and promised to dishonor God, and serve him with all your might. Do you believe this? It is true whether you believe it or not, Some of you to excuse yourselves, may plead the example of others, and say that you hear a great many white-people, who know more, than such poor ignorant negroes, as you are, and some who are rich and great gentlemen, swear, and talk profanely; and some of you may say this of your masters, and say no more than is true, But all this is not a sufficient excuse for you. You know that murder is wicked. If you saw your master kill a man, do you suppose this would be any excuse for you, if you should commit the same crime? You must know it would not; nor will your hearing him curse and swear, and take the name of God in vain, or any other man, be he ever so great or rich, excuse you. God is greater than all other beings, and him we are bound to obey. To him we must give an account for every idle word that we speak. He will bring us all, rich and poor, white and black, to his judgment seat. If we are found among those who feared his name, and trembled at his word, we shall be called good and faithful servants. Our slavery will be at an end, and though ever so mean, low, and despited in this world, we shall sit with God in his kingdom as Kings and Priests, and rejoice forever, and ever. Do not then, my dear friends, take God's holy name in vain, or speak profanely in any way. Let not the example of others lead you into the sin, but reverence and fear that great and fearful name, the Lord our God. I might now caution you against other sins to which you are exposed; but as I meant only to mention those you were exposed to, more than others, by your being slaves, I will conclude what I have to say to you, by advising you to become religious, and to make religion the great business of your lives.

Now I acknowledge that liberty is a great thing, and worth seeking for, if we can get it honestly, and by our good conduct, prevail on our masters to set us free: Though for my own part I do not wish to be free, yet I should be glad, if others, especially the young negroes were to be free, for many of us, who are grown up slaves, and have always had masters to take care of us, should hardly know how to take care of ourselves; and it may be more for our own comfort to remain as we are. That liberty is a great thing we may know from our own feelings, and we may likewise Judge so from the conduct of the white-people, in the late war. How much money has been spent, and how many lives has been lost, to defend their liberty. I must say that I have hoped that God would open their eyes, when they were so much engaged for liberty, to think of the state of the poor blacks, and to pity us. He has done it in some measure, and has raised us up many friends, for which we have reason to be thankful, and to hope in his mercy. What may be done further, he only knows, for known unto God are all his ways from the beginning. But this my dear brethren Is by no means, the greatest thing we have to be concerned about. Getting our liberty in this world, is nothing to our having the liberty of the children of God. Now the Bible tells us that we are all by nature, sinners, that we are slaves to sin and Satan, and that unless we are converted, or born again, we must be miserable forever. Christ says, except a man be born again, he cannot see the kingdom of God, and all that do not see the kingdom of God, must be in the kingdom of darkness.

There are but two places where all go after death, white and black, rich and poor; those places are Heaven and Hell. Heaven is a place made for those, who are born again, and who love God, and it is a place where they will be happy for ever. Hell is a place made for those who hate God, and are his enemies, and where they will be miserable to all eternity. Now you may think you are not enemies to God, and do not hate him: But if your heart has not been changed, and you have not become true Christians, you certainly are enemies to God, and have been opposed to him ever since you were born. Many of you, I suppose, never think of this, and are almost as ignorant as the beasts that perish. Those of you who can read I must beg you to read the Bible, and whenever you can get time, study the Bible, and if you can get no other time, spare some of your time from sleep, and learn what the mind and will of God is. But what shall I say to them who cannot read. This lay with great weight on my mind, when I thought of writing to my poor brethren, but I hope that those who can read will take pity on them and read what I have to say to them. In hopes of this I will beg of you to spare no pains in trying to learn to read. If you are once engaged you may learn. Let all the time you can get be spent in trying to learn to read. Get those who can read to learn you, but remember, that what you learn for, is to read the Bible. If there was no Bible, it would be no matter whether you could read or not. Reading other books would do you no good. But the Bible is the word of God, and tells you what you must do to please God; it tells you how you may escape misery, and be happy for ever. If you see most people neglect the Bible, and many that can read never look into it, let it not harden you and make you think lightly of it, and that it is a book of no worth. All those who are really good, love the Bible, and meditate on it day and night. In the Bible God has told us every thing it is necessary we should know, in order to be happy here and hereafter. The Bible is a revelation of the mind and will of God to men. Therein we may learn, what God is. That he made all things by the power of his word; and that he made all things for his own glory, and not for our glory. That he is over all, and above all his creatures, and more above them that we can think or conceive—that they can do nothing without him—that he upholds them all, and will over-rule all things for his own glory. In the Bible likewise we are told what man is. That he was at first made holy, in the image of God, that he fell from that state of holiness, and became an enemy to God, and that since the fall, all the imaginations of the thoughts of his heart, are evil and only evil, and that continually. That the carnal mind is not subject to the law of God, neither indeed can be. And that all mankind, were under the wrath, and curse of God, and must have been for ever miserable, if they had been left to suffer what their sins deserved. It tells us that God, to save some of mankind, sent his Son into this world to die, in the room and stead of sinners, and that now God can save from eternal misery, all that believe in his Son, and take him for their saviour, and that all are called upon to repent, and believe in Jesus Christ. It tells us that those who do repent, and believe, and are friends to Christ, shall have many trials and sufferings in this world, but that they shall be happy forever, after death, and reign with Christ to all eternity. The Bible tells us that this world is a place of trial, and that there is no other time or place for us to alter, but in this life. If we are Christians when we die, we shall awake to the resurrection of life; if not, we shall awake to the resurrection of damnation. It tells us, we must all live in Heaven or Hell, be happy or miserable, and that without end. The Bible does not tell us of but two places, for all to go to. There is no place for innocent folks, that are not Christians. There is no place for ignorant folks, that did not know how to be Christians. What I mean is, that there is no place besides Heaven and Hell. These two places, will receive all mankind, for Christ says, there are but two sorts, he that is not with me is against me, and he that gathereth not with me, scattereth abroad.—The Bible likewise tells us that this world, and all things in it shall be burnt up—and that "God has appointed a day in which he will judge the world, and that he will bring every secret thing whether it be good or bad into judgment that which is done in secret shall be declared on the house top." I do not know, nor do I think any can tell, but that the day of judgment may last a thousand years. God could tell the state of all his creatures in a moment, but then every thing that every one has done, through his whole life is to be told, before the whole world of angels, and men. There, Oh how solemn is the thought! You, and I, must stand, and hear every thing we have thought or done, however secret, however wicked and vile, told before all the men and women that ever have been, or ever will be, and before all the angels, good and bad.

Now my dear friends seeing the Bible is the word of God, and every thing in it is true, and it reveals such awful and glorious things, what can be more important than that you should learn to read it; and when you have learned to read, that you should study it day and night. There are some things very encouraging in God's word for such ignorant creatures as we are; for God hath not chosen the rich of this world. Not many rich, not many noble are called, but God hath chosen the weak things of this world, and things which are not, to confound the things that are: And when the great and the rich refused coming to the gospel feast, the servant was told, to go into the highways, and hedges, and compel those poor creatures that he found there to come in. Now my brethren it seems to me, that there are no people that ought to attend to the hope of happiness in another world so much as we do. Most of us are cut off from comfort and happiness here in this world, and can expect nothing from it. Now seeing this is the case, why should we not take care to be happy after death. Why should we spend our whole lives in sinning against God: And be miserable in this world, and in the world to come. If we do thus, we shall certainly be the greatest fools. We shall be slaves here, and slaves forever. We cannot plead so great temptations to neglect religion as others. Riches and honours which drown the greater part of mankind, who have the gospel, in perdition, can be little or no temptations to us.

We live so little time in this world that it is no matter how wretched and miserable we are, if it prepares us for heaven. What is forty, fifty, or sixty years, when compared to eternity. When thousands and millions of years have rolled away, this eternity will be no nigher coming to an end. Oh how glorious is an eternal life of happiness! And how dreadful, an eternity of misery. Those of us who have had religious masters, and have been taught to read the Bible, and have been brought by their example and teaching to a sense of divine things, how happy shall we be to meet them in heaven, where we shall join them in praising God forever. But if any of us have had such masters, and yet have lived and died wicked, how will it add to our misery to think of Our folly. If any of us, who have wicked and profane masters should become religious, how will our estates be changed in another world. Oh my friends, let me entreat of you to think on these things, and to live as if you believed them to be true. If you become Christians you will have reason to bless God forever, that you have been brought into a land where you have heard the gospel, though you have been slaves. If we should ever get to Heaven, we shall find nobody to reproach us for being black, or for being slaves. Let me beg of you my dear African brethren, to think very little of your bondage in this life, for your thinking of it will do you no good. If God designs to set us free, he will do it, in his own time, and way; but think of your bondage to sin and Satan, and do not rest, until you are delivered from it. We cannot be happy if we are ever so free or ever so rich, while we are servants of sin, and slaves to Satan. We must be miserable here, and to all eternity. I will conclude what I have to say with a few words to those negroes who have their liberty. The most of what I have said to those who are slaves may be of use to you, but you have more advantages, on some accounts, if you will improve your freedom, as you may do, than they. You have more time to read God's holy word, and to take care of the salvation of your souls. Let me beg of you to spend your time in this way, or it will be better for you, if you had always been slaves. If you think seriously of the matter, you must conclude, that if you do not use your freedom, to promote the salvation of your souls, it will not be of any lasting good to you. Besides all this, if you are idle, and take to bad courses, you will hurt those of your brethren who are slaves, and do all in your power to prevent their being free. Our great reason that is given by some for not freeing us, I understand is, that we should not know how to take care of ourselves, and should take to bad courses. That we should be lazy and idle, and get drunk and steal. Now all those of you, who follow any bad courses, and who do not take care to get an honest living by your labour and industry, are doing more to prevent our being free, than any body else. Let me beg of you then for the sake of your own good and happiness, in time, and for eternity, and for the sake of your poor brethren, who are still in bondage "to lead quiet and peaceable lives in all Godliness and honesty," and may God bless you, and bring yo to his kingdom, for Christ's sake, Amen.

Why Sit Ye Here and Die

Why sit ye here and die? If we say we will go to a foreign land, the famine and the pestilence are there, and there we shall die. If we sit here, we shall die. Come let us plead our cause before the whites: if they save us alive, we shall live—and if they kill us, we shall but die.

Methinks I heard a spiritual interrogation—"Who shall go forward, and take off the reproach that is cast upon the people of color? Shall it be a woman?" And my heart made this reply—"If it is thy will, be it even so, Lord Jesus!"

I have heard much respecting the horrors of slavery; but may Heaven forbid that the generality of my color throughout these United States should experience any more of its horrors than to be a servant of servants, or hewers of wood and drawers of water! Tell us no more of southern slavery; for with few exceptions, although I may be very erroneous in my opinion, yet I consider our condition but little better than that. Yet, after all, methinks there are no chains so galling as the chains of ignorance—no fetters so binding as those that bind the soul, and exclude it from the vast field of useful and scientific knowledge. O, had I received the advantages of early education, my ideas would, ere now, have expanded far and wide; but, alas! I possess nothing but moral capability—no teachings but the teachings of the Holy spirit.

I have asked several individuals of my sex, who transact business for themselves, if providing our girls were to give them the most satisfactory references, they would not be willing to grant them an equal opportunity with others? Their reply has been—for their own part, they had no objection; but as it was not the custom, were they to take them into their employ, they would be in danger of losing the public patronage.

And such is the powerful force of prejudice. Let our girls possess what amiable qualities of soul they may; let their characters be fair and spotless as innocence itself; let their natural taste and ingenuity be what they may; it is impossible for scarce an individual of them to rise above the condition of servants. Ah! why is this cruel and unfeeling distinction? Is it merely because God has made our complexion to vary? If it be, O, shame to soft, relenting humanity! "Tell it not in Gath! publish it not in the streets of Askelon!" Yet, after all, methinks were the American free people of color to turn their attention more assiduously to moral worth and intellectual improvement, this would be the result: prejudice would gradually diminish, and the whites would be compelled to say, unloose those fetters!

Though black their skins as shades of night, Their hearts are pure, their souls are white.

Few white persons of either sex, who are calculated for anything else, are willing to spend their lives and bury their talents in performing mean, servile labor. And such is the horrible idea that I entertain respecting a life of servitude, that if I conceived of there being no possibility of my rising above the condition of a servant, I would gladly hail death as a welcome messenger. O, horrible idea, indeed! to possess noble souls aspiring after high and honorable acquirements, yet confined by the chains of ignorance and poverty to lives of continual drudgery and toil. Neither do I know of any who have enriched themselves by spending their lives as house-domestics, washing windows, shaking carpets, brushing boots, or tending upon gentlemen's tables. I can but die for expressing my sentiments; and I am as willing to die by the sword as the pestilence; for I and a true born American; your blood flows in my veins, and your spirit fires my breast.

I observed a piece in the Liberator a few months since, stating that the colonizationists had published a work respecting us, asserting that we were lazy and idle. I confute them on that point. Take us generally as a people, we are neither lazy nor idle; and considering how little we have to excite or stimulate us, I am almost astonished that there are so many industrious and ambitious ones to be found; although I acknowledge, with extreme sorrow, that there are some who never were and never will be serviceable to society. And have you not a similar class among yourselves?

Again. It was asserted that we were "a ragged set, crying for liberty." I reply to it, the whites have so long and so loudly proclaimed the theme of equal rights and privileges, that our souls have caught the flame also, ragged as we are. As far as our merit deserves, we feel a common desire to rise above the condition of servants and drudges. I have learnt, by bitter experience, that continual hard labor deadens the energies of the soul, and benumbs the faculties of the mind; the ideas become confined, the mind barren, and, like the scorching sands of Arabia, produces nothing; or, like the uncultivated soil, brings forth thorns and thistles.

Again, continual hard labor irritates our tempers and sours our dispositions; the whole system becomes worn out with toil and failure; nature herself becomes almost exhausted, and we care but little whether we live or die. It is true, that the free people of color throughout these United States are neither bought nor sold, nor under the lash of the cruel driver; many obtain a comfortable support; but few, if any, have an opportunity of becoming rich and independent; and the employments we most pursue are as unprofitable to us as the spider's web or the floating bubbles that vanish into air. As servants, we are respected; but let us presume to aspire any higher, our employer regards us no longer. And where it not that the King eternal has declared that Ethiopia shall stretch forth her hands unto God, I should indeed despair.

I do not consider it derogatory, my friends, for persons to live out to service. There are many whose inclination leads them to aspire no higher; and I would highly commend the performance of almost anything for an honest livelihood; but where constitutional strength is wanting, labor of this kind, in its mildest form, is painful. And doubtless many are the prayers that have ascended to Heaven from Africa's daughters for strength to perform their work. Oh, many are the tears that have been shed for the want of that strength! Most of our color have dragged out a miserable existence of servitude from the cradle to the grave. And what literary acquirements can be made, or useful knowledge derived, from either maps, books or charm, by those who continually drudge from Monday morning until Sunday noon? O, ye fairer sisters, whose hands are never soiled, whose nerves and muscles are never strained, go learn by experience! Had we had the opportunity that you have had, to improve our moral and mental faculties, what would have hindered our intellects from being as bright, and our manners from being as dignified as yours? Had it been our lot to have been nursed in the lap of affluence and ease, and to have basked beneath the smiles and sunshine of fortune, should we not have naturally supposed that we were never made to toil? And why are not our forms as delicate, and our constitutions as slender, as yours? Is not the workmanship as curious and complete? Have pity upon us, have pity upon us, O ye who have hearts to feel for other's woes; for the hand of God has touched us. Owing to the disadvantages under which we labor, there are many flowers among us that are . . . born to bloom unseen, and waste their fragrance on the desert air.

My beloved brethren, as Christ has died in vain for those who will not accept of offered mercy, so will it be vain for the advocates of freedom to spend their breath in our behalf, unless with united hearts and souls you make some mighty efforts to raise your sons, and daughters from the horrible state of servitude and degradation in which they are placed.

It is upon you that woman depends; she can do but little besides using her influence; and it is for her sake and yours that I have come forward and made myself a hissing and a reproach among the people; for I am also one of the wretched and miserable daughters of the descendants of fallen Africa. Do you ask, why are you wretched and miserable? I reply, look at many of the most worthy and interesting of us doomed to spend our lives in gentlemen's kitchens. Look at our young men, smart, active and energetic, with souls filled with ambitious fire; if they look forward, alas! what are their prospects? They can be nothing but the humblest laborers, on account of their dark complexions; hence many of them lose their ambition, and become worthless. Look at our middle-aged men, clad in their rusty plaids and coats; in winter, every cent they earn goes to buy their wood and pay their rents; their poor wives also toil beyond their strength, to help support their families. Look at our aged sires, whose heads are whitened with the front of seventy winters, with their old wood-saws on their backs. Alas, what keeps us so? Prejudice, ignorance and poverty. But ah! methinks our oppression is soon to come to an end; yes, before the Majesty of heaven, our groans and cries have reached the ears of the Lord of Sabaoth (James 5:4). As the prayers and tears of Christians will avail the finally impenitent nothing; neither will the prayers and tears of the friends of humanity avail us anything, unless we possess a spirit of virtuous emulation within our breasts. Did the pilgrims, when they first landed on these shores, quietly compose themselves, and say, "the Britons have all the money and all the power, and we must continue their servants forever?" Did they sluggishly sigh and say, "our lot is hard, the Indians own the soil, and we cannot cultivate it?" No; they first made powerful efforts to raise themselves and then God raised up those illustrious patriots WASHINGTON and LAFAYETTE, to assist and defend them. And, my brethren, have you made a powerful effort? Have you prayed the Legislature for mercy's sake to grant you all the rights and privileges of free citizens, that your daughters may raise to that degree of respectability which true merit deserves, and your sons above the servile situations which most of them fill?

EDUCATION FOR AFRICAN AMERICAN WOMEN

Oh, do not say you cannot make anything of your children; but say, with the help and assistance of God, we will try. Perhaps you will say that you cannot send them to high schools and academies. You can have them taught in the first rudiments of useful knowledge, and then you can have private teachers, who will instruct them in the higher branches.

It is of no use for us to sit with our hands folded, hanging our heads like bulrushes lamenting our wretched condition; but let us make a mighty effort and arise. Let every female heart become united, and let us raise a fund ourselves; and at the end of one year and a half, we might be able to lay the cornerstone for the building of a high school, that the higher branches of knowledge might be enjoyed by us.

Do you ask, what can we do? Unite and build a store of your own. Fill one side with dry goods and the other with groceries. Do you ask, where is the money? We have spent more than enough for nonsense to do what building we should want. We have never had an opportunity of displaying our talents; therefore the world thinks we know nothing. . .

Few white persons of either sex are willing to spend their lives and bury their talents in performing mean, servile labor. And such is the horrible idea I entertain respecting a life of servitude, that if I conceived of there being no possibility of my rising above the condition of servant, I would gladly hail death as a welcome messenger. Oh, horrible idea, indeed to possess noble souls, aspiring after high and honorable acquirements, yet confined by the chains of ignorance and poverty to lives of continual drudgery and toil.

Neither do I know of any who have enriched themselves by spending their lives as house domestics, washing windows, shaking carpets, brushing boots or tending upon gentlemen's tables. I have learned, by bitter experience, that continued hard labor deadens the energies of the soul, and benumbs the faculties of the mind; the ideas become confined, the mind barren. Continual hard labor irritates our tempers and sours our dispositions; the whole system becomes worn out with toil and fatigue, and we care but little whether we live or die.

I do not consider it derogatory, my friends, for persons to live out to service. There are many whose inclination leads them to aspire no higher: and I would highly commend the performance of almost anything for an honest livelihood; but where constitutional strength is wanting, labor of this kind in its mildest form is painful: and, doubtless, many are the prayers that have ascended to heaven from Afric's daughters for strength to perform their work. Most of our color have dragged out a miserable existence of servitude from the cradle to the grave. And what literary acquirements can be made, or useful knowledge derived, from either maps, books, or charts, by those who continually drudge from Monday morning until Sunday noon? . . .

O ye fairer sisters, whose hands are never soiled, whose nerves and muscles are never strained, go learn by experience! Had we had the opportunity that you have had to improve our moral and mental faculties, what would have hindered our intellects from being as bright, and our manners from being as dignified, as yours? Had it been our lot to have been nursed in the lap of affluence and ease, and to have basked beneath the smiles and sunshine of fortune, should we not have naturally supposed that we were never made to toil? And why are not our forms as delicate and our constitutions as slender as yours? Is not the workmanship as curious and complete? . . .

Look at our young men smart, active, and energetic, with souls filled with ambitious fire; if they look forward, alas! What are their prospects? They can be nothing but the humblest laborer, on account of their dark complexion; hence many of them lose their ambition and become worthless.

Look at our middle aged men, clad in their rusty plaids and coats. In winter, every cent they earn goes to buy their wood and pay their rent; their poor wives also toil beyond their strength, to help support their families.

Look at our aged sires, whose heads are whitened with the frosts of seventy winters, with their old wood saws on their backs. Alas, what keeps us so? Prejudice, ignorance and poverty.

But ah! Did the pilgrims, when they first landed on these shores, quietly compose themselves, and say, "The Britons have all the money and all the power, and we must continue their servants forever?" Did they sigh and say, "Our lot is hard; the Indians own the soil, and we cannot cultivate it?" No, they first made powerful efforts to raise themselves. And, my brethren have you made a powerful effort? Have you prayed the legislature for mercy's sake to grant you all the rights and privileges of free citizens, that your daughters may rise to that degree of respectability which true merit deserves, and your sons above the servile situations which most of them fill?

An Address at the African Masonic Hall

African Rights and liberty is a subject that ought to fire the breast of every free man of color in these United States, and excite in his bosom a lively, deep, decided and heart-felt interest. When I cast my eyes on the long list of illustrious names that are enrolled on the bright annals of fame amongst the whites, I turn my eyes within, and ask my thoughts, "Where are the names of our illustrious ones?" It must certainly have been for the want of energy on the part of the free people of color that they have been long willing to bear the yoke of oppression. It must have been the want of ambition and force that has given the whites occasion to say, that our natural abilities are not as good, and our capacities by nature inferior to theirs. They boldly assert, that, did we possess a natural independence of soul, and feel a love for liberty within our breasts, some one of our sable race, long before this, would have testified it, notwithstanding the disadvantages under which we labor. We have made ourselves appear altogether unqualified to speak in our own defence, and are therefore looked upon as objects of pity and commiseration. We have been imposed upon, insulted and derided on every side; and now, if we complain, it is considered as the height of impertinenance. We have suffered ourselves to be considered as dastards, cowards, mean, faint-hearted wretches; and on this account, (not because of our complexion), many despise us and would gladly spurn us from their presence.

These things have fired my soul with a holy indignation, and compelled me thus to come forward, and endeavor to turn their attention to knowledge and improvement; for knowledge is power. I would ask, is it blindness of mind, or stupidity of soul, or the want of education, that has caused our men who are 60 or 70 years of age, never to let their voices be heard nor their hands be raised in behalf of their color? Or has it been for the fear of offending the whites? If it has, a ye fearful ones, throw off your fearfulness, and come forth in the name of the Lord, and in the strength of the God of Justice, and make yourselves useful and active members in society; for they admire a noble and patriotic spirit in others—and should they not admire it in us? If you are men, convince them that you possess the spirit of men; and as your day, so shall your strength be. Have the sons of Africa no souls? Feel they no ambitious desires? Shall the chains of ignorance forever confine them? Shall the insipid appellation of "clever negroes," or "good creatures;" any longer content them? Where can we find amongst ourselves the man of science, or a philosopher, or an able statesman, or a counselor at law? Show me our fearless and brave, our noble and gallant ones. Where are our lecturers on natural history, and our critics in useful knowledge? There may be a few such men amongst us, but they are rare. It is true, our fathers bled and died in the revolutionary war, and others fought bravely under the command of Jackson, in defence of liberty. But where is the man that has distinguished himself in these modern days by acting wholly in the defence of African rights and liberty? There was one—although he sleeps, his memory lives.

I am sensible that there are many highly intelligent gentlemen of color in these United States, in the force of whose arguments, doubtless, I should discover my inferiority; but if they are blest with wit and talent, friends and fortune, why have they not made themselves men of eminence, by striving to take all the reproach that is cast upon the people of color, and in endeavoring to alleviate the woes of their brethren in bondage? Talk, without effort, is nothing; you are abundantly capable, gentlemen, of making yourselves men of distinction; and this gross neglect, on your part, causes my blood to boil within me. Here is the grand cause which hinders the rise and progress of the people of color. It is their want of laudable ambition and requisite courage.

Individuals have been distinguished according to their genius and talents, ever since the first formation of man, and will continue to be whilst the world stands. The different grades rise to honor and respectability as their merits may deserve. History informs us that we sprung from one of the most learned nations of the whole earth—from the seat, if not the parent of science; yes, poor, despised Africa was once the resort of sages and legislators of other nations, was esteemed the school for learning, and the most illustrious men in Greece flocked thither for instruction. But it was our gross sins and abominations that provoked the Almighty to frown thus heavily upon us, and give our glory unto others. Sin and prodigality have caused the downfall of nations, kings and emperors; and were it not that God in wrath remembers mercy, we might indeed despair; but a promise is left us; "Ethiopia shall again stretch forth her hands unto God."

But it is of no use for us to boast that we sprung from this learned and enlightened nation, for this day a thick mist of moral gloom hangs over millions of our race. Our condition as a people has been low for hundreds of years, and it will continue to be so, unless, by the true piety and virtue we strive, to regain that which we have lost. White Americans, by their prudence, economy and exertions, have sprung up and become one of the most flourishing nations in the world, distinguished for their knowledge of the arts and sciences, for their polite literature. Whilst our minds are vacant and starving for want of knowledge, theirs are filled to overflowing. Most of our color have been taught to stand in fear of the white man from their earliest infancy, to work as soon as they could walk, and call "master" before they scarce could lisp the name of mother. Continual fear and laborious servitude have in some degree lessened in us that natural force and energy which belong to man; or else, in defiance of opposition, our men, before this would have nobly and boldly contended for their rights. But give the man of color an equal opportunity with the white, from the cradle to manhood, and from manhood to the grave, and you would discover the dignified statesman, the man of science, and the philosopher. But there is no such opportunity for the sons of Africa, and I fear that our powerful ones are fully determined that there never shall be. Forbid, ye Powers on High, that it should any longer be said that our men possess no force. 0 ye sons of Africa, when will your voices be heard in our legislative halls, in defiance of your enemies, contending for equal rights and liberty? How can you, when you reflect from what you have fallen, refrain from crying mightily unto God, to turn away from us the fierceness of his anger, and remember our transgressions against us no more forever? But a God of infinite purity will not regard the prayers of those who hold religion in one hand, and prejudice, sin and pollution in the other; he will not regard the prayers of self-righteousness and hypocrisy. Is it possible, I exclaim, that for the want of knowledge, we have labored for hundreds of years to support others, and been content to receive what they chose to give us in return? Cast your eyes about—look as far as you can see—all, all is owned by the lordly white, except here and there a lowly dwelling which the man of color, midst deprivations, fraud and opposition, has been scarce able to procure. Like King Solomon, who put neither nail nor hammer to the temple, yet received the praise; so also have the white Americans gained themselves a name, like the names of the great men that are in the earth, whilst in reality we have been their principal foundation and support. We have pursued the shadow, they have obtained the substance; we have performed the labor, they have received the profits; we have planted the vines, they have eaten the fruits of them.

I would implore our men, and especially our rising youth, to flee from the gambling board and the dance hall; for we are poor, and have no money to throwaway. I do not consider dancing as criminal in itself, but it is astonishing to me that our young men are so blind to their own interest and the future welfare of their children, as to spend their hard earnings for this frivolous amusement; for it has been carried on among us to such an unbecoming extent that it has become absolutely disgusting. "Faithful are the wounds of a friend, but the kisses of an enemy are deceitful." Had those men amongst us, who have had an opportunity, turned their attention as assiduously to mental and moral improvement as they have to gambling and dancing, I might have remained quietly at home, and they stood contending in my place. These polite accomplishments will never enroll your names on the bright annals of fame, who admire the belle void of intellectual knowledge, or applaud the dandy that talks largely on politics, without striving to assist his fellow in the revolution, when the nerves and muscles of every other man forced him into the field of action. You have a right to rejoice, and to let your hearts cheer you in the days of your youth; yet remember that for all these things God will bring you into judgment. Then, 0 ye sons of Africa, turn your mind from these perishable objects, and contend for the cause of God and the rights of man. Form yourselves into temperance societies. There are temperate men amongst you; then why will you any longer neglect to strive, by your example, to suppress vice in all its abhorrent forms? You have been told repeatedly of the glorious results arising from temperance, and can you bear to see the whites arising in honor and respectability also?

But I forbear. Let our money, instead of being thrown away as heretofore, be appropriated for schools and seminaries of learning for our children and youth. We ought to follow the example of the whites in this respect. Nothing would raise our respectability, add to our peace and happiness and reflect so much honor upon us, as to be ourselves the promoters of temperance, and the supporters, as far as we are able, of useful and scientific knowledge. The rays of light and knowledge have been hid from our view; we have been taught to consider ourselves as scarce superior to the brute creation; and have performed the most laborious part of American drudgery. Had we as people received one half the early advantages the whites have received, I would defy the government of these United States to deprive us any longer of our rights.

I am informed that the agent of the Colonization Society has recently formed an association of young men, for the purpose of influencing those of us to go to Liberia who may feel disposed. The colonizationists are blind to their own interest, for should the nations of the earth make war with America, they would find their forces much weakened by our absence; or should we remain here, can our "brave soldiers" and "fellow citizens," as they were termed in time of calamity, condescend to defend the rights of the whites, and be again deprived of their own, or sent to Liberia in return? 0, if the colonizationists are real friends to Africa, let them expend the money which they collect in erecting a college to educate her inured sons in this land of gospel light and liberty; for it would be most thankfully received on our part, and convince us of the truth of their professions, and save time, expense and anxiety. Let them place before us noble objects, worthy of pursuit, and see if we prove ourselves to be those unambitious negroes they term us. But ah! Methinks their hearts are so frozen towards us, they had rather their money should be sunk in the ocean than to administer it to our relief; and I fear, if they dared, like Pharaoh king of Egypt, they would order every male child amongst us to be drowned. But the most high God is still as able to subdue the lofty pride of these white Americans, as He was the heart of that ancient rebel. They say though we are looked upon as things, yet we sprang from a scientific people. Had our men the requisite force and energy, they would soon convince them, by their efforts both in public and private, that they were men, or things in the shape of men. Well may the colonizationists laugh us to scorn for our negligence; well may they cry, "Shame to the sons of Africa." As the burden of the Israelites was too great for Moses to bear, so also is our burden too great for our noble advocate to bear. You must feel interested, my brethren, in what he undertakes, and hold up his hands by your good words, or in spite of himself his soul will become discouraged, and his heart will die within him; for he has, as it were, the strong bulls of Bashan to contend with.

Prejudice Against the Colored Man

Mr. President, with much feeling do I rise to address the society on this resolution, and I should hardly have been induced to have done it had I not been requested. I confess I am personally interested in this resolution. But were it not for the fact that none can feel the lash but those who have it upon them, that none know where the chain galls but those who wear it, I would not address you.

This is a serious business, sir. The prejudice which exists against the colored man, the free man is like the atmosphere, everywhere felt by him. It is true that in these United States and in this State, there are men, like myself, colored with the skin like my own, who are not subjected to the lash, who are not liable to have their wives and their infants torn from them; from whose hand the Bible is not taken. It is true that we may walk abroad; we may enjoy our domestic comforts, our families; retire to the closet; visit the sanctuary, and may be permitted to urge on our children and our neighbors in well doing. But sir, still we are slaves—everywhere we feel the chain galling us. It is by that prejudice which the resolution condemns, the spirit of slavery, the law which has been enacted here, by a corrupt public sentiment, through the influence of slavery which treats moral agents different from the rule of God, which treats them irrespective of their morals or intellectual cultivation. This spirit is withering all our hopes, and ofttimes causes the colored parent as he looks upon his child, to wish he had never been born. Often is the heart of the colored mother, as she presses her child to her bosom, filled with sorrow to think that, by reason of this prejudice, it is cut off from all hopes of usefulness in this land. Sir, this prejudice is wicked.

If the nation and church understood this matter, I would not speak a word about that killing influence that destroys the colored man's reputation. This influence cuts us off from everything; it follows us up from childhood to manhood; it excludes us from all stations of profit, usefulness and honor; takes away from us all motive for pressing forward in enterprises, useful and important to the world and to ourselves.

In the first place, it cuts us off from the advantages of the mechanic arts almost entirely. A colored man can hardly learn a trade, and if he does it is difficult for him to find any one who will employ him to work at that trade, in any part of the State. In most of our large cities there are associations of mechanics who legislate out of their society colored men. And in many cases where our young men have learned trades, they have had to come to low employments for want of encouragement in those trades.

It must be a matter of rejoicing to know that in this vicinity colored fathers and mothers have the privileges of education. It must be a matter of rejoicing that in this vicinity colored parents can have their children trained up in schools.—At present, we find the colleges barred against them.

I will say nothing about the inconvenience which I have experienced myself, and which every man of color experiences, though made in the image of God. I will say nothing about the inconvenience of traveling; how we are frowned upon and despised. No matter how we may demean ourselves, we find embarrassments everywhere.

But sir, this prejudice goes further. It debars men from heaven. While sir, slavery cuts off the colored portion of the community from religious privileges, men are made infidels. What, they demand, is your Christianity? How do you regard your brethren? How do you treat them at the Lord's table? Where is your consistency in talking about the heathen, transversing the ocean to circulate the Bible everywhere, while you frown upon them at the door? These things meet us and weigh down our spirits.

And, sir, the constitution of society, molded by this prejudice, destroys souls. I have known extensively, that in revivals which have been blessed and enjoyed in this part of the country, the colored population were overlooked. I recollect an instance. The Lord God was pouring out His Spirit. He was entering every house, and sinners were converted. I asked, Where is the colored man? Who is weeping for them? Who is endeavoring to pull them out of the fire? No reply was made.—I was asked to go round with one of the elders and visit them. We went and they humbled themselves. The Church commenced efficient efforts, and God blessed them as soon as they began to act for these people as though they had souls.

And sir, the manner in which our churches are regulated destroys souls. Whilst the church is thrown open to everybody, and one says come, come in and share the blessings of the sanctuary, this is the gate of heaven—he says to the colored man, be careful where you take your stand. I know an efficient church in this State, where a respectable colored man went to the house of God, and was going to take a seat in the gallery, and one of the officers contended with him, and said, "you cannot go there, sir."

In one place the people had come together to the house of the Lord. The sermon was preached—the emblems were about to be administered—and all at once the person who managed the church thought the value of the pews would be diminished if the colored people sat in them. They objected to their sitting there, and the colored people left and went into the gallery, and that, too, when they were thinking of handling the memorials of the broken body and shed blood of the Savior! And, sir, this prejudice follows the colored man everywhere, and depresses his spirits.

Thanks be to God, there is a buoyant principle which elevates the poor down-trodden colored man above all this:—It is that there is society which regards man according to his worth; it is the fact, that when he looks up to Heaven he knows that God treats him like a moral agent, irrespective of caste or the circumstances in which he may be placed. Amid the embarrassments which he has to meet, and the scorn and contempt that is heaped upon him, he is cheered by the hope that he will be disenthralled, and soon, like a bird set forth from its cage, wing his flight to Jesus, where he can be happy, and look down with pity on the man who despises the poor slave for being what God made him, and who despises him because he is identified with the poor slave. Blessed be God for the principles of the Gospel. Were it not for these, and for the fact that a better day is dawning, I would not wish to live.—Blessed be God for the antislavery movement. Blessed be God there is a war waging with slavery, that the granite rock is about to be rolled from its base. But as long as the colored man is to be looked upon as an inferior caste, so long will they disregard his cries, his groans, his shrieks.

I rejoice, sir, in this Society; and I deem the day when I joined this Society as one of the proudest days of my life. And I know I can die better, in more peace today, to know there are men who will plead the cause of my children.

Let me, through you, sir, request this delegation to take hold of this subject. This will silence the slave holder, when he says where is your love for the slave? Where is your love for the colored man who is crushed at your feet? Talking to us about emancipating our slaves when you are enslaving them by your feelings, and doing more violence to them by your prejudice, than we are to our slaves by our treatment. They call on us to evince our love for the slave, by treating man as man, the colored man as a man, according to his worth.

We Must Assert Our Rightful Claims
and Plead Our Own Cause

GENTLEMEN: I consider this a most happy period in our history, when we as a people are in some degree awake to a sense of our condition and are determined no longer to submit tamely and silently to wear the galling yoke of oppression, under which we have so long suffered—oppression riveted upon us, as well by an unholy and cruel prejudice, as by unjust and unequal legislation. More particularly do I consider it ominous of good, when I see here collected, so much of wisdom and talent, from different parts of this great nation, collected here to deliberate upon the wisest and best methods by which we may seek a redress of those grievances which most sorely oppress us as a people.

Gentlemen, in behalf of my fellow citizens of Buffalo, I bid you welcome, from the East and West, the North and South, to our city. Among you are the men who are lately from that part of our country where they see our brethren bound and manacled, suffering and bleeding, under the hand of the tyrant, who holds in one hand the Constitution of the United States, which guarantees freedom and equal rights to every citizen, and in the other "the scourge dripping with gore," drawn from the veins of his fellow man. Here also are those who live in my native New England, among the "descendants of the pilgrims," whose laws are more in accordance with the principles of freedom and equal rights, so that but few laws are found recorded on their statute books of which we need complain. But though their laws are not marked with such palpable and flagrant injustice toward the colored man as those of the South, yet there we are proscribed, by a fixed and cruel prejudice little less oppressive. Our grievances are many and great, but it is not my intention to enumerate or to enlarge upon them. I will simply say, however, that we wish to secure for ourselves, in common with other citizens, the privilege of seeking our own happiness in any part of the country we may choose, which right is now unjustly and, we believe, unconstitutionally denied us in a part of this Union. We wish also to secure the elective franchise in those states where it is denied us, where our rights are legislated away, and our voice neither heard nor regarded. We also wish to secure, for our children especially, the benefits of education, which in several States are entirely denied us, and in others are enjoyed only in name. These, and many other things, of which we justly complain, bear most heavily upon us as a people; and it is our right and our duty to seek for redress, in that way which will be most likely to secure the desired end.

In your wisdom, you will, I doubt not, take into consideration these and the many other grievances which we suffer, and form such organizations and recommend such measures as shall, in your wisdom, seem most likely to secure our enfranchisement, the benefits of education to our children, and all our rights in common with other citizens of this republic.

Two objects should distinctly and constantly be borne in mind, in all our deliberations. One is the diffusion of truth, and the other the elevation of our own people. By the diffusion of truth I mean that we must take a bold and elevated stand for the truth. We must determine, in the strength of God, to do everything that will advance the great and holy cause of freedom, and nothing that will in the least retard its progress. We must, by every means in our power, strive to persuade the white people to act with more confidence in their own principles of liberty—to make laws just and equal for all the people.

But while the color of the skin is made the criterion of the law, it is our right, our duty and, I hope I may say, our fixed determination, to make known our wrongs to the world and to our oppressors; to cease not day nor night to "tell, in burning words, our tale of woe," and pour a flood of living light on the minds and consciences of the oppressor, till we change their thoughts, feelings, and actions toward us as men and citizens of this land. We must convince our fellow men that slavery is unprofitable; that it is for the well-being and prosperity of this nation, the peace and happiness of our common country, that slavery and oppression be abolished within its borders, and that laws be enacted equal and just for all its citizens.

Proscription is not in accordance with equal rights, no more than is oppression with holy freedom, or slavery with the spirit of free institutions. The present system of laws, in this our country, enacted in reference to us, the oppressed and downtrodden descendants of Africa, do, and will continue to, operate like the canker worm in the root of the tree of liberty, preventing its growth and ultimately destroying its vitality. We may well say, in the language of a distinguished statesman and patriot of our own land, "We tremble for our country when we reflect that God is just, and that his justice will not always sleep." By the example of other nations, who have gone before, whose history should be a warning to this people, we learn that slavery and oppression has nowhere prospered long; it blasts a nation's glory and prosperity, divides her power, weakens her strength, and grows like a corroding consumption in her very vitals. "God's judgments will not sleep forever, but he will visit the nations of the earth in justice." We love our common country—"With all her faults, we love her still." This is the land where we all drew our first breath; where we have grown up to strength and manhood. "Here is deposited the ashes of our fathers"; here we have contracted the most sacred engagements, the dearest relations of life; here we have found the companions of our childhood, the friends of our youth, the gentle partners of our lives; here are the haunts of our infancy, the scenes of every endearing hour—in a word, this is our own native land. I repeat it, then: We love our country, we love our fellow citizens—but we love liberty more. . .

It is time that we were more awake to our own interests, more united in our efforts, and more efficient in our measures. We must profit by the example of our oppressors. We must act on their principles in resisting tyranny. We must adopt their resolutions in favor of liberty. "They have taught us a lesson, in their struggle for independence, that should never be forgotten. They have taught the world emphatically that a people united in the cause of liberty are invincible to those who would enslave them, and that heaven will ever frown on the cause of injustice, and ultimately grant success to those who oppose it." Shall we, then, longer submit in silence to our accumulated wrongs? Forbid it, heaven, that we should longer stand in silence, "hugging the delusive phantom of hope," when every gale that sweeps from the South, bears on its wings, to our ears, the dismal sound of slavery's clanking chains, now riveted on three millions of our brethren, and we ourselves are aliens and outcasts in our native land.

Is the question asked, what shall we do? Shall we petition for our rights? I do not pretend to dictate the course that should be pursued; but I have very little hope in petitioning longer. We have petitioned again and again, and what has been the result? Our humblest prayers have not been permitted a hearing. We could not even state our grievances. Our petitions were disregarded, our applications slighted, and we spurned from the mercy seat, insulted, abused and slandered. And this day finds us in the same unhappy and hopeless condition in which we have been for our whole lives; no other hope is let us, but in our own exertions and an "appeal to the god of armies." From what other source can we expect that help will come? Shall we appeal to the Christian community—to the church of our own land? What is her position? Behold her gigantic form, with hands upraised to heaven! See her increased and made rich by the toil and sweat and blood of slaves! View her arrayed in her pontifical robes, screening the horrid monster, slavery, with her very bosom—within her most sacred enclosures, that the world may not gaze on its distorted visage or view its hellish form! Yes, throwing around this accursed system, the very drapery of heaven, to cover this damning sin and give it character and respectability in the eyes of the country and in the eyes of the world. We cannot, therefore, look to her for help, for she has taken sides against us and on the side of slavery. Shall we turn to either of the great political parties of the day? What are our prospects there? Is there any hope of help? No, they are but the slaves of slavery, too, contending which shall be most faithful in supporting the foul system of slavery, that they may secure the vote of the slaveholder himself, and of his scores of human cattle. Shall we, then, look to the abolitionists and wait for them to give us our rights? I would not say a word that would have a tendency to discourage them in their noble efforts in behalf of the poor slave, or their exertions to advance the cause of truth and humanity. Some of them have made great sacrifices and have labored with a zeal and fidelity that justly entitle them to our confidence and gratitude. But if we sit down in idleness and sloth, waiting for them—or any other class of men—to do our own work, I fear it will never be done. If we are not willing to rise up and assert our rightful claims, and plead our own cause, we have no reason to look for success. We ourselves must be willing to contend for the rich boon of freedom and equal rights, or we shall never enjoy that boon. It is found only of them that seek.

An Address to the Slaves of the United States

Brethren and Fellow Citizens:—Your brethren of the North, East, and West have been accustomed to meet together in National Conventions, to sympathize with each other, and to weep over your unhappy condition. In these meetings we have addressed all classes of the free, but we have never, until this time, sent a word of consolation and advice to you. We have been contented in sitting still and mourning over your sorrows, earnestly hoping that before this day your sacred liberty would have been restored. But, we have hoped in vain. Years have rolled on, and tens of thousands have been borne on streams of blood and tears, to the shores of eternity. While you have been oppressed, we have also been partakers with you; nor can we be free while you are enslaved. We, therefore, write to you as being bound with you. Many of you are bound to us, not only by the ties of a common humanity, but we are connected by the more tender relations of parents, wives, husbands, children, brothers, and sisters, and friends. As such we most affectionately address you.

Slavery has fixed a deep gulf between you and us, and while it shuts out from you the relief and consolation which your friends would willingly render, it affects and persecutes you with a fierceness which we might not expect to see in the fiends of hell. But still the Almighty Father of mercies has left to us a glimmering ray of hope, which shines out like a lone star in a cloudy sky. Mankind are becoming wiser, and better— the oppressor's power is fading, and you, everyday, are becoming better informed, and more numerous. Your grievances, brethren, are many. We shall not attempt, in this short address, to present to the world all the dark catalogue of this nation's sins, which have been committed upon an innocent people. Nor is it indeed necessary, for you feel them from day to day, and all the civilized world look upon them with amazement.

Two hundred and twenty seven years ago, the first of our injured race were brought to the shores of America. They came not with glad spirits to select their homes in the New World. They came not with their own consent, to find an unmolested enjoyment of the blessings of this fruitful soil. The first dealings they had with men calling themselves Christians, exhibited to them the worst features of corrupt and sordid hearts; and convinced them that no cruelty is too great, no villainy and no robbery too abhorrent for even enlightened men to perform, when influenced by avarice and lust. Neither did they come flying upon the wings of Liberty, to a land of freedom. But they came with broken hearts, from their beloved native land, and were doomed to unrequited toil and deep degradation. Nor did the evil of their bondage end at their emancipation by death. Succeeding generations inherited their chains, and millions have come from eternity into time, and have returned again to the world of spirits, cursed and ruined by American slavery.

The propagators of the system, or their immediate ancestors, very soon discovered its growing evil, and its tremendous wickedness, and secret promises were made to destroy it. The gross inconsistency of a people holding slaves, who had themselves "ferried o'er the wave" for freedom's sake, was too apparent to be entirely overlooked. The voice of Freedom cried, "Emancipate yourselves." Humanity supplicated with tears for the deliverance of the children of Africa. Wisdom urged her solemn plea. The bleeding captive plead his innocence, and pointed to Christianity who stood weeping at the cross. Jehovah frowned upon the nefarious institution, and thunderbolts, red with vengeance, struggled to leap forth to blast the guilty wretches who maintained it. But all was in vain. Slavery had stretched its dark wings of death over the land, the Church stood silently by the priests prophesied falsely, and the people loved to have it so. Its throne is established, and now it reigns triumphant.

Nearly three millions of your fellow citizens are prohibited by law and public opinion, (which in this country is stronger than law,) from reading the Book of Life. Your intellect has been destroyed as much as possible, and every ray of light they have attempted to shut out from your minds. The oppressors themselves have become involved in the ruin. They have become weak, sensual, and rapacious—they have cursed you—they have cursed themselves—they have cursed the earth which they have trod.

The colonists threw the blame upon England. They said that the mother country entailed the evil upon them, and that they would rid themselves of it if they could. The world thought they were sincere, and the philanthropic pitied them. But time soon tested their sincerity.

In a few years the colonists grew strong, and severed themselves from the British Government. Their independence was declared, and they took their station among the sovereign powers of the earth. The declaration was a glorious document. Sages admired it, and the patriotic of every nation reverenced the God like sentiments which it contained. When the power of Government returned to their hands, did they emancipate the slaves? No; they rather added new links to our chains. Were they ignorant of the principles of Liberty? Certainly they were not. The sentiments of their revolutionary orators fell in burning eloquence upon their hearts, and with one voice they cried, Liberty or Death. Oh, what a sentence was that! It ran from soul to soul like electric fire, and nerved the arm of thousands to fight in the holy cause of Freedom. Among the diversity of opinions that are entertained in regard to physical resistance, there are but a few found to gainsay that stern declaration. We are among those who do not. Slavery! How much misery is comprehended in that single word. What mind is there that does not shrink from its direful effects? Unless the image of God be obliterated from the soul, all men cherish the love of Liberty. The nice discerning political economist does not regard the sacred right more than the untutored African who roams in the wilds of Congo. Nor has the one more right to the full enjoyment of his freedom than the other. In every man's mind the good seeds of liberty are planted, and he who brings his fellow down so low, as to make him contented with a condition of slavery, commits the highest crime against God and man. Brethren, your oppressors aim to do this. They endeavor to make you as much like brutes as possible. When they have blinded the eyes of your mind when they have embittered the sweet waters of life then, and not till then, has American slavery done its perfect work.

TO SUCH DEGREDATION IT IS SINFUL IN THE EXTREME FOR YOU TO MAKE VOLUNTARY SUBMISSION. The divine commandments you are in duty bound to reverence and obey. If you do not obey them, you will surely meet with the displeasure of the Almighty. He requires you to love him supremely, and your neighbor as yourself—to keep the Sabbath day holy—to search the Scriptures—and bring up your children with respect for his laws, and to worship no other God but him. But slavery sets all these at nought, and hurls defiance in the face of Jehovah. The forlorn condition in which you are placed, does not destroy your moral obligation to God. You are not certain of heaven, because you suffer yourselves to remain in a state of slavery, where you cannot obey the commandments of the Sovereign of the universe. If the ignorance of slavery is a passport to heaven, then it is a blessing, and no curse, and you should rather desire its perpetuity than its abolition. God will not receive slavery, nor ignorance, nor any other state of mind, for love and obedience to him. Your condition does not absolve you from your moral obligation. The diabolical injustice by which your liberties are cloven down, NEITHER GOD, NOR ANGELS, OR JUST MEN, COMMAND YOU TO SUFFER FOR A SINGLE MOMENT. THEREFORE IT IS YOUR SOLEMN AND IMPERATIVE DUTY TO USE EVERY MEANS, BOTH MORAL, INTELLECTUAL, AND PHYSICAL THAT PROMISES SUCCESS. If a band of heathen men should attempt to enslave a race of Christians, and to place their children under the influence of some false religion, surely Heaven would frown upon the men who would not resist such aggression, even to death. If, on the other hand, a band of Christians should attempt to enslave a race of heathen men, and to entail slavery upon them, and to keep them in heathenism in the midst of Christianity, the God of heaven would smile upon every effort which the injured might make to disenthral themselves. Brethren, it is as wrong for your lordly oppressors to keep you in slavery, as it was for the man thief to steal our ancestors from the coast of Africa. You should therefore now use the same manner of resistance, as would have been just in our ancestors when the bloody foot prints of the first remorseless soul thief was placed upon the shores of our fatherland. The humblest peasant is as free in the sight of God as the proudest monarch that ever swayed a sceptre. Liberty is a spirit sent out from God, and like its great Author, is no respecter of persons.

Brethren, the time has come when you must act for yourselves. It is an old and true saying that, "if hereditary bondmen would be free, they must themselves strike the blow." You can plead your own cause, and do the work of emancipation better than any others. The nations of the world are moving in the great cause of universal freedom, and some of them at least will, ere long, do you justice. The combined powers of Europe have placed their broad seal of disapprobation upon the African slave trade. But in the slaveholding parts of the United States, the trade is as brisk as ever. They buy and sell you as though you were brute beasts. The North has done much—her opinion of slavery in the abstract is known. But in regard to the South, we adopt the opinion of the New York Evangelist— We have advanced so far, that the cause apparently waits for a more effectual door to be thrown open than has been yet. We are about to point out that more effectual door. Look around you, and behold the bosoms of your loving wives heaving with untold agonies! Hear the cries of your poor children! Remember the stripes your fathers bore. Think of the torture and disgrace of your noble mothers. Think of your wretched sisters, loving virtue and purity, as they are driven into concubinage and are exposed to the unbridled lusts of incarnate devils. Think of the undying glory that hangs around the ancient name of Africa—and forget not that you are native born American citizens, and as such, you are justly entitled to all the rights that are granted to the freest. Think how many tears you have poured out upon the soil which you have cultivated with unrequited toil and enriched with your blood; and then go to your lordly enslavers and tell them plainly, that you are determined to be free. Appeal to their sense of justice, and tell them that they have no more right to oppress you, than you have to enslave them. Entreat them to remove the grievous burdens which they have imposed upon you, and to remunerate you for your labor. Promise them renewed diligence in the cultivation of the soil, if they will render to you an equivalent for your services. Point them to the increase of happiness and prosperity in the British West Indies since the Act of Emancipation. Tell them in language which they cannot misunderstand, of the exceeding sinfulness of slavery, and of a future judgment, and of the righteous retributions of an indignant God. Inform them that all you desire is FREEDOM, and that nothing else will suffice. Do this, and for ever after cease to toil for the heartless tyrants, who give you no other reward but stripes and abuse. If they then commence the work of death, they, and not you, will be responsible for the consequences. You had better all die die immediately, than live slaves and entail your wretchedness upon your posterity. If you would be free in this generation, here is your only hope. However much you and all of us may desire it, there is not much hope of redemption without the shedding of blood. If you must bleed, let it all come at once—rather die freemen, than live to be slaves. It is impossible like the children of Israel, to make a grand exodus from the land of bondage. The Pharaohs are on both sides of the blood red waters! You cannot move en masse, to the dominions of the British Queen—nor can you pass through Florida and overrun Texas, and at last find peace in Mexico. The propagators of American slavery are spending their blood and treasure, that they may plant the black flag in the heart of Mexico and riot in the halls of the Montezumas. In the language of the Rev. Robert Hall, when addressing the volunteers of Bristol, who were rushing forth to repel the invasion of Napoleon, who threatened to lay waste the fair homes of England, "Religion is too much interested in your behalf, not to shed over you her most gracious influences."

You will not be compelled to spend much time in order to become inured to hardships. From the first moment that you breathed the air of heaven, you have been accustomed to nothing else but hardships. The heroes of the American Revolution were never put upon harder fare than a peck of corn and a few herrings per week. You have not become enervated by the luxuries of life. Your sternest energies have been beaten out upon the anvil of severe trial. Slavery has done this, to make you subservient, to its own purposes; but it has done more than this, it has prepared you for any emergency. If you receive good treatment, it is what you could hardly expect; if you meet with pain, sorrow, and even death, these are the common lot of slaves.

Fellow men! Patient sufferers! behold your dearest rights crushed to the earth! See your sons murdered, and your wives, mothers and sisters doomed to prostitution. In the name of the merciful God, and by all that life is worth, let it no longer be a debatable question whether it is better to choose Liberty or death.

In 1822, Denmark Veazie (Vesey), of South Carolina, formed a plan for the liberation of his fellow men. In the whole history of human efforts to overthrow slavery, a more complicated and tremendous plan was never formed. He was betrayed by the treachery of his own people, and died a martyr to freedom. Many a brave hero fell, but history, faithful to her high trust, will transcribe his name on the same monument with Moses, Hampden, Tell, Bruce and Wallace, Toussaint L'Ouverture, Lafayette and Washington. That tremendous movement shook the whole empire of slavery. The guilty soul thieves were overwhelmed with fear. It is a matter of fact, that at that time, and in consequence of the threatened revolution, the slave States talked strongly of emancipation. But they blew but one blast of the trumpet of freedom and then laid it aside. As these men became quiet, the slaveholders ceased to talk about emancipation; and now behold your condition today! Angels sigh over it, and humanity has long since exhausted her tears in weeping on your account!

The patriotic Nathaniel Turner followed Denmark Veazie (Vesey). He was goaded to desperation by wrong and injustice. By despotism, his name has been recorded on the list of infamy, and future generations will remember him among the noble and brave.

Next arose the immortal Joseph Cinque, the hero of the Amistad. He was a native African, and by the help of God he emancipated a whole ship load of his fellow men on the high seas. And he now sings of liberty on the sunny hills of Africa and beneath his native palm trees, where he hears the lion roar and feels himself as free as that king of the forest.

Next arose Madison Washington that bright star of freedom, and took his station in the constellation of true heroism. He was a slave on board the brig Creole, of Richmond, bound to New Orleans, that great slave mart, with a hundred and four others. Nineteen struck for liberty or death. But one life was taken, and the whole were emancipated, and the vessel was carried into Nassau, New Providence.

Noble men! Those who have fallen in freedom's conflict, their memories will be cherished by the true hearted and the God fearing in all future generations; those who are living, their names are surrounded by a halo of glory.

Brethren, arise, arise! Strike for your lives and liberties. Now is the day and the hour. Let every slave throughout the land do this, and the days of slavery are numbered. You cannot be more oppressed than you have been—you cannot suffer greater cruelties than you have already. Rather die freemen than live to be slaves. Remember that you are FOUR MILLIONS!

It is in your power so to torment the God cursed slaveholders that they will be glad to let you go free. If the scale was turned, and black men were the masters and white men the slaves, every destructive agent and element would be employed to lay the oppressor low. Danger and death would hang over their heads day and night. Yes, the tyrants would meet with plagues more terrible than those of Pharaoh. But you are a patient people. You act as though, you were made for the special use of these devils. You act as though your daughters were born to pamper the lusts of your masters and overseers. And worse than all, you tamely submit while your lords tear your wives from your embraces and defile them before your eyes. In the name of God, we ask, are you men? Where is the blood of your fathers? Has it all run out of your veins? Awake, awake; millions of voices are calling you! Your dead fathers speak to you from their graves. Heaven, as with a voice of thunder, calls on you to arise from the dust.

Let your motto be resistance! resistance! RESISTANCE! No oppressed people have ever secured their liberty without resistance. What kind of resistance you had better make, you must decide by the circumstances that surround you, and according to the suggestion of expediency. Brethren, adieu! Trust in the living God. Labor for the peace of the human race, and remember that you are FOUR MILLIONS.

My Slave Experience in Maryland

I do not know that I can say anything to the point. My habits and early life have done much to unfit me for public speaking, and I fear that your patience has already been wearied by the lengthened remarks of other speakers, more eloquent than I can possibly be, and better prepared to command the attention of the audience. And I can scarcely hope to get your attention even for a longer period than fifteen minutes.

Before coming to this meeting, I had a sort of desire I don't know but it was vanity to stand before a New York audience in the Tabernacle. But when I came in this morning, and looked at those massive pillars, and saw the vast throng which had assembled, I got a little frightened, and was afraid that I could not speak; but now that the audience is not so large and I have recovered from my fright, I will venture to say a word on Slavery.

I ran away from the South seven years ago passing through this city in no little hurry, I assure you and lived about three years in New Bedford, Massachusetts, before I became publicly known to the anti-slavery people. Since then I have been engaged for three years in telling the people what I know of it. I have come to this meeting to throw in my mite, and since no fugitive slave has preceded me, I am encouraged to say a word about the sunny South. I thought, when the eloquent female who addressed this audience a while ago, was speaking of the horrors of Slavery, that many an honest man would doubt the truth of the picture which she drew; and I can unite with the gentleman from Kentucky in saying, that she came far short of describing them.

I can tell you what I have seen with my own eyes, felt on my own person, and know to have occurred in my own neighborhood. I am not from any of those States where the slaves are said to be in their most degraded condition; but from Maryland, where Slavery is said to exist in its mildest form; yet I can stand here and relate atrocities which would make your blood to boil at the statement of them. I lived on the plantation of Col. Lloyd, on the eastern shore of Maryland, and belonged to that gentleman's clerk. He owned, probably, not less than a thousand slaves.

I mention the name of this man, and also of the persons who perpetrated the deeds which I am about to relate, running the risk of being hurled back into interminable bondage for I am yet a slave; yet for the sake of the cause for the sake of humanity, I will mention the names, and glory in running the risk. I have the gratification to know that if I fall by the utterance of truth in this matter, that if I shall be hurled back into bondage to gratify the slaveholder to be killed by inches that every drop of blood which I shall shed, every groan which I shall utter, every pain which shall rack my frame, every sob in which I shall indulge, shall be the instrument, under God, of tearing down the bloody pillar of Slavery, and of hastening the day of deliverance for three millions of my brethren in bondage.

I therefore tell the names of these bloody men, not because they are worse than other men would have been in their circumstances. No, they are bloody from necessity. Slavery makes it necessary for the slaveholder to commit all conceivable outrages upon the miserable slave. It is impossible to hold the slaves in bondage without this.

We had on the plantation an overseer, by the name of Austin Gore, a man who was highly respected as an overseer proud, ambitious, cruel, artful, obdurate. Nearly every slave stood in the utmost dread and horror of that man. His eye flashed confusion amongst them. He never spoke but to command, nor commanded but to be obeyed. He was lavish with the whip, sparing with his word. I have seen that man tie up men by the two hands, and for two hours, at intervals, ply the lash. I have seen women stretched up on the limbs of trees, and their bare backs made bloody with the lash. One slave refused to be whipped by him I need not tell you that he was a man, though black his features, degraded his condition. He had committed some trifling offence for they whip for trifling offences the slave refused to be whipped, and ran he did not stand to and fight his master as I did once, and might do again though I hope I shall not have occasion to do so he ran and stood in a creek, and refused to come out. At length his master told him he would shoot him if he did not come out. Three calls were to be given him. The first, second, and third, were given, at each of which the slave stood his ground. Gore, equally determined and firm, raised his musket, and in an instant poor Derby was no more. He sank beneath the waves, and naught but the crimsoned waters marked the spot. Then a general outcry might be heard amongst us. Mr. Lloyd asked Gore why he had resorted to such a cruel measure. He replied, coolly, that he had done it from necessity; that the slave was setting a dangerous example, and that if he was permitted to be corrected and yet save his life, that the slaves would effectually rise and be freemen, and their masters be slaves. His defence was satisfactory. He remained on the plantation, and his fame went abroad. He still lives in St. Michaels, Talbot county, Maryland, and is now, I presume, as much respected, as though his guilty soul had never been stained with his brother's blood.

I might go on and mention other facts if time would permit. My own wife had a dear cousin who was terribly mangled in her sleep, while nursing the child of a Mrs. Hicks. Finding the girl asleep, Mrs. Hicks beat her to death with a billet of wood, and the woman has never been brought to justice. It is not a crime to kill a negro in Talbot county, Maryland, farther than it is a deprivation of a man's property. I used to know of one who boasted that he had killed two slaves, and with an oath would say, "I'm the only benefactor in the country."

Now, my friends, pardon me for having detained you so long; but let me tell you with regard to the feelings of the slave. The people at the North say "Why don't you rise? If we were thus treated we would rise and throw off the yoke. We would wade knee deep in blood before we would endure the bondage." You'd rise up! Who are these that are asking for manhood in the slave, and who say that he has it not, because he does not rise? The very men who are ready by the Constitution to bring the strength of the nation to put us down! You, the people of New York, the people of Massachusetts, of New England, of the whole Northern States, have sworn under God that we shall be slaves or die! And shall we three millions be taunted with a want of the love of freedom, by the very men who stand upon us and say, submit, or be crushed?

We don't ask you to engage in any physical warfare against the slaveholder. We only ask that in Massachusetts, and the several non slaveholding States which maintain a union with the slaveholder who stand with your heavy heels on the quivering heart strings of the slave, that you will stand off. Leave us to take care of our masters. But here you come up to our masters and tell them that they ought to shoot us to take away our wives and little ones to sell our mothers into interminable bondage, and sever the tenderest ties. You say to us, if you dare to carry out the principles of our fathers, we'll shoot you down. Others may tamely submit; not I You may put the chains upon me and fetter me, but I am not a slave, for my master who puts the chains upon me, shall stand in as much dread of me as I do of him. I ask you in the name of my three millions of brethren at the South. We know that we are unable to cope with you in numbers; you are numerically stronger, politically stronger, than we are but we ask you if you will rend asunder the heart and (crush) the body of the slave? If so, you must do it at your own expense.

While you continue in the Union, you are as bad as the slaveholder. If you have thus wronged the poor black man, by stripping him of his freedom, how are you going to give evidence of your repentance? Undo what you have done. Do you say that the slave ought not to be free? These hands are they not mine? This body is it not mine? Again, I am your brother, white as you are. I'm your blood kin. You don't get rid of me so easily. I mean to hold on to you. And in this land of liberty, I'm a slave. The twenty six States that blaze forth on your flag, proclaim a compact to return me to bondage if I run away, and keep me in bondage if I submit. Wherever I go, under the aegis of your liberty, there I'm a slave. If I go to Lexington or Bunker Hill, there I'm a slave, chained in perpetual servitude. I may go to your deepest valley, to your highest mountain, I'm still a slave, and the bloodhound may chase me down.

Now I ask you if you are willing to have your country the hunting ground of the slave. God says thou shalt not oppress: the Constitution says oppress: which will you serve, God or man? The American Anti-Slavery Society says God, and I am thankful for it. In the name of my brethren, to you, Mr. President, and the noble band who cluster around you, to you, who are scouted on every hand by priest, people, politician, Church, and State, to you I bring a thankful heart, and in the name of three millions of slaves, I offer you their gratitude for your faithful advocacy in behalf of the slave.

On Woman Suffrage

Mrs. President, Ladies and Gentlemen:—I come to this platform with unusual diffidence. Although I have long been identified with the Woman's Suffrage movement, and have often spoken in its favor, I am somewhat at a loss to know what to say on this really great and uncommon occasion, where so much has been said.

When I look around on this assembly, and see the many able and eloquent women, full of the subject, ready to speak, and who only need the opportunity to impress this audience with their views and thrill them with "thoughts that breathe and words that burn," I do not feel like taking up more than a very small space of your time and attention, and shall not. I would not, even now, presume to speak, but for the circumstance of my early connection with the cause, and of having been called upon to do so by one whose voice in this Council we all gladly obey. Men have very little business here as speakers, anyhow; and if they come here at all they should take back benches and wrap themselves in silence. For this is an International Council, not of men, but of women, and woman should have all the say in it. This is her day in court. I do not mean to exalt the intellect of woman above man's; but I have heard many men speak on this subject, some of them the most eloquent to be found anywhere in the country; and I believe no man, however gifted with thought and speech, can voice the wrongs and present the demands of women with the skill and effect, with the power and authority of woman herself. The man struck is the man to cry out. Woman knows and feels her wrongs as man cannot know and feel them, and she also knows as well as he can know, what measures are needed to redress them. I grant all the claims at this point. She is her own best representative. We can neither speak for her, nor vote for her, nor act for her, nor be responsible for her; and the thing for men to do in the premises is just to get out of her way and give her the fullest opportunity to exercise all the powers inherent in her individual personality, and allow her to do it as she herself shall elect to exercise them. Her right to be and to do is as full, complete and perfect as the right of any man on earth. I say of her, as I say of the colored people, "Give her fair play, and hands off." There was a time when, perhaps, we men could help a little. It was when this woman suffrage cause was in its cradle, when it was not big enough to go alone, when it had to be taken in the arms of its mother from Seneca

Falls, N.Y., to Rochester, N.Y., for baptism. I then went along with it and offered my services to help it, for then it needed help; but now it can afford to dispense with me and all of my sex. Then its friends were few—now its friends are many. Then it was wrapped in obscurity—now it is lifted in sight of the whole civilized world, and people of all lands and languages give it their hearty support. Truly the change is vast and wonderful.

I though my eye of faith was tolerably clear when I attended those meetings in Seneca Falls and Rochester, but it was far too dim to see at the end of forty years a result so imposing as this International Council, and to see yourself (Elizabeth Cady Stanton) and Miss Anthony alive and active in its proceedings. Of course, I expected to be alive myself, and am not surprised to find myself so; for such is, perhaps, the presumption and arrogance common to my sex. Nevertheless, I am very glad to see you here today, and to see this great assembly of women. I am glad that you are its president. No manufactured "boom," or political contrivance, such as make presidents elsewhere, has made you president of this assembly of women in this Capital of the Nation. You hold your place by reason of eminent fitness, and I give you joy that your life and labors in the cause of woman are thus crowned with honor and glory. This I say in spite of the warning given us by Miss Anthony's friend against mutual admiration.

There may be some well-meaning people in this audience who have never attended a woman suffrage convention, never heard a woman suffrage speech, never read a woman suffrage newspaper, and they may be surprised that those who speak here do not argue the question. It may be kind to tell them that our cause has passed beyond the period of arguing. The demand of the hour is not argument, but assertion, firm and inflexible assertion, assertion which has more than the force of an argument. If there is any argument to be made, it must be made by opponents, not by the friends of woman suffrage. Let those who want argument examine the ground upon which they base their claim to the right to vote. They will find that there is not one reason, not one consideration, which they can urge in support of man's claim to vote, which does not equally support the right of woman to vote.

There is today, however, a special reason for omitting argument. This is the end of the fought decade of the woman suffrage movement, a kind of jubilee which naturally turns our minds to the past.

Ever since this Council has been in session, my thoughts have been reverting to the past. I have been thinking more or less, of the scene presented forty years ago in the little Methodist church at Seneca Falls, the manger in which this organized suffrage movement was born. It was very small thing then. It was not then big enough to be abused, or loud enough to make itself heard outside, and only a few of those who saw it had any notion that the little thing would live. I have been thinking, too, of the strong conviction, the noble courage, the sublime faith in God and man it required at that time to set this suffrage ball in motion. The history of the world has given to us many sublime undertakings, but none more sublime than this. It was a great thing for the friends of peace to organize in opposition to war; it was a great thing for the friends of temperance to organize against intemperance; it was a great thing for humane people to organize in opposition to slavery; but it was a much greater thing, in view of all the circumstances, for woman to organize herself in opposition to her exclusion from participation in government. The reason is obvious. War, intemperance and slavery are open, undisguised, palpable evils. The best feelings of human nature revolt at them. We could easily make men see the misery, the debasement, the terrible suffering caused by intemperance; we could easily make men see the desolation wrought by war and the hell-black horrors of chattel slavery; but the case was different in the movement for woman suffrage. Men took for granted all that could be said against intemperance, war and slavery. But no such advantage was found in the beginning of the cause of suffrage for women. On the contrary, everything in her condition was supposed to be lovely, just as it should be. She had no rights denied, no wrongs to redress. She herself had no suspicion but that all was going well with her. She floated along on the tide of life as her mother and grandmother had done before her, as in a dream of Paradise. Her wrongs, if she had any, were too occult to be seen, and too light to be felt. It required a daring voice and a determined hand to awake her from this delightful dream and call the nation to account for the rights and opportunities of which it was depriving her. It was well understood at the beginning that woman would not thank us for disturbing her by this call to duty, and it was known that man would denounce and scorn us for such a daring innovation upon the established order of things. But this did not appall or delay the word and work.

At this distance of time from that convention at Rochester, and in view of the present position of the question, it is hard to realize the moral courage it required to launch this unwelcome movement. Any man can be brave when the danger is over, go to the front when there is no resistance, rejoice when the battle is fought and the victory is won; but it is not so easy to venture upon a field untried with one-half the whole world against you, as these women did.

Then who were we, for I count myself in, who did this thing? We were few in numbers, moderate in resources, and very little known in the world. The most that we had to commend us was a firm conviction that we were in the right, and a firm faith that the right must ultimately prevail. But the case was well considered. Let no man imagine that the step was taken recklessly and thoughtlessly. Mrs. Stanton had dwelt upon it at least six years before she declared it in the Rochester convention. Walking with her from the house of Joseph and Thankful Southwick, two of the noblest people I ever knew, Mrs. Stanton, with an earnestness that I shall never forget, unfolded her view on this woman question precisely as she had in this Council. This was six and forty years ago, and it was not until six years after, that she ventured to make her formal, pronounced and startling demand for the ballot. She had, as I have said, considered well, and knew something of what would be the cost of the reform she was inaugurating. She knew the ridicule, the rivalry, the criticism and the bitter aspersions which she and her co-laborers would have to meet and to endure. But she saw more clearly than most of us that the vital point to be made prominent, and the one that included all others, was the ballot, and she bravely said the word. It was not only necessary to break the silence of woman and make her voice heard, but she must have a clear, palpable and comprehensive measure set before her, one worthy of her highest ambition and her best exertions, and hence the ballot was brought to the front.

There are few facts in my humble history to which I look back with more satisfaction than to the fact, recorded in the history of the woman-suffrage movement, that I was sufficiently enlightened at that early day, and when only a few years from slavery, to support your resolution for woman suffrage. I have done very little in this world in which to glory except this one act—and I certainly glory in that. When I ran away form slavery, it was for myself; when I advocated emancipation, it was for my people; but when I stood up for the rights of woman, self was out of the question, and I found a little nobility in the act.

In estimating the forces with which this suffrage cause has had to contend during these forty years, the fact should be remembered that relations of long standing beget a character in the parties to them in favor of their continuance. Time itself is a conservative power—a very conservative power. One shake of his hoary locks will sometimes paralyze the hand and palsy the tongue of the reformer. The relation of man to woman has the advantage tell us that what is always was and always will be, world without end. But we have heard this old argument before, and if we live very long we shall hear it again. When any aged error shall be assailed, and any old abuse is to be removed, we shall meet this same old argument. Man has been so long the king and woman the subject—man has been so long accustomed to command and woman to obey—that both parties to the relation have been hardened into their respective places, and thus has been piled up a mountain of iron against woman's enfranchisement.

The same thing confronted us in our conflicts with slavery. Long years ago Henry Clay said, on the floor of the American Senate, "I know there is a visionary dogma that man cannot hold property in man," and, with a brow of defiance, he said, "That is property which the law makes property. Two hundred years of legislation has sanctioned and sanctified Negro slaves as property." But neither the power of time nor the might of legislation has been able to keep life in that stupendous barbarism.

The universality of man's rule over woman is another factor in the resistance to the woman-suffrage movement. We are pointed to the fact that men have not only always ruled over women, but that they do so rule everywhere, and they easily think that a thing that is done everywhere must be right. Though the fallacy of this reasoning is too transparent to need refutation, it still exerts a powerful influence. Even our good Brother Jasper yet believes, with the ancient Church, that the sun "do move," notwithstanding all the astronomers of the world are against him. One year ago I stood on the Pincio in Rome and witnessed the unveiling of the statue of Galileo. It was an imposing sight. At no time before had Rome been free enough to permit such a statue to be placed within her walls. It is now there, not with the approval of the Vatican. No priest took part in the ceremonies. It was all the work of laymen. One or two priests passed the statue with averted eyes, but the great truths of the solar system were not angry at the sight, and the same will be true when woman shall be clothed, as she will yet be, with all the rights of American citizenship.

All good causes are mutually helpful. The benefits accruing from this movement for the equal rights of woman are not confined or limited to woman only. They will be shared by every effort to promote the progress and welfare of mankind everywhere and in all ages. It was an example and a prophecy of what can be accomplished against strongly opposing forces, against time-hallowed abuses, against deeply entrenched error, against worldwide usage, and against the settled judgment of mankind, by a few earnest women, clad only in the panoply of truth, and determined to live and die in what they considered a righteous cause.

I do not forget the thoughtful remark of our president in the opening address to this International Council, reminding us of the incompleteness of our work. The remark was wise and timely. Nevertheless, no man can compare the present with the past, the obstacles that then opposed us, and the influences that now favor us, the meeting in the little Methodist chapel forty years ago, and the Council in this vast theater today, without admitting that woman's cause is already a brilliant success. But, however this may be and whatever the future may have in store for us, one thing is certain—this new revolution in human thought will never go backward. When a great truth once gets abroad in the world, no power on earth can imprison it, or prescribe its limits, or suppress it. It is bound to go on till it becomes the thought of the world. Such a truth is woman's right to equal liberty with man. She was born with it. It was hers before she comprehended it. It is inscribed upon all the powers and faculties of her soul, and no custom, law or usage can ever destroy it. Now that it has got fairly fixed in the minds of the few, it is bound to become fixed in the minds of the many, and be supported at last by a great cloud of witnesses, which no man can number and no power can withstand.

The women who have thus far carried on this agitation have already embodied and illustrated Theodore Parker's three grades of human greatness. The first is greatness in executive and administrative ability; second, greatness in the ability to organize; and, thirdly, in the ability to discover truth. Wherever these three elements of power are combined in any movement, there is a reasonable ground to believe in its final success; and these elements of power have been manifest in the women who have had the movement in hand from the beginning. They are seen in the order which has characterized the proceedings of this Council. They are seen in the depth and are seen in the fervid eloquence and downright earnestness with which women advocate their cause. They are seen in the profound attention with which woman is heard in her own behalf. They are seen in the steady growth and onward march of the movement, and they will be seen in the final triumph of woman's cause, not only in this country, but throughout the world.

A Plea for the Oppressed

When I forget you, Oh my people, may my tongue cleave to the roof of my mouth, and may my right hand forget her cunning! Dark hover the clouds. The Anti-Slavery pulse beats faintly. The right of suffrage is denied. The colored man is still crushed by the weight of oppression. He may possess talents of the highest order, yet for him is no path of fame or distinction opened. He can never hope to attain those privileges while his brethren remain enslaved. Since, therefore, the freedom of the slave and the gaining of our rights, social and political, are inseparably connected, let all the friends of humanity plead for those who may not plead their own cause.

Reformers, ye who have labored long to convince man that happiness is found alone in doing good to others, that humanity is a unit, that he who injures one individual wrongs the race;—that to love one's neighbor as one's self is the sum of human virtue—ye that advocate the great principles of Temperance, Peace, and Moral Reform will you not raise your voice in behalf of these stricken ones!—will you not plead the cause of the Slave?

Slavery is the combination of all crime. It is War.

Those who rob their fellow-men of home, of liberty, of education, of life, are really at war against them as though they cleft them down upon the bloody field. It is intemperance; for there is an intoxication when the fierce passions rage in man's breast, more fearful than the madness of the drunkard, which if let loose upon the moral universe would sweep away everything pure and holy, leaving but the wreck of man's nobler nature. Such passions does Slavery foster—yea, they are a part of herself. It is full of pollution. Know you not that to a slave, virtue is a sin counted worthy of death? That many, true to the light within, notwithstanding the attempts to shut out the truth, feeling that a consciousness of purity is dearer than life, have nobly died? Their blood crieth to God, a witness against the oppressor.

Statesmen, you who have bent at ambition's shrine, who would leave your names on the page of history, to be venerated by coming generations as among those of the great and good, will you advocate the cause of the down-trodden, remembering that the spirit of liberty is abroad in the land? The precious seed is sown in the heart of the people, and though the fruit does not appear, the germ is there, and the harvest will yet be gathered. Truly is this an age of reform. The world is going on, not indeed keeping pace with the rapid tread of its leaders, but none the less progressing. As the people take a step in one reform, the way is prepared for another. Now while other evils in man's social and political condition are being remedied, think you that Slavery can stand the searching test—an enlightened people's sense of justice? Then speak the truth boldly; fear not loss of property or station. It is a higher honor to embalm your name in the hearts of a grateful people than to contend for the paltry honors of party preferment.

Woman, I turn to thee. Is it not thy mission to visit the poor? To shed the tear of sympathy? To relieve the wants of the suffering? Where wilt thou find objects more needing sympathy than among the slaves!

Mother, hast thou a precious gem in thy charge, like those that make up the Savior's jewels? Has thy heart, trembling with its unutterable joyousness, bent before the throne of the Giver with the prayer that thy child might be found in his courts? Thou hast seen the dawning of intelligence in its bright eye, and watched with interest the unfolding of its powers. Its gentle, winning ways have doubly endeared it to thee. Death breathes upon the flower, and it is gone. Now thou canst feel for the slave-mother who has bent with the same interest over her child, whose heart is entwined around it even more firmly than thine own around thine, for to her it is the only ray of joy in a dreary world. She returns weary and sick at heart from the labors of the field; the child's beaming smile of welcome half banishes the misery of her lot. Would she not die for it? Ye who know the depths of a mother's love, answer! Hark! Strange footsteps are near her dwelling! The door is thrown rudely open! Her master says—"There is the woman!" She comprehends it all—she is sold! From her trembling lips escape the words—"my child!" She throws herself at the feet of those merciless men, and pleads permission to keep her babe, but in vain. What is she more than any other slave, that she should be permitted this favor? They are separated.

Sister, have you ever had a kind and loving brother? How often would he lay aside his book to relieve you from some difficulty? How have you hung upon the words of wisdom that he has uttered? How earnestly have you studied that you might stand his companion—his equal. You saw him suddenly stricken by the destroyer. Oh! How your heart ached!

There was a slave-girl who had a brother kind and noble as your own. He had scarcely any advantages: yet stealthily would he draw an old volume from his pocket, and through the long night would pore over its contents. His soul thirsted for knowledge. He yearned for freedom, but free-soil was far away. That sister might not go, he staid with her. They say that slaves do not feel for or love each other; I fear that there are few brothers with a pale face who would have stood that test. For her he tamed the fire of his eye, toiled for that which profited him not, and labored so industriously that the overseer had no apology for applying the lash to his back. Time passed on: that brother stood in his manhood's prime as tenderly kind and as dearly beloved as ever. That sister was insulted;—the lash was applied to her quivering back; her brother rushed to save her! He tore away the fastenings which bound her to the whipping post, he held her on his arm—she was safe. She looked up, encountered the ferocious gaze of the overseer, heard the report of a pistol, and felt the heart's blood of a brother gushing over her. But we draw the veil.

Mother, sister, by thy own deep sorrow of heart; by the sympathy of thy woman's nature, plead for the downtrodden of thy own, of every land. Instill the principles of love, of common brotherhood, in the nursery, in the social circle. Let these be the prayer of thy life.

Christians, you whose souls are filled with love for your fellow men, whose prayer to the Lord is, "Oh! that I may see thy salvation among the children of men!" Does the battle wax warm? dost thou faint with the burden and heat of the day? Yet a little longer; the arm of the Lord is mighty to save those who trust in him. Truth and right must prevail. The bondsman shall go free. Look to the future! Hark! the shout of joy gushes from the heart of earth's freed millions! It rushes upward. The angels on heaven's outward battlements catch the sound on their golden lyres, and send it thrilling through the echoing arches of the upper world. How sweet, how majestic, from those starry isles float those deep inspiring sounds over the ocean of space! Softened and mellowed they reach earth, filing the soul with harmony, and breathing of God— of love—and of universal freedom.

I Won't Obey the Fugitive Slave Law

I was a slave; I knew the dangers I was exposed to. I had made up my mind as to the course I was to take. On that score I needed no counsel, nor did the colored citizens generally. They had taken their stand—they would not be taken back to slavery. If to shoot down their assailants should forfeit their lives, such result was the least of the evil. They will have their liberties or die in their defense. What is life to me if I am to be a slave in Tennessee? My neighbors! I have lived with you many years, and you know me. My home is here, and my children were born here. I am bound to Syracuse by pecuniary interests, and social and family bonds. And do you think I can be taken away from you and from my wife and children, and be a slave in Tennessee? Has the President and his Secretary sent this enactment up here, to you, Mr. Chairman, to enforce on me in Syracuse?—and will you obey him? Did I think so meanly of you—did I suppose the people of Syracuse, strong as they are in numbers and love of liberty—or did I believe their love of liberty was so selfish, unmanly and unchristian—did I believe them so sunken and servile and degraded as to remain at their homes and labors, or, with none of that spirit which smites a tyrant down, to surround a United States Marshal to see me torn from my home and family, and hurled back to bondage—I say did I think so meanly of you, I could never come to live with you. Nor should I have stopped, on my return from Troy, twenty-four hours since, but to take my family and movables to a neighborhood which would take fire, and arms, too, to resist the least attempt to execute this diabolical law among them. Some kind and good friends advise me to quit my country, and stay in Canada, until this tempest is passed. I doubt not the sincerity of such counsellors. But my conviction is strong, that their advice comes from a lack of knowledge of themselves and the case in hand. I believe that their own bosoms are charged to the brim with qualities that will smite to the earth the villains who may interfere to enslave any man in Syracuse. I apprehend the advice is suggested by the perturbation of the moment, and not by the tranquil spirit that rules above the storm, in the eternal home of truth and wisdom. Therefore I have hesitated to adopt this advice, at least until I have the opinion of this meeting. Those friends have not canvassed this subject. I have. They are called suddenly to look at it. I have looked at it steadily, calmly, resolutely, and at length defiantly, for a long time. I tell you the people of Syracuse and of the whole North must meet this tyranny and crush it by force, or be crushed by it. This hellish enactment has precipitated the conclusion that white men must live in dishonorable submission, and colored men be slaves, or they must give their physical as well as intellectual powers to the defense of human rights. The time has come to change the tones of submission into tones of defiance,—and to tell Mr. Fillmore and Mr. Webster, if they propose to execute this measure upon us, to send on their bloodhounds. Mr. President, long ago I was beset by over-prudent and good men and women to purchase my freedom. Nay, I was frequently importuned to consent that they purchase it, and present it as evidence of their partiality to my person and character. Generous and kind as those friends were, my heart recoiled from the proposal. I owe my freedom to the God who made me, and who stirred me to claim it against all other beings in God's universe. I will not, nor will I consent, that anybody else shall countenance the claims of a vulgar despot to my soul and body. Were I in chains, and did these kind people come to buy me out of prison, I would acknowledge the boon with inexpressible thankfulness. But I feel no chains, and am in no prison. I received my freedom from Heaven, and with it came the command to defend my title to it. I have long since resolved to do nothing and suffer nothing that can, in any way, imply that I am indebted to any power but the Almighty for my manhood and personality.

Now, you are assembled here, the strength of this city is here to express their sense of this fugitive act, and to proclaim to the despots at Washington whether it shall be enforced here—whether you will permit the government to return me and other fugitives who have sought asylum among you, to the Hell of slavery. The question is with you. If you will give us up, say so, and we will shake the dust from our feet and leave you. But we believe better things. We know you are taken by surprise. The immensity of this meeting testifies to the general consternation that has brought it together, necessarily, precipitately, to decide the most stirring question that can be presented, to wit, whether, the government having transgressed Constitutional and natural limits, you will bravely resist its aggressions, and tell its soulless agents that no slaveholder shall make your city and county a hunting field for slaves.

Whatever may be your decision, my ground is taken. I have declared it everywhere. It is known over the state and out of the state—over the line in the North, and over the line in the South. I don't respect this law—I don't fear it—I won't obey it! It outlaws me, and I outlaw it, and the men who attempt to enforce it on me. I place the governmental officials on the ground that they place me. I will not live a slave, and if force is employed to reenslave me, I shall make preparations to meet the crisis as becomes a man. If you will stand by me—and I believe you will do it, for your freedom and honor are involved as well as mine—it requires no microscope to see that—I say if you will stand with us in resistance to this measure, you will be the saviors of your country. Your decision tonight in favor of resistance will give vent to the spirit of liberty, and it will break the bands of party, and shout for joy all over the North. Your example only is needed to be the type of popular action in Auburn, and Rochester, and Utica, and Buffalo, and all the West, and eventually in the Atlantic cities. Heaven knows that this act of noble daring will break out somewhere—and may God grant that Syracuse be the honored spot, whence it shall send an earthquake voice through the land!

Ar'nt I a Woman?

Well, children, where there is so much racket there must be something out of kilter. I think that 'twixt the negroes of the South and the women at the North, all talking about rights, the white men will be in a fix pretty soon. But what's all this here talking about?

That man over there says women need to be helped into carriages, and lifted over ditches, and to have the best place everywhere. Nobody ever helps me into carriages, or over mud-puddles, or gives me any best place! And arn't I a woman? Look at me! Look at my arm! I have ploughed, and planted, and gathered into barns, and no man could head me! And arn't I woman? I could work as much and eat as much as a man—when I could get it—and bear the lash as well! And arn't I a woman? I have borne thirteen children, and seen them most all sold off to slavery, and when I cried out with my mother's grief, none but Jesus heard me! And aren't I a woman?

Then they talk about this thing in the head; what's this they call it? ("Intellect," whispered someone near.) That's it, honey. What's that got to do with women's rights or negro rights? If my cup won't hold but a pint, and yours holds a quart, wouldn't you be mean not to let me have my little half-measure full? Then that little man in black there, he says women can't have as much rights as men, because Christ wasn't a woman! Where did your Christ come from? From God and a woman! Man had nothing to do with Him. . .

If the first woman God ever made was strong enough to turn the world upside down all alone, these women together ought to be able to turn it back, and get it right side up again! And now they are asking to do it, the men better let them.

What, To the Slave, Is the Fourth of July?

Mr. President, Friends and Fellow Citizens: He who could address this audience without a quailing sensation, has stronger nerves than I have. I do not remember ever to have appeared as a speaker before any assembly more shrinkingly, nor with greater distrust of my ability, than I do this day. A feeling has crept over me, quite unfavorable to the exercise of my limited powers of speech. The task before me is one which requires much previous thought and study for its proper performance. I know that apologies of this sort are generally considered flat and unmeaning. I trust, however, that mine will not be so considered. Should I seem at ease, my appearance would much misrepresent me. The little experience I have had in addressing public meetings, in country schoolhouses, avails me nothing on the present occasion.

The papers and placards say, that I am to deliver a 4th (of) July oration. This certainly sounds large, and out of the common way, for it is true that I have often had the privilege to speak in this beautiful Hall, and to address many who now honor me with their presence. But neither their familiar faces, nor the perfect gage I think I have of Corinthian Hall, seems to free me from embarrassment.

The fact is, ladies and gentlemen, the distance between this platform and the slave plantation, from which I escaped, is considerable—and the difficulties to be overcome in getting from the latter to the former, are by no means slight. That I am here today is, to me, a matter of astonishment as well as of gratitude. You will not, therefore, be surprised, if in what I have to say, I evince no elaborate preparation, nor grace my speech with any high sounding exordium. With little experience and with less learning, I have been able to throw my thoughts hastily and imperfectly together; and trusting to your patient and generous indulgence, I will proceed to lay them before you.

This, for the purpose of this celebration, is the 4th of July. It is the birthday of your National Independence, and of your political freedom. This, to you, is what the Passover was to the emancipated people of God. It carries your minds back to the day, and to the act of your great deliverance; and to the signs, and to the wonders, associated with that act, and that day. This celebration also marks the beginning of another year of your national life; and reminds you that the Republic of America is now 76 years old. I am glad, fellow-citizens, that your nation is so young. Seventy-six years, though a good old age for a man, is but a mere speck in the life of a nation. Three score years and ten is the allotted time for individual men; but nations number their years by thousands. According to this fact, you are, even now, only in the beginning of your national career, still lingering in the period of childhood. I repeat, I am glad this is so. There is hope in the thought, and hope is much needed, under the dark clouds which lower above the horizon. The eye of the reformer is met with angry flashes, portending disastrous times; but his heart may well beat lighter at the thought that America is young, and that she is still in the impressible stage of her existence. May he not hope that high lessons of wisdom, of justice and of truth, will yet give direction to her destiny? Were the nation older, the patriot's heart might be sadder, and the reformer's brow heavier. Its future might be shrouded in gloom, and the hope of its prophets go out in sorrow. There is consolation in the thought that America is young. Great streams are not easily turned from channels, worn deep in the course of ages. They may sometimes rise in quiet and stately majesty, and inundate the land, refreshing and fertilizing the earth with their mysterious properties. They may also rise in wrath and fury, and bear away, on their angry waves, the accumulated wealth of years of toil and hardship. They, however, gradually flow back to the same old channel, and flow on as serenely as ever. But, while the river may not be turned aside, it may dry up, and leave nothing behind but the withered branch, and the unsightly rock, to howl in the abyss-sweeping wind, the sad tale of departed glory. As with rivers so with nations.

Fellow-citizens, I shall not presume to dwell at length on the associations that cluster about this day. The simple story of it is that, 76 years ago, the people of this country were British subjects. The style and title of your "sovereign people" (in which you now glory) was not then born. You were under the British Crown. Your fathers esteemed the English Government as the home government; and England as the fatherland. This home government, you know, although a considerable distance from your home, did, in the exercise of its parental prerogatives, impose upon its colonial children, such restraints, burdens and limitations, as, in its mature judgment, it deemed wise, right and proper.

But, your fathers, who had not adopted the fashionable idea of this day, of the infallibility of government, and the absolute character of its acts, presumed to differ from the home government in respect to the wisdom and the justice of some of those burdens and restraints. They went so far in their excitement as to pronounce the measures of government unjust, unreasonable, and oppressive, and altogether such as ought not to be quietly submitted to. I scarcely need say, fellow citizens, that my opinion of those measures fully accords with that of your fathers. Such a declaration of agreement on my part would not be worth much to anybody. It would, certainly, prove nothing, as to what part I might have taken, had I lived during the great controversy of 1776. To say now that America was right, and England wrong, is exceedingly easy. Everybody can say it; the dastard, not less than the noble brave, can flippantly discant on the tyranny of England towards the American Colonies. It is fashionable to do so; but there was a time when to pronounce against England, and in favor of the cause of the colonies, tried men's souls. They who did so were accounted in their day, plotters of mischief, agitators and rebels, dangerous men. To side with the right, against the wrong, with the weak against the strong, and with the oppressed against the oppressor! here lies the merit, and the one which, of all others, seems unfashionable in our day. The cause of liberty may be stabbed by the men who glory in the deeds of your fathers. But, to proceed.

Feeling themselves harshly and unjustly treated by the home government, your fathers, like men of honesty, and men of spirit, earnestly sought redress. They petitioned and remonstrated; they did so in a decorous, respectful, and loyal manner. Their conduct was wholly unexceptionable. This, however, did not answer the purpose. They saw themselves treated with sovereign indifference, coldness and scorn. Yet they persevered. They were not the men to look back.

As the sheet anchor takes a firmer hold, when the ship is tossed by the storm, so did the cause of your fathers grow stronger, as it breasted the chilling blasts of kingly displeasure. The greatest and best of British statesmen admitted its justice, and the loftiest eloquence of the British Senate came to its support. But, with that blindness which seems to be the unvarying characteristic of tyrants, since Pharaoh and his hosts were drowned in the Red Sea, the British Government persisted in the exactions complained of.

The madness of this course, we believe, is admitted now, even by England; but we fear the lesson is wholly lost on our present ruler.

Oppression makes a wise man mad. Your fathers were wise men, and if they did not go mad, they became restive under this treatment.

They felt themselves the victims of grievous wrongs, wholly incurable in their colonial capacity. With brave men there is always a remedy for oppression. Just here, the idea of a total separation of the colonies from the crown was born! It was a startling idea, much more so, than we, at this distance of time, regard it. The timid and the prudent (as has been intimated) of that day, were, of course, shocked and alarmed by it. Such people lived then, had lived before, and will, probably, ever have a place on this planet; and their course, in respect to any great change, (no matter how great the good to be attained, or the wrong to be redressed by it), may be calculated with as much precision as can be the course of the stars. They hate all changes, but silver, gold and copper change! Of this sort of change they are always strongly in favor.

These people were called Tories in the days of your fathers; and the appellation, probably, conveyed the same idea that is meant by a more modern, though a somewhat less euphonious term, which we often find in our papers, applied to some of our old politicians.

Their opposition to the then dangerous thought was earnest and powerful; but, amid all their terror and affrighted vociferations against it, the alarming and revolutionary idea moved on, and the country with it.

On the second of July, 1776, the old Continental Congress, to the dismay of the lovers of ease, and the worshipers of property, clothed that dreadful idea with all the authority of national sanction. They did so in the form of a resolution; and as we seldom hit upon resolutions, drawn up in our day whose transparency is at all equal to this, it may refresh your minds and help my story if I read it.

(We) solemnly publish and declare, that these United Colonies are, and of right, ought to be free and Independent States; that they are Absolved from all Allegiance to the British Crown; and that all political connection between them and the State of Great Britain is and ought to be (totally) dissolved.

Citizens, your fathers made good that resolution. They succeeded; and today you reap the fruits of their success. The freedom gained is yours; and you, therefore, may properly celebrate this anniversary. The 4th of July is the first great fact in your nation's history—the very ring—bolt in the chain of your yet undeveloped destiny.

Pride and patriotism, not less than gratitude, prompt you to celebrate and to hold it in perpetual remembrance. I have said that the Declaration of Independence is the ring-bolt to the chain of your nation's destiny; so, indeed, I regard it. The principles contained in that instrument are saving principles. Stand by those principles, be true to them on all occasions, in all places, against all foes, and at whatever cost.

From the round top of your ship of state, dark and threatening clouds may be seen. Heavy billows, like mountains in the distance, disclose to the leeward huge forms of flinty rocks! That bolt drawn, that chain broken, and all is lost. Cling to this day—cling to it, and to its principles, with the grasp of a storm-tossed mariner to a spar at midnight.

The coming into being of a nation, in any circumstances, is an interesting event. But, besides general considerations, there were peculiar circumstances which make the advent of this republic an event of special attractiveness.

The whole scene, as I look back to it, was simple, dignified and sublime.

The population of the country, at the time, stood at the insignificant number of three millions. The country was poor in the munitions of war. The population was weak and scattered, and the country a wilderness unsubdued. There were then no means of concert and combination, such as exist now. Neither steam nor lightning had then been reduced to order and discipline. From the Potomac to the Delaware was a journey of many days. Under these, and innumerable other disadvantages, your fathers declared for liberty and independence and triumphed.

Fellow Citizens, I am not wanting in respect for the fathers of this republic. The signers of the Declaration of Independence were brave men. They were great men too—great enough to give fame to a great age. It does not often happen to a nation to raise, at one time, such a number of truly great men. The point from which I am compelled to view them is not, certainly, the most favorable; and yet I cannot contemplate their great deeds with less than admiration. They were statesmen, patriots and heroes, and for the good they did, and the principles they contended for, I will unite with you to honor their memory.

They loved their country better than their own private interests; and, though this is not the highest form of human excellence, all will concede that it is a rare virtue, and that when it is exhibited, it ought to command respect. He who will, intelligently, lay down his life for his country, is a man whom it is not in human nature to despise. Your fathers staked their lives, their fortunes, and their sacred honor, on the cause of their country. In their admiration of liberty, they lost sight of all other interests.

They were peace men; but they preferred revolution to peaceful submission to bondage. They were quiet men; but they did not shrink from agitating against oppression. They showed forbearance; but that they knew its limits. They believed in order; but not in the order of tyranny. With them, nothing was "settled" that was not right. With them, justice, liberty and humanity were "final;" not slavery and oppression. You may well cherish the memory of such men. They were great in their day and generation. Their solid manhood stands out the more as we contrast it with these degenerate times.

How circumspect, exact and proportionate were all their movements! How unlike the politicians of an hour! Their statesmanship looked beyond the passing moment, and stretched away in strength into the distant future. They seized upon eternal principles, and set a glorious example in their defense. Mark them!

Fully appreciating the hardship to be encountered, firmly believing in the right of their cause, honorably inviting the scrutiny of an on-looking world, reverently appealing to heaven to attest their sincerity, soundly comprehending the solemn responsibility they were about to assume, wisely measuring the terrible odds against them, your fathers, the fathers of this republic, did, most deliberately, under the inspiration of a glorious patriotism, and with a sublime faith in the great principles of justice and freedom, lay deep the corner-stone of the national superstructure, which has risen and still rises in grandeur around you.

Of this fundamental work, this day is the anniversary. Our eyes are met with demonstrations of joyous enthusiasm. Banners and pennants wave exultingly on the breeze. The din of business, too, is hushed. Even Mammon seems to have quitted his grasp on this day. The ear-piercing fife and the stirring drum unite their accents with the ascending peal of a thousand church bells. Prayers are made, hymns are sung, and sermons are preached in honor of this day; while the quick martial tramp of a great and multitudinous nation, echoed back by all the hills, valleys and mountains of a vast continent, bespeak the occasion one of thrilling and universal interests nation's jubilee.

Friends and citizens, I need not enter further into the causes which led to this anniversary. Many of you understand them better than I do. You could instruct me in regard to them. That is a branch of knowledge in which you feel, perhaps, a much deeper interest than your speaker. The causes which led to the separation of the colonies from the British crown have never lacked for a tongue. They have all been taught in your common schools, narrated at your firesides, unfolded from your pulpits, and thundered from your legislative halls, and are as familiar to you as household words. They form the staple of your national poetry and eloquence.

I remember also that as a people Americans are remarkably familiar with all facts which make in their own favor. This is esteemed by some as a national trait—perhaps a national weakness. It is a fact, that whatever makes for the wealth or for the reputation of Americans, and can be had cheap will be found by Americans. I shall not be charged with slandering Americans if I say I think the American side of any question may be safely left in American hands.

I leave, therefore, the great deeds of your fathers to other gentlemen whose claim to have been regularly descended will be less likely to be disputed than mine!

My business, if I have any here today, is with the present. The accepted time with God and his cause is the ever-living now.

Trust no future, however pleasant, Let the dead past bury its dead; Act, act in the living present, Heart within, and God overhead.

We have to do with the past only as we can make it useful to the present and to the future. To all inspiring motives, to noble deeds which can be gained from the past, we are welcome. But now is the time, the important time. Your fathers have lived, died, and have done their work, and have done much of it well. You live and must die, and you must do your work. You have no right to enjoy a child's share in the labor of your fathers, unless your children are to be blest by your labors. You have no right to wear out and waste the hard-earned fame of your fathers to cover your indolence. Sydney Smith tells us that men seldom eulogize the wisdom and virtues of their fathers, but to excuse some folly or wickedness of their own. This truth is not a doubtful one. There are illustrations of it near and remote, ancient and modern. It was fashionable, hundreds of years ago, for the children of Jacob to boast, we have "Abraham to our father," when they had long lost Abraham's faith and spirit. That people contented themselves under the shadow of Abraham's great name, while they repudiated the deeds which made his name great. Need I remind you that a similar thing is being done all over this country today? Need I tell you that the Jews are not the only people who built the tombs of the prophets, and garnished the sepulchres of the righteous? Washington could not die till he had broken the chains of his slaves. Yet his monument is built up by the price of human blood, and the traders in the bodies and souls of men, shout—"We have Washington to our father."—Alas! that it should be so; yet so it is.

The evil that men do, lives after them, The good is oft interred with their bones.

Fellow-citizens, pardon me, allow me to ask, why am I called upon to speak here today? What have I, or those I represent, to do with your national independence? Are the great principles of political freedom and of natural justice, embodied in that Declaration of Independence, extended to us? and am I, therefore, called upon to bring our humble offering to the national altar, and to confess the benefits and express devout gratitude for the blessings resulting from your independence to us?

Would to God, both for your sakes and ours, that an affirmative answer could be truthfully returned to these questions! Then would my task be light, and my burden easy and delightful. For who is there so cold, that a nation's sympathy could not warm him? Who so obdurate and dead to the claims of gratitude, that would not thankfully acknowledge such priceless benefits? Who so stolid and selfish, that would not give his voice to swell the hallelujahs of a nation's jubilee, when the chains of servitude had been torn from his limbs? I am not that man. In a case like that, the dumb might eloquently speak, and the "lame man leap as an hart."

But, such is not the state of the case. I say it with a sad sense of the disparity between us. I am not included within the pale of this glorious anniversary! Your high independence only reveals the immeasurable distance between us. The blessings in which you, this day, rejoice, are not enjoyed in common. The rich inheritance of justice, liberty, prosperity and independence, bequeathed by your fathers, is shared by you, not by me. The sunlight that brought life and healing to you, has brought stripes and death to me. This Fourth of July is yours, not mine. You may rejoice, I must mourn. To drag a man in fetters into the grand illuminated temple of liberty, and call upon him to join you in joyous anthems, were inhuman mockery and sacrilegious irony. Do you mean, citizens, to mock me, by asking me to speak today? If so, there is a parallel to your conduct. And let me warn you that it is dangerous to copy the example of a nation whose crimes, lowering up to heaven, were thrown down by the breath of the Almighty, burying that nation in irrecoverable ruin! I can today take up the plaintive lament of a peeled and woe-smitten people!

"By the rivers of Babylon, there we sat down. Yea! we wept when we remembered Zion. We hanged our harps upon the willows in the midst thereof. For there, they that carried us away captive, required of us a song; and they who wasted us required of us mirth, saying, Sing us one of the songs of Zion. How can we sing the Lord's song in a strange land? If I forget thee, O Jerusalem, let my right hand forget her cunning. If I do not remember thee, let my tongue cleave to the roof of my mouth."

Fellow-citizens; above your national, tumultuous joy, I hear the mournful wail of millions! whose chains, heavy and grievous yesterday, are, today, rendered more intolerable by the jubilee shouts that reach them. If I do forget, if I do not faithfully remember those bleeding children of sorrow this day, "may my right hand forget her cunning, and may my tongue cleave to the roof of my mouth!" To forget them, to pass lightly over their wrongs, and to chime in with the popular theme, would be treason most scandalous and shocking, and would make me a reproach before God and the world. My subject, then fellow-citizens, is American slavery. I shall see, this day, and its popular characteristics, from the slave's point of view. Standing, there, identified with the American bondman, making his wrongs mine, I do not hesitate to declare, with all my soul, that the character and conduct of this nation never looked blacker to me than on this 4th of July! Whether we turn to the declarations of the past, or to the professions of the present, the conduct of the nation seems equally hideous and revolting.

America is false to the past, false to the present, and solemnly binds herself to be false to the future.

Standing with God and the crushed and bleeding slave on this occasion, I will, in the name of humanity which is outraged, in the name of liberty which is fettered, in the name of the constitution and the Bible, which are disregarded and trampled upon, dare to call in question and to denounce, with all the emphasis I can command, everything that serves to perpetuate slavery—the great sin and shame of America! "I will not equivocate; I will not excuse;" I will use the severest language I can command; and yet not one word shall escape me that any man, whose judgment is not blinded by prejudice, or who is not at heart a slaveholder, shall not confess to be fight and just.

But I fancy I hear some one of my audience say, it is just in this circumstance that you and your brother abolitionists fail to make a favorable impression on the public mind. Would you argue more, and denounce less, would you persuade more, and rebuke less, your cause would be much more likely to succeed.

But, I submit, where all is plain there is nothing to be argued. What point in the anti-slavery creed would you have me argue? On what branch of the subject do the people of this country need light? Must I undertake to prove that the slave is a man? That point is conceded already. Nobody doubts it. The slaveholders themselves acknowledge it in the enactment of laws for their government. They acknowledge it when they punish disobedience on the part of the slave. There are seventy-two crimes in the State of Virginia, which, if committed by a black man, (no matter how ignorant he be), subject him to the punishment of death; while only two of the same crimes will subject a white man to the like punishment. What is this but the acknowledgement that the slave is a moral, intellectual and responsible being? The manhood of the slave is conceded.

It is admitted in the fact that Southern statute books are covered with enactments forbidding, under severe fines and penalties, the teaching of the slave to read or to write. When you can point to any such laws, in reference to the beasts of the field, then I may consent to argue the manhood of the slave. When the dogs in your streets, when the fowls of the air, when the cattle on your hills, when the fish of the sea, and the reptiles that crawl, shall be unable to distinguish the slave from a brute, their will I argue with you that the slave is a man!

For the present, it is enough to affirm the equal manhood of the Negro race. Is it not astonishing that, while we are ploughing, planting and reaping, using all kinds of mechanical tools, erecting houses, constructing bridges, building ships, working in metals of brass, iron, copper, silver and gold; that, while we are reading, writing and cyphering, acting as clerks, merchants and secretaries, having among us lawyers, doctors, ministers, poets, authors, editors, orators and teachers; that, while we are engaged in all manner of enterprises common to other men, digging gold in California, capturing the whale in the Pacific, feeding sheep and cattle on the hill-side, living, moving, acting, thinking, planning, living in families as husbands, wives and children, and, above all, confessing and worshipping the Christian's God, and looking hopefully for life and immortality beyond the grave, we are called upon to prove that we are men!

Would you have me argue that man is entitled to liberty? That he is the rightful owner of his own body? You have already declared it. Must

I argue the wrongfulness of slavery? Is that a question for Republicans? Is it to be settled by the rules of logic and argumentation, as a matter beset with great difficulty, involving a doubtful application of the principle of justice, hard to be understood? How should I look today, in the presence of Americans, dividing, and subdividing a discourse, to show that men have a natural right to freedom? speaking of it relatively, and positively, negatively, and affirmatively. To do so, would be to make myself ridiculous, and to offer an insult to your understanding. There is not a man beneath the canopy of heaven, that does not know that slavery is wrong for him.

What, am I to argue that it is wrong to make men brutes, to rob them of their liberty, to work them without wages, to keep them ignorant of their relations to their fellow men, to beat them with sticks, to flay their flesh with the lash, to load their limbs with irons, to hunt them with dogs, to sell them at auction, to sunder their families, to knock out their teeth, to bum their flesh, to starve them into obedience and submission to their masters? Must I argue that a system thus marked with blood and stained with pollution is wrong? No! I will not. I have better employments for my time and strength than such arguments would imply.

What, then, remains to be argued? Is it that slavery is not divine; that God did not establish it; that our doctors of divinity are mistaken? There is blasphemy in the thought. That which is inhuman, cannot be divine! Who can reason on such a proposition? They that can, may; I cannot. The time for such argument is past.

At a time like this, scorching irony, not convincing argument, is needed. O! had I the ability, and could I reach the nation's ear, I would, today, pour out a fiery stream of biting ridicule, blasting reproach, withering sarcasm, and stern rebuke. For it is not light that is needed, but fire; it is not the gentle shower, but thunder. We need the storm, the whirlwind, and the earthquake. The feeling of the nation must be quickened; the conscience of the nation must be roused; the propriety of the nation must be startled; the hypocrisy of the nation must be exposed; and its crimes against God and man must be proclaimed and denounced.

What, to the American slave, is your Fourth of July? I answer: a day that reveals to him, more than all other days in the year, the gross injustice and cruelly to which he is the constant victim. To him, your celebration is a sham; your boasted liberty, an unholy license; your national greatness, swelling vanity; your sounds of rejoicing are empty and heartless; your denunciations of tyrants, brass fronted impudence; your shouts of liberty and equality, hollow mockery; your prayers and hymns, your sermons and thanksgivings, with all your religious parade, and solemnity, are, to him, mere bombast, fraud, deception, impiety, and hypocrisy—a thin veil to cover up crimes which would disgrace a nation of savages. There is not a nation on the earth guilty of practices, more shocking and bloody, than are the people of these United States, at this very hour.

Go where you may, search where you will, roam through all the monarchies and despotisms of the old world, travel through South America, search out every abuse, and when you have found the last, lay your facts by the side of the everyday practices of this nation, and you will say with me, that, for revolting barbarity and shameless hypocrisy, America reigns without a rival. Take the American slave-trade, which, we are told by the papers, is especially prosperous just now. Ex-Senator Benton tells us that the price of men was never higher than now. He mentions the fact to show that slavery is in no danger. This trade is one of the peculiarities of American institutions. It is carried on in all the large towns and cities in one-half of this confederacy; and millions are pocketed every year, by dealers in this horrid traffic. In several states, this trade is a chief source of wealth. It is called (in contradistinction to the foreign slave-trade) "the internal slave trade." It is, probably, called so, too, in order to divert from it the horror with which the foreign slave-trade is contemplated. That trade has long since been denounced by this government, as piracy. It has been denounced with burning words, from the high places of the nation, as an execrable traffic. To arrest it, to put an end to it, this nation keeps a squadron, at immense cost, on the coast of Africa. Everywhere, in this country, it is safe to speak of this foreign slave-trade, as a most inhuman traffic, opposed alike to the laws of God and of man. The duty to extirpate and destroy it, is admitted even by our doctors of divinity. In order to put an end to it, some of these last have consented that their colored brethren (nominally free) should leave this country, and establish themselves on the western coast of Africa! It is, however, a notable fact that, while so much execration is poured out by Americans upon those engaged in the foreign slave-trade, the men engaged in the slave-trade between the states pass without condemnation, and their business is deemed honorable.

Behold the practical operation of this internal slave-trade, the American slave-trade, sustained by American politics and America religion. Here you will see men and women reared like swine for the market. You know what is a swine-drover? I will show you a man-drover. They inhabit all our Southern States. They perambulate the country, and crowd the highways of the nation, with droves of human stock. You will see one of these human flesh-jobbers, armed with pistol, whip and bowie-knife, driving a company of a hundred men, women, and children, from the Potomac to the slave market at New Orleans. These wretched people are to be sold singly, or in lots, to suit purchasers. They are food for the cotton-field, and the deadly sugar-mill. Mark the sad procession, as it moves wearily along, and the inhuman wretch who drives them. Hear his savage yells and his blood-chilling oaths, as he hurries on his affrighted captives! There, see the old man, with locks thinned and gray. Cast one glance, if you please, upon that young mother, whose shoulders are bare to the scorching sun, her briny tears falling on the brow of the babe in her arms. See, too, that girl of thirteen, weeping, yes! weeping, as she thinks of the mother from whom she has been torn! The drove moves tardily. Heat and sorrow have nearly consumed their strength; suddenly you hear a quick snap, like the discharge of a rifle; the fetters clank, and the chain rattles simultaneously; your ears are saluted with a scream, that seems to have torn its way to the center of your soul! The crack you heard, was the sound of the slave-whip; the scream you heard, was from the woman you saw with the babe. Her speed had faltered under the weight of her child and her chains! that gash on her shoulder tells her to move on. Follow the drove to New Orleans. Attend the auction; see men examined like horses; see the forms of women rudely and brutally exposed to the shocking gaze of American slave-buyers. See this drove sold and separated forever; and never forget the deep, sad sobs that arose from that scattered multitude. Tell me citizens, where, under the sun, you can witness a spectacle more fiendish and shocking. Yet this is but a glance at the American slave-trade, as it exists, at this moment, in the ruling part of the United States.

I was born amid such sights and scenes. To me the American slave-trade is a terrible reality. When a child, my soul was often pierced with a sense of its horrors. I lived on Philpot Street, Fell's Point, Baltimore, and have watched from the wharves, the slave ships in the Basin, anchored from the shore, with their cargoes of human flesh, waiting for favorable winds to waft them down the Chesapeake. There was, at that time, a grand slave mart kept at the head of Pratt Street, by Austin Woldfolk. His agents were sent into every town and county in Maryland, announcing their arrival, through the papers, and on flaming hand-bills headed "Cash for Negroes." These men were generally well dressed men, and very captivating in their manners. Ever ready to drink, to treat, and to gamble. The fate of many a slave has depended upon the turn of a single card; and many a child has been snatched from the arms of its mother by bargains arranged in a state of brutal drunkenness.

The flesh-mongers gather up their victims by dozens, and drive them, chained, to the general depot at Baltimore. When a sufficient number have been collected here, a ship is chartered, for the purpose of conveying the forlorn crew to Mobile, or to New Orleans. From the slave prison to the ship, they are usually driven in the darkness of night; for since the antislavery agitation, a certain caution is observed.

In the deep, still darkness of midnight I have been often aroused by the dead heavy footsteps, and the piteous cries of the chained gangs that passed our door. The anguish of my boyish heart was intense; and I was often consoled, when speaking to my mistress in the morning, to hear her say that the custom was very wicked; that she hated to hear the rattle of the chains, and the heart-rending cries. I was glad to find one who sympathized with me in my horror. Fellow-citizens, this murderous traffic is, today, in active operation in this boasted republic. In the solitude of my spirit, I see clouds of dust raised on the highways of the South; I see the bleeding footsteps; I hear the doleful wail of fettered humanity, on the way to the slave markets, where the victims are to be sold like horses, sheep and swine, knocked off to the highest bidder. There I see the tenderest ties ruthlessly broken, to gratify the lust, caprice and rapacity of the buyers and sellers of men. My soul sickens at the sight.

Is this the land your Fathers loved, The freedom which they toiled to win? Is this the earth whereon they moved? Are these the graves they slumber in?

But a still more inhuman, disgraceful, and scandalous state of things remains to be presented. By an act of the American Congress, not yet two years old, slavery has been nationalized in its most horrible and revolting form. By that act, Mason & Dixon's line has been obliterated; New York has become as Virginia; and the power to hold, hunt, and sell men, women, and children as slaves remains no longer a mere state institution, but is now an institution of the whole United States. The power is co-extensive with the Star-Spangled Banner and American Christianity. Where these go, may also go the merciless slave-hunter. Where these are, man is not sacred. He is a bird for the sportsman's gun. By that most foul and fiendish of all human decrees, the liberty and person of every man are put in peril. Your broad republican domain is hunting ground for men. Not for thieves and robbers, enemies of society, merely, but for men guilty of no crime. Your lawmakers have commanded all good citizens to engage in this hellish sport. Your President, your Secretary of State, your lords, nobles and ecclesiastics enforce, as a duty you owe to your free and glorious country, and to your God, that you do this accursed thing. Not fewer than forty Americans have, within the past two years, been hunted down and, without a moment's warning, hurried away in chains, and consigned to slavery and excruciating torture. Some of these have had wives and children, dependent on them for bread; but of this, no account was made. The right of the hunter to his prey stands superior to the right of marriage, and to all rights in this republic, the rights of God included! For black men there are neither law, justice, humanity, not religion. The Fugitive Slave Law makes makes mercy to them a crime; and bribes the judge who tries them. An American judge gets ten dollars for every victim he consigns to slavery, and five, when he fails to do so. The oath of any two villains is sufficient, under this hell-black enactment, to send the most pious and exemplary black man into the remorseless jaws of slavery! His own testimony is nothing. He can bring no witnesses for himself. The minister of American justice is bound by the law to hear but one side; and that side, is the side of the oppressor. Let this damning fact be perpetually told. Let it be thundered around the world, that, in tyrant-killing, king-hating, people-loving, democratic, Christian America, the seats of justice are filled with judges, who hold their offices under an open and palpable bribe, and are bound, in deciding in the case of a man's liberty, to hear only his accusers!

In glaring violation of justice, in shameless disregard of the forms of administering law, in cunning arrangement to entrap the defenseless, and in diabolical intent, this Fugitive Slave Law stands alone in the annals of tyrannical legislation. I doubt if there be another nation on the globe, having the brass and the baseness to put such a law on the statute-book. If any man in this assembly thinks differently from me in this matter, and feels able to disprove my statements, I will gladly confront him at any suitable time and place he may select.

I take this law to be one of the grossest infringements of Christian Liberty, and, if the churches and ministers of our country were not stupidly blind, or most wickedly indifferent, they, too, would so regard it.

At the very moment that they are thanking God for the enjoyment of civil and religious liberty, and for the right to worship God according to the dictates of their own consciences, they are utterly silent in respect to a law which robs religion of its chief significance, and makes it utterly worthless to a world lying in wickedness. Did this law concern the "mint, anise and cummin"—abridge the fight to sing psalms, to partake of the sacrament, or to engage in any of the ceremonies of religion, it would be smitten by the thunder of a thousand pulpits. A general shout would go up from the church, demanding repeal, repeal, instant repeal! And it would go hard with that politician who presumed to solicit the votes of the people without inscribing this motto on his banner. Further, if this demand were not complied with, another Scotland would be added to the history of religious liberty, and the stern old Covenanters would be thrown into the shade. A John Knox would be seen at every church door, and heard from every pulpit, and Fillmore would have no more quarter than was shown by Knox, to the beautiful, but treacherous queen Mary of Scotland. The fact that the church of our country, (with fractional exceptions), does not esteem "the Fugitive Slave Law" as a declaration of war against religious liberty, implies that that church regards religion simply as a form of worship, an empty ceremony, and not a vital principle, requiring active benevolence, justice, love and good will towards man. It esteems sacrifice above mercy; psalm-singing above right doing; solemn meetings above practical righteousness. A worship that can be conducted by persons who refuse to give shelter to the houseless, to give bread to the hungry, clothing to the naked, and who enjoin obedience to a law forbidding these acts of mercy, is a curse, not a blessing to mankind. The Bible addresses all such persons as "scribes, Pharisees, hypocrites, who pay tithe of mint, anise, and cummin, and have omitted the weightier matters of the law, judgment, mercy and faith." But the church of this country is not only indifferent to the wrongs of die slave, it actually takes sides with the oppressors. It has made itself the bulwark of American slavery, and the shield of American slave-hunters. Many of its most eloquent Divines. who stand as the very lights of the church, have shamelessly given the sanction of religion and the Bible to the whole slave system. They have taught that man may, properly, be a slave; that the relation of master and slave is ordained of God; that to send back an escaped bondman to his master is clearly the duty of all the followers of the Lord Jesus Christ; and this horrible blasphemy is palmed off upon the world for Christianity.

For my part, I would say, Welcome infidelity! welcome atheism! welcome anything—in preference to the gospel, as preached by those divines. They convert the very name of religion into an engine of tyranny, and barbarous cruelty, and serve to confirm more infidels, in this age, than all the infidel writings of Thomas Paine, Voltaire, and Bolingbroke, put together, have done! These ministers make religion a cold and flinty-hearted thing, having neither principles of right action, nor bowels of compassion. They strip the love of God of its beauty, and leave the throng of religion a huge, horrible, repulsive form. It is a religion for oppressors, tyrants, man-stealers, and thugs. It is not that "pure and undefiled religion" which is from above, and which is "first pure, then peaceable, easy to be entreated, full of mercy and good fruits, without partiality and without hypocrisy." But a religion which favors the rich against the poor; which exalts the proud above the humble; which divides mankind into two classes, tyrants and slaves; which says to the man in chains, stay there; and to the oppressor, oppress on; it is a religion which may be professed and enjoyed by all the robbers and enslavers of mankind; it makes God a respecter of persons, denies his fatherhood of the race, and tramples in the dust the great truth of the brotherhood of man. All this we affirm to be true of the popular church, and the popular worship of our land and nation—a religion, a church, and a worship which, on the authority of inspired wisdom, we pronounce to be an abomination in the sight of God. In the language of Isaiah, the American church might be well addressed, "Bring no more vain ablations; incense is an abomination unto me: the new moons and Sabbaths, the calling of assemblies, I cannot away with; it is iniquity even the solemn meeting. Your new moons and your appointed feasts my soul hateth. They are a trouble to me; I am weary to bear them; and when ye spread forth your hands I will hide mine eyes from you. Yea! when ye make many prayers, I will not hear. Your hands are full of blood; cease to do evil, learn to do well; seek judgment; relieve the oppressed; judge for the fatherless; plead for the widow."

The American church is guilty, when viewed in connection with what it is doing to uphold slavery; but it is superlatively guilty when viewed in connection with its ability to abolish slavery.

The sin of which it is guilty is one of omission as well as of commission. Albert Barnes but uttered what the common sense of every man at all observant of the actual state of the case will receive as truth, when he declared that "There is no power out of the church that could sustain slavery an hour, if it were not sustained in it."

Let the religious press, the pulpit, the Sunday school, the conference meeting, the great ecclesiastical, missionary, Bible and tract associations of the land array their immense powers against slavery and slave-holding; and the whole system of crime and blood would be scattered to the winds; and that they do not do this involves them in the most awful responsibility of which the mind can conceive.

In prosecuting the anti-slavery enterprise, we have been asked to spare the church, to spare the ministry; but how, we ask, could such a thing be done? We are met on the threshold of our efforts for the redemption of the slave, by the church and ministry of the country, in battle arrayed against us; and we are compelled to fight or flee. From what quarter, I beg to know, has proceeded a fire so deadly upon our ranks, during the last two years, as from the Northern pulpit? As the champions of oppressors, the chosen men of American theology have appeared—men, honored for their so-called piety, and their real learning. The Lords of Buffalo, the Springs of New York, the Lathrops of Auburn, the Coxes and Spencers of Brooklyn, the Gannets and Sharps of Boston, the Deweys of Washington, and other great religious lights of the land, have, in utter denial of the authority of Him, by whom the professed to he called to the ministry, deliberately taught us, against the example or the Hebrews and against the remonstrance of the Apostles, they teach "that we ought to obey man's law before the law of God."

My spirit wearies of such blasphemy; and how such men can be supported, as the "standing types and representatives of Jesus Christ," is a mystery which I leave others to penetrate. In speaking of the American church, however, let it be distinctly understood that I mean the great mass of the religious organizations of our land. There are exceptions, and I thank God that there are. Noble men may be found, scattered all over these Northern States, of whom Henry Ward Beecher of Brooklyn, Samuel J. May of Syracuse, and my esteemed friend (Rev. R. R. Raymond) on the platform, are shining examples; and let me say further, that upon these men lies the duty to inspire our ranks with high religious faith and zeal, and to cheer us on in the great mission of the slave's redemption from his chains.

One is struck with the difference between the attitude of the American church towards the anti-slavery movement, and that occupied by the churches in England towards a similar movement in that country. There, the church, true to its mission of ameliorating, elevating, and improving the condition of mankind, came forward promptly, bound up the wounds of the West Indian slave, and restored him to his liberty. There, the question of emancipation was a high(ly) religious question. It was demanded, in the name of humanity, and according to the law of the living God. The Sharps, the Clarksons, the Wilberforces, the Buxtons, and Burchells and the Knibbs, were alike famous for their piety, and for their philanthropy. The anti-slavery movement there was not an anti-church movement, for the reason that the church took its full share in prosecuting that movement: and the anti-slavery movement in this country will cease to be an anti-church movement, when the church of this country shall assume a favorable instead or a hostile position towards that movement.

Americans! your republican politics, not less than your republican religion, are flagrantly inconsistent. You boast of your love of liberty, your superior civilization, and your pure Christianity, while the whole political power of the nation (as embodied in the two great political parties) is solemnly pledged to support and perpetuate the enslavement of three millions of your countrymen. You hurl your anathemas at the crowned headed tyrants of Russia and Austria, and pride yourselves on your Democratic institutions, while you yourselves consent to be the mere tools and bodyguards of the tyrants of Virginia and Carolina. You invite to your shores fugitives of oppression from abroad, honor them with banquets, greet them with ovations, cheer them, toast them, salute them, protect them, and pour out your money to them like water; but the fugitives from your own land you advertise, hunt, arrest, shoot and kill. You glory in your refinement and your universal education yet you maintain a system as barbarous and dreadful as ever stained the character of a nation—a system begun in avarice, supported in pride, and perpetuated in cruelty. You shed tears over fallen Hungary, and make the sad story of her wrongs the theme of your poets, statesmen and orators, till your gallant sons are ready to fly to arms to vindicate her cause against her oppressors; but, in regard to the ten thousand wrongs of the American slave, you would enforce the strictest silence, and would hail him as an enemy of the nation who dares to make those wrongs the subject of public discourse! You are all on fire at the mention of liberty for France or for Ireland; but are as cold as an iceberg at the thought of liberty for the enslaved of America. You discourse eloquently on the dignity of labor; yet, you sustain a system which, in its very essence, casts a stigma upon labor. You can bare your bosom to the storm of British artillery to throw off a threepenny tax on tea; and yet wring the last hard-earned farthing from the grasp of the black laborers of your country. You profess to believe "that, of one blood,

God made all nations of men to dwell on the face of all the earth," and hath commanded all men, everywhere to love one another; yet you notoriously hate, (and glory in your hatred), all men whose skins are not colored like your own. You declare, before the world, and are understood by the world to declare, that you "hold these truths to be self evident, that all men are created equal; and are endowed by their Creator with certain inalienable rights; and that, among these are, life, liberty, and the pursuit of happiness;" and yet, you hold securely, in a bondage which, according to your own Thomas Jefferson, "is worse than ages of that which your fathers rose in rebellion to oppose," a seventh part of the inhabitants of your country.

Fellow-citizens! I will not enlarge further on your national inconsistencies. The existence of slavery in this country brands your republicanism as a sham, your humanity as a base pretence, and your Christianity as a lie. It destroys your moral power abroad; it corrupts your politicians at home. It saps the foundation of religion; it makes your name a hissing, and a by word to a mocking earth. It is the antagonistic force in your government, the only thing that seriously disturbs and endangers your Union. It fetters your progress; it is the enemy of improvement, the deadly foe of education; it fosters pride; it breeds insolence; it promotes vice; it shelters crime; it is a curse to the earth that supports it; and yet, you cling to it, as if it were the sheet anchor of all your hopes. Oh! be warned! be warned! a horrible reptile is coiled up in your nation's bosom; the venomous creature is nursing at the tender breast of your youthful republic; for the love of God, tear away, and fling from you the hideous monster, and let the weight of twenty millions crush and destroy it forever!

But it is answered in reply to all this, that precisely what I have now denounced is, in fact, guaranteed and sanctioned by the Constitution of the United States; that the right to hold and to hunt slaves is a part of that Constitution framed by the illustrious Fathers of this Republic. Then, I dare to affirm, notwithstanding all I have said before, your fathers stooped, basely stooped

To palter with us in a double sense: And keep the word of promise to the ear, But break it to the heart.

And instead of being the honest men I have before declared them to be, they were the veriest imposters that ever practiced on mankind. This is the inevitable conclusion, and from it there is no escape. But I differ from those who charge this baseness on the framers of the Constitution of the United States. It is a slander upon their memory, at least, so I believe. There is not time now to argue the constitutional question at length—nor have I the ability to discuss it as it ought to be discussed. The subject has been handled with masterly power by Lysander Spooner, Esq., by William Goodell, by Samuel E. Sewall, Esq., and last, though not least, by Gerritt Smith, Esq. These gentlemen have, as I think, fully and clearly vindicated the Constitution from any design to support slavery for an hour.

Fellow-citizens! there is no matter in respect to which, the people of the North have allowed themselves to be so ruinously imposed upon, as that of the pro-slavery character of the Constitution. In that instrument I hold there is neither warrant, license, nor sanction of the hateful thing; but, interpreted as it ought to be interpreted, the Constitution is a glorious liberty document. Read its preamble, consider its purposes. Is slavery among them? Is it at the gateway? Or is it in the temple? It is neither. While I do not intend to argue this question on the present occasion, let me ask, if it be not somewhat singular that, if the Constitution were intended to be, by its framers and adopters, a slave-holding instrument, why neither slavery, slaveholding, nor slave can anywhere be found in it. What would be thought of an instrument, drawn up, legally drawn up, for the purpose of entitling the city of Rochester to a track of land, in which no mention of land was made? Now, there are certain rules of interpretation, for the proper understanding of all legal instruments. These rules are well established. They are plain, common-sense rules, such as you and I, and all of us, can understand and apply, without having passed years in the study of law. I scout the idea that the question of the constitutionality or unconstitutionality of slavery is not a question for the people. I hold that every American citizen has a fight to form an opinion of the constitution, and to propagate that opinion, and to use all honorable means to make his opinion the prevailing one. Without this fight, the liberty of an American citizen would be as insecure as that of a Frenchman. Ex-Vice-President Dallas tells us that the constitution is an object to which no American mind can be too attentive, and no American heart too devoted. He further says, the constitution, in its words, is plain and intelligible, and is meant for the home-bred, unsophisticated understandings of our fellow-citizens. Senator Berrien tell us that the Constitution is the fundamental law, that which controls all others. The charter of our liberties, which every citizen has a personal interest in understanding thoroughly. The testimony of Senator Breese, Lewis Cass, and many others that might be named, who are everywhere esteemed as sound lawyers, so regard the constitution. I take it, therefore, that it is not presumption in a private citizen to form an opinion of that instrument.

Now, take the constitution according to its plain reading, and I defy the presentation of a single pro-slavery clause in it. On the other hand it will be found to contain principles and purposes, entirely hostile to the existence of slavery.

I have detained my audience entirely too long already. At some future period I will gladly avail myself of an opportunity to give this subject a full and fair discussion. Allow me to say, in conclusion, notwithstanding the dark picture I have this day presented of the state of the nation, I do not despair of this country."

Allow me to say, in conclusion, notwithstanding the dark picture I have this day presented of the state of the nation, I do not despair of this country. There are forces in operation, which must inevitably work the downfall of slavery. "The arm of the Lord is not shortened," and the doom of slavery is certain. I, therefore, leave off where I began, with hope. While drawing encouragement from the Declaration of Independence, the great principles it contains, and the genius of American Institutions, my spirit is also cheered by the obvious tendencies of the age. Nations do not now stand in the same relation to each other that they did ages ago. No nation can now shut itself up from the surrounding world, and trot round in the same old path of its fathers without interference. The time was when such could be done. Long established customs of hurtful character could formerly fence themselves in, and do their evil work with social impunity. Knowledge was then confined and enjoyed by the privileged few, and the multitude walked on in mental darkness. But a change has now come over the affairs of mankind. Walled cities and empires have become unfashionable. The arm of commerce has borne away the gates of the strong city. Intelligence is penetrating the darkest corners of the globe. It makes its pathway over and under the sea, as well as on the earth. Wind, steam, and lightning are its chartered agents. Oceans no longer divide, but link nations together. From Boston to London is now a holiday excursion. Space is comparatively annihilated. Thoughts expressed on one side of the Atlantic are, distinctly heard on the other.

The far-off and almost fabulous Pacific rolls in grandeur at our feet. The Celestial Empire, the mystery of ages, is being solved. The fiat of the Almighty, "Let there be Light," has not yet spent its force. No abuse, no outrage whether in taste, sport or avarice, can now hide itself from the all-pervading light. The iron shoe, and crippled foot of China must be seen, in contrast with nature. Africa must rise and put on her yet unwoven garment. "Ethiopia shall stretch out her hand unto God." In the fervent aspirations of William Lloyd Garrison, I say, and let every heart join in saying it.

God speed the year of jubilee The wide world o'er When from their galling chains set free, Th' oppress'd shall vilely bend the knee, And wear the yoke of tyranny Like brutes no more. That year will come, and freedom's reign, To man his plundered fights again Restore.

God speed the day when human blood Shall cease to flow! In every clime be understood, The claims of human brotherhood, And each return for evil, good, Not blow for blow; That day will come all feuds to end. And change into a faithful friend Each foe.

God speed the hour, the glorious hour, When none on earth Shall exercise a lordly power, Nor in a tyrant's presence cower; But all to manhood's stature tower, By equal birth! That hour will com, to each, to all, And from his prison-house, the thrall Go forth.

Until that year, day, hour, arrive, With head, and heart, and hand I'll strive, To break the rod, and rend the gyve, The spoiler of his prey deprive—So witness Heaven! And never from my chosen post, Whate'er the peril or the cost, Be driven.

If There is No Struggle, There
is No Progress

The general sentiment of mankind is that a man who will not fight for himself, when he has the means of doing so, is not worth being fought for by others, and this sentiment is just. For a man who does not value freedom for himself will never value it for others, or put himself to any inconvenience to gain it for others. Such a man, the world says, may lie down until he has sense enough to stand up. It is useless and cruel to put a man on his legs, if the next moment his head is to be brought against a curbstone.

A man of that type will never lay the world under any obligation to him, but will be a moral pauper, a drag on the wheels of society, and if he too be identified with a peculiar variety of the race he will entail disgrace upon his race as well as upon himself. The world in which we live is very accommodating to all sorts of people. It will cooperate with them in any measure which they propose; it will help those who earnestly help themselves, and will hinder those who hinder themselves. It is very polite, and never offers its services unasked. Its favors to individuals are measured by an unerring principle in this—viz., respect those who respect themselves, and despise those who despise themselves. It is not within the power of unaided human nature to persevere in pitying a people who are insensible to their own wrongs and indifferent to the attainment of their own rights. The poet was as true to common sense as to poetry when he said,

Who would be free, themselves must strike the blow.

When O'Connell, with all Ireland at his back, was supposed to be contending for the just rights and liberties of Ireland, the sympathies of mankind were with him, and even his enemies were compelled to respect his patriotism. Kossuth, fighting for Hungary with his pen long after she had fallen by the sword, commanded the sympathy and support of the liberal world till his own hopes died out. The Turks, while they fought bravely for themselves and scourged and drove back the invading legions of Russia, shared the admiration of mankind. They were standing up for their own rights against an arrogant and powerful enemy; but as soon as they let out their fighting to the Allies, admiration gave way to contempt. These are not the maxims and teachings of a coldhearted world. Christianity itself teaches that man shall provide for his own house. This covers the whole ground of nations as well as individuals. Nations no more than individuals can innocently be improvident. They should provide for all wants—mental, moral and religious—and against all evils to which they are liable as nations. In the great struggle now progressing for the freedom and elevation of our people, we should be found at work with all our might, resolved that no man or set of men shall be more abundant in labors, according to the measure of our ability, than ourselves.

I know, my friends, that in some quarters the efforts of colored people meet with very little encouragement. We may fight, but we must fight like the Sepoys of India, under white officers. This class of Abolitionists don't like colored celebrations, they don't like colored conventions, they don't like colored antislavery fairs for the support of colored newspapers. They don't like any demonstrations whatever in which colored men take a leading part. They talk of the proud Anglo-Saxon blood as flippantly as those who profess to believe in the natural inferiority of races. Your humble speaker has been branded as an ingrate, because he has ventured to stand up on his own and to plead our common cause as a colored man, rather than as a Garrisonian. I hold it to be no part of gratitude to allow our white friends to do all the work, while we merely hold their coats. Opposition of the sort now referred to is partisan position, and we need not mind it. The white people at large will not largely be influenced by it. They will see and appreciate all honest efforts on our part to improve our condition as a people.

Let me give you a word of the philosophy of reform. The whole history of the progress of human liberty shows that all concessions yet made to her august claims have been born of earnest struggle. The conflict has been exciting, agitating, all-absorbing, and for the time being, putting all other tumults to silence. It must do this or it does nothing. If there is no struggle there is no progress. Those who profess to favor freedom and yet deprecate agitation are men who want crops without plowing up the ground; they want rain without thunder and lightning. They want the ocean without the awful roar of its many waters.

This struggle may be a moral one, or it may be a physical one, and it may be both moral and physical, but it must be a struggle. Power concedes nothing without a demand. It never did and it never will. Find out just what any people will quietly submit to and you have found out the exact measure of injustice and wrong which will be imposed upon them, and these will continue till they are resisted with either words or blows, or with both. The limits of tyrants are prescribed by the endurance of those whom they oppress. In the light of these ideas, Negroes will be hunted at the North and held and flogged at the South so long as they submit to those devilish outrages and make no resistance, either moral or physical. Men may not get all they pay for in this world, but they must certainly pay for all they get. If we ever get free from the oppressions and wrongs heaped upon us, we must pay for their removal. We must do this by labor, by suffering, by sacrifice, and if needs be, by our lives and the lives of others.

Hence, my friends, every mother who, like Margaret Garner, plunges a knife into the bosom of her infant to save it from the hell of our Christian slavery, should be held and honored as a benefactress. Every fugitive from slavery who, like the noble William Thomas at Wilkes Barre, prefers to perish in a river made red by his own blood to submission to the hell hounds who were hunting and shooting him should be esteemed as a glorious martyr, worthy to be held in grateful memory by our people. The fugitive Horace, at Mechanicsburgh, Ohio, the other day, who taught the slave catchers from Kentucky that it was safer to arrest white men than to arrest him, did a most excellent service to our cause. Parker and his noble band of fifteen at Christiana, who defended themselves from the kidnappers with prayers and pistols, are entitled to the honor of making the first successful resistance to the Fugitive Slave Bill. But for that resistance, and the rescue of Jerry and Shadrack, the man hunters would have hunted our hills and valleys here with the same freedom with which they now hunt their own dismal swamps.

There was an important lesson in the conduct of that noble Krooman in New York the other day, who, supposing that the American Christians were about to enslave him, betook himself to the masthead and with knife in hand said he would cut his throat before he would be made a slave. Joseph Cinque, on the deck of the Amistad, did that which should make his name dear to us. He bore nature's burning protest against slavery. Madison Washington who struck down his oppressor on the deck of the Creole, is more worthy to be remembered than the colored man who shot Pitcairn at Bunker Hill.

My friends, you will observe that I have taken a wide range, and you think it is about time that I should answer the special objection to this celebration. I think so too. This, then, is the truth concerning the inauguration of freedom in the British West Indies. Abolition was the act of the British government. The motive which led the government to act no doubt was mainly a philanthropic one, entitled to our highest admiration and gratitude. The national religion, the justice and humanity cried out in thunderous indignation against the foul abomination, and the government yielded to the storm. Nevertheless a share of the credit of the result falls justly to the slaves themselves. "Though slaves, they were rebellious slaves." They bore themselves well. They did not hug their chains, but according to their opportunities, swelled the general protest against oppression. What Wilberforce was endeavoring to win from the British senate by his magic eloquence the slaves themselves were endeavoring to gain by outbreaks and violence. The combined action of one and the other wrought out the final result. While one showed that slavery was wrong, the other showed that it was dangerous as well as wrong. Mr. Wilberforce, peace man though he was, and a model of piety, availed himself of this element to strengthen his case before the British Parliament, and warned the British government of the danger of continuing slavery in the West Indies. There is no doubt that the fear of the consequences, acting with a sense of the moral evil of slavery, led to its abolition. The spirit of freedom was abroad in the Islands. Insurrection for freedom kept the planters in a constant state of alarm and trepidation. A standing army was necessary to keep the slaves in their chains. This state of facts could not be without weight in deciding the question of freedom in these countries.

I am aware that the rebellious disposition of the slaves was said to arise out of the discussion which the Abolitionists were carrying on at home, and it is not necessary to refute this alleged explanation. All that I contend for is this: that the slaves of the West Indies did fight for their freedom, and that the fact of their discontent was known in England, and that it assisted in bringing about that state of public opinion which finally resulted in their emancipation. And if this be true, the objection is answered.

Again, I am aware that the insurrectionary movements of the slaves were held by many to be prejudicial to their cause. This is said now of such movements at the South. The answer is that abolition followed close on the heels of insurrection in the West Indies, and Virginia was never nearer emancipation than when General Turner kindled the fires of insurrection at Southampton.

Sir, I have now more than filled up the measure of my time. I thank you for the patient attention given to what I have had to say. I have aimed, as I said at the beginning, to express a few thoughts having some relation to the great interest of freedom both in this country and in the British West Indies, and I have said all that I mean to say, and the time will not permit me to say more.

LIBERTY FOR SLAVES

Could we trace the record of every human heart, the aspirations of every immortal soul, perhaps we would find no man so imbruted and degraded that we could not trace the word liberty either written in living characters upon the soul or hidden away in some nook or corner of the heart. The law of liberty is the law of God, and is antecedent to all human legislation. It existed in the mind of Deity when He hung the first world upon its orbit and gave it liberty to gather light from the central sun.

Some people say, set the slaves free. Did you ever think, if the slaves were free, they would steal everything they could lay their hands on from now till the day of their death—that they would steal more than two thousand millions of dollars? (applause) Ask Maryland, with her tens of thousands of slaves, if she is not prepared for freedom, and hear her answer: "I help supply the coffee-gangs of the South." Ask Virginia, with her hundreds of thousands of slaves, if she is not weary with her merchandise of blood and anxious to shake the gory traffic from her hands, and hear her reply: "Though fertility has covered my soil, through a genial sky bends over my hills and vales, though I hold in my hand a wealth of water-power enough to turn the spindles to clothe the world, yet, with all these advantages, on of my chief staples has been the sons and daughters I send to the human market and human shambles." (applause) Ask the farther South, and all the cotton-growing States chime in, "We have need of fresh supplies to fill the ranks of those whose lives have gone out in unrequited toil on our distant plantations."

A hundred thousand new-born babes are annually added to the victims of slavery; twenty thousand lives are annually sacrificed on the plantations of the South. Such a sight should send a thrill of horror through the nerves of civilization and impel the heart of humanity to lofty deeds. So it might, if men had not found out a fearful alchemy by which this blood can be transformed into gold. Instead of listening to the cry of agony, they listen to the ring of dollars and stoop down to pick up the coin. (applause)

But a few months since a man escaped from bondage and found a temporary shelter almost beneath the shadow of Bunker Hill. Had that man stood upon the deck of an Austrian ship, beneath the shadow of the house of the Hapsburgs, he would have found protection. Had he been wrecked upon an island or colony of Great Britain, the waves of the tempest-lashed ocean would have washed him deliverance. Had he landed upon the territory of vine-encircled France and a Frenchman had reduced him to a thing and brought him here beneath the protection of our institutions and our laws, for such a nefarious deed that Frenchman would have lost his citizenship in France. Beneath the feebler light which glimmers from the Koran, the Bey of Tunis would have granted him freedom in his own dominions. Beside the ancient pyramids of Egypt he would have found liberty, for the soil laved by the glorious Nile is now consecrated to freedom. But from Boston harbour, made memorable by the infusion of three-penny taxed tea, Boston in its proximity to the plains of Lexington and Concord, Boston almost beneath the shadow of Bunker Hill and almost in sight of Plymouth Rock, he is thrust back from liberty and manhood and reconverted into a chattel. You have heard that, down South, they keep bloodhounds to hunt slaves. Ye bloodhounds, go back to your kennels; when you fail to catch the flying fugitive, when his stealthy tread is heard in the place where the bones of the revolutionary sires repose, the ready North is base enough to do your shameful service. (applause)

Slavery is mean, because it tramples on the feeble and weak. A man comes with his affidavits from the South and hurries me before a commissioner; upon that evidence ex parte and alone he hitches me to the car of slavery and trails my womanhood in the dust. I stand at the threshold of the Supreme Court and ask for justice, simple justice. Upon my tortured heart is thrown the mocking words, "You are a negro; you have no rights which white men are bound to respect"! (loud and long-continued applause) Had it been my lot to have lived beneath the Crescent instead of the Cross, had injustice and violence been heaped upon my head as a Mohammedan woman, as a member of a common faith, I might have demanded justice and been listened to by the Pasha, the Bey or the Vizier; but when I come here to ask for justice, me tell me, "We have no higher law than the Constitution." (applause)

But I will not dwell on the dark side of the picture. God is on the side of freedom; and any cause that has God on its side, I care not how much it may be trampled upon, how much it may be trailed in the dust, is sure to triumph. The message of Jesus Christ is on the side of freedom, "I come to preach deliverance to the captives, the opening of the prison doors to them that are bound." The truest and noblest hearts in the land are on the side of freedom. They may be hissed at by slavery's minions, their names cast out as evil, their characters branded with fanaticism, but O, "to side with Truth is noble when we share her humble crust Ere the cause bring fame and profit and it's prosperous to be just."

May I not, in conclusion, ask every honest, noble heart, every seeker after truth and justice, if they will not also be on the side of freedom. Will you not resolve that you will abate neither heart nor hope till you hear the death-knell of human bondage sounded, and over the black ocean of slavery shall be heard a song, more exulting than the song of Miriam when it floated o'er Egypt's dark sea, the requiem of Egypt's ruined hosts and the anthem of the deliverance of Israel's captive people?

The Mission of the War

Ladies and Gentlemen: By the mission of the war I mean nothing occult, arbitrary or difficult to be understood, but simply those great moral changes in the fundamental conditions of the people, demanded by the situation of the country plainly involved in the nature of the war, and which, if the war is conducted in accordance with its true character, it is naturally and logically fitted to accomplish.

Speaking in the name of Providence, some men tell me that slavery is already dead, that it expired with the first shot at Sumter. This may be so, but I do not share the confidence with which it is asserted. In a grand crisis like this, we should all prefer to look facts sternly in the face and to accept their verdict whether it bless or blast us. I look for no miraculous destruction of slavery. The war looms before me simply as a great national opportunity, which may be improved to national salvation, or neglected to national ruin. I hope much from the bravery of our soldiers, but in vain is the might of armies if our rulers fail to profit by experience and refuse to listen to the suggestions of wisdom and justice. The most hopeful fact of the hour is that we are now in a salutary school—the school of affliction. If sharp and signal retribution, long protracted, wide-sweeping and overwhelming, can teach a great nation respect for the long-despised claims of justice, surely we shall be taught now and for all time to come. But if, on the other hand, this potent teacher, whose lessons are written in characters of blood and thundered to us from a hundred battlefields shall fail, we shall go down as we shall deserve to go down, as a warning to all other nations which shall come after us. It is not pleasant to contemplate the hour as one of doubt and danger. We naturally prefer the bright side, but when there is a dark side it is folly to shut our eyes to it or deny its existence.

I know that the acorn involves the oak, but I know also that the commonest accident may destroy its potential character and defeat its natural destiny. One wave brings its treasure from the briny deep, but another often sweeps it back to its primal depths. The saying that revolutions never go backward must be taken with limitations. The Revolution of 1848 was one of the grandest that ever dazzled a gazing world. It overturned the French throne, sent Louis Philippe into exile, shook every throne in Europe, and inaugurated a glorious Republic. Looking from a distance, the friends of democratic liberty saw in the convulsion the death of kingcraft in Europe and throughout the world. Great was their disappointment. Almost in the twinkling of an eye, the latent forces of despotism rallied. The Republic disappeared. Her noblest defenders were sent into exile, and the hopes of democratic liberty were blasted in the moment of their bloom. Politics and perfidy proved too strong for the principles of liberty and justice in that contest. I wish I could say that no such liabilities darken the horizon around us. But the same elements are plainly involved here as there. Though the portents are that we shall flourish, it is too much to say that we cannot fail and fall. Our destiny is to be taken out of our own hands. It is cowardly to shuffle our responsibilities upon the shoulders of Providence. I do not intend to argue but to state facts.

We are now wading into the third year of conflict with a fierce and sanguinary rebellion, one which, at the beginning of it, we were hopefully assured by one of our most sagacious and trusted political prophets would be ended in less than ninety days; a rebellion which, in its worst features, stands alone among rebellions a solitary and ghastly horror, without a parallel in the history of any nation, ancient or modern; a rebellion inspired by no love of liberty and by no hatred of oppression, as most other rebellions have been, and therefore utterly indefensible upon any moral or social grounds; a rebellion which openly and shamelessly sets at defiance the world's judgment of right and wrong, appeals from light to darkness, from intelligence to ignorance, from the ever-increasing prospects and blessings of a high and glorious civilization to the cold and withering blasts of a naked barbarism; a rebellion which even at this unfinished stage of it counts the number of its slain not by thousands nor by tens of thousands, but by hundreds of thousands; a rebellion which in the destruction of human life and property has rivaled the earthquake, the whirlwind and the pestilence that waketh in darkness and wasteth at noonday. It has planted agony at a million hearthstones, thronged our streets with the weeds of mourning, filled our land with mere stumps of men, ridged our soil with two hundred thousand rudely formed graves and mantled it all over with the shadow of death. A rebellion which, while it has arrested the wheels of peaceful industry and checked the flow of commerce, has piled up a debt heavier than a mountain of gold to weigh down the necks of our children's children. There is no end to the mischief wrought. It has brought ruin at home, contempt abroad, has cooled our friends, heated our enemies and endangered our existence as nation.

Now, for what is all this desolation, ruin, shame suffering and sorrow? Can anybody want the answer? Can anybody be ignorant of the answer? It has been given a thousand times from this and other platforms. We all know it is slavery. Less than a half a million of Southern slaveholders— holding in bondage four million slaves—finding themselves outvoted in the effort to get possession of the United States government, in order to serve the interests of slavery, have madly resorted to the sword—have undertaken to accomplish by bullets what they failed to accomplish by ballots. That is the answer.

It is worthy of remark that secession was an afterthought with the rebels. Their aim was higher; secession was only their second choice. Who was going to fight for slavery in the Union? It was not separation, but subversion. It was not Richmond, but Washington. It was not the Confederate rag, but the glorious Star-Spangled Banner.

Whence came the guilty ambition equal to this atrocious crime. A peculiar education was necessary to this bold wickedness. Here all is plain again. Slavery—the peculiar institution—is aptly fitted to produce just such patriots, who first plunder and then seek to destroy their country. A system which rewards labor with stripes and chains, which robs the slave of his manhood and the master of all just consideration for the rights of his fellow man—has prepared the characters, male and female, the figure in this rebellion—and for all its cold-blooded and hellish atrocities. In all the most horrid details of torture, starvation and murder in the treatment of our prisoners, I behold the features of the monster in whose presence I was born, and that is slavery. From no sources less foul and wicked could such a rebellion come. I need not dwell here. The country knows the story by heart. But I am one of those who think this rebellion—inaugurated and carried on for a cause so unspeakably guilty and distinguished by barbarities which would extort a cry of shame from the painted savage— is quite enough for the whole lifetime of any one nation, though the lifetime should cover the space of a thousand years. We ought not to want a repetition of it. Looking at the matter from no higher ground than patriotism—the American considerations of justice, liberty, progress and civilization—the American people should resolve that this shall be the last slaveholding rebellion that shall ever curse this continent. Let the War cost more or cost little, let it be long or short, the work now begun should suffer no pause, no abatement, until it is done and done forever.

I know that many are appalled and disappointed by the apparently interminable character this war. I am neither appalled nor disappointed without pretending to any higher wisdom than other men. I knew well enough and often said it: once let the North and South confront each other on the battlefield, and slavery and freedom be the inspiring motives of the respective sections, the contest will be fierce, long and sanguinary. Governor Seymour charges us with prolonging the war, and I say the longer the better if it must be so—in order to put an end to the hell-black cause out of which the rebellion has risen.

Say not that I am indifferent to the horrors and hardships of the war. I am not indifferent. In common with the American people generally, I feel the prolongation of the war a heavy calamity, private as well as public. There are vacant space at my hearthstone which I shall rejoice to see filled again by the boys who once occupied them, but which cannot be thus filled while the war lasts, for they have enlisted "during the war."

But even from the length of this struggle, we who mourn over it may well enough draw some consolation when we reflect upon the vastness and grandeur of its mission. The world has witnessed many wars—and history records and perpetuates their memory—but the world has not seen a nobler and grander war than that which the loyal people of this country are now waging against the slaveholding rebels. The blow we strike is not merely to free a country or continent, but the whole world, from slavery; for when slavery fails here, it will fall everywhere. We have no business to mourn over our mission. We are writing the statutes of eternal justice and liberty in the blood of the worst of tyrants as a warning to all aftercomers. We should rejoice that there was normal life and health enough in us to stand in our appointed place, and do this great service for mankind.

It is true that the war seems long. But this very slow progress is an essential element of its effectiveness. Like the slow convalescence of some patients the fault is less chargeable to the medicine than to the deep-seated character of the disease. We were in a very low condition before the remedy was applied. The whole head was sick and the whole heart faint. Dr. Buchanan and his Democratic friends had given us up and were preparing to celebrate the nations' funeral. We had been drugged nearly to death by proslavery compromises. A radical change was needed in our whole system. Nothing is better calculated to effect the desired change than the slow, steady and certain progress of the war.

I know that his view of the case is not very consoling to the peace Democracy. I was not sent and am not come to console this breach of our political church. They regard this grand moral revolution I the mind and heart of the nation as the most distressing attribute of the war, and howl over it like certain characters of whom we read—who thought themselves tormented before their time.

Upon the whole, I like their mode of characterizing the war. They charge that it is no longer conducted upon constitutional principles. The same was said by Breckinridge and Vallandigham. They charge that it is not waged to establish the Union as it was. The same idea has occurred to Jefferson Davis. They charge that his is a war for the subjugation of the South. In a word, that is, an Abolition war.

For one, I am not careful to deny this charge. But it is instructive to observe how this charge is brought and how it is met. Both warn us of danger. Why is this war fiercely denounced as an Abolition war? I answer, because the nation has long bitterly hated Abolition and the enemies of the war confidently rely upon this hatred to serve the ends of treason. Why do the loyal people deny the charge? I answer, because they know that Abolition, though now a vast power, is still odious. Both the charge and the denial tell how the people hate and despise the only measure that can save the country.

An Abolition war! Well, let us thank the Democracy for teaching us this word. The charge in a comprehensive sense is most true, and it is a pity that it is true, but it would be a vast pity if it were not true. Would that it were more true than it is. When our government and people shall bravely avow this to be an Abolition war, then the country will be safe. Then our work will be fairly mapped out. Then the uplifted arm of the nation will swing unfettered to its work, and the spirit and power of the rebellion will be broken. Had slavery been abolished in the Border States at the very beginning of the war, as it ought to have been—had it been abolished in Missouri, as it would have been but for Presidential interference—there would now be no rebellion in the Southern states, for, instead of having to watch these Border States, as they have done, our armies would have marched in overpowering numbers directly upon the rebels and overwhelmed them. I now hold that a sacred regard for truth, as well as sound policy, makes it our duty to own and avow before heaven and earth that this war is, and of right ought to be, and Abolition War.

The abolition of slavery is the comprehensive and logical object of the war, for it includes everything else which the struggle involves. It is a war for the Union, a war for the Constitution, I admit; but it is logically such a war only in the sense that the greater includes the lesser. Slavery has proved itself the strong man of our national house.

In every rebel state it proved itself stronger than the Union, stronger than the Constitution, and stronger than the Republican institutions can become possible. An Abolition war, therefore, includes Union, Constitution, Republican institutions, and all else that goes to make up the greatness and glory of our common country. On the other hand, exclude Abolition, and you exclude all else for which you are fighting.

The position of the Democratic party in relation to the war ought to surprise nobody. It is consistent with the history of the party for thirty years. Slavery, and only slavery, has been its recognized master during all that time. It early won for itself the title of being the natural ally of the South and of slavery. It has always been for peace or against peace, for war and against war, precisely as dictated by slavery. Ask why it was for the Florida War, and it answers, slavery. Ask why it was for the Mexican War, and it answers, slavery. Ask why it was for the annexation of Texas, and it answers, slavery. Ask why it was opposed to habeas corpus when a Negro was the applicant, and it answers slavery. Ask why it is now in favor of the habeas corpus, when rebels and traitors are the applicants for its benefits, and it answers, slavery. Ask why it was for mobbing down freedom of speech a few years ago, when that freedom was claimed by the Abolitionists, and it answers, slavery. Ask why it now asserts freedom of speech, when sympathizers with traitors claim that freedom, and again slavery is the answer. Ask why it denied the right of a state to protect itself against possible abuses of the fugitive Slave Bill, and you have the same old answer. Ask why it now asserts the sovereignty of the states separately as against the states united, and again slavery is the answer. Ask why it was opposed to giving persons claimed as fugitive slaves a jury trial before returning them to slavery; ask why it is now in favor of giving jury trial to traitors before sending them to the forts for safekeeping; ask why it was for war at the beginning of the Rebellion; ask why it has attempted to embarrass and hinder the loyal government at every step of its progress, and you have but one answer, slavery.

The fact is, the party in question—I say nothing of individual men who were once members of it—has had but one vital and animating principle for thirty years, and that has been the same old horrible and hell-born principle of Negro slavery.

It has now assumed a saintly character. Its members would receive the benediction due to peacemakers. At one time they would stop bloodshed at the South by inaugurating bloody revolution at the North. The livery of peace is a beautiful livery, but in this case it is a stolen livery and sits badly on the wearer. These new apostles of peace call themselves Peace Democrats, and boast that they belong to the only party which can restore the country to peace. I neither dispute their title nor the pretensions founded upon it. The best that can be said of the peacemaking ability of this class of men is their bitterest condemnation. It consists in their known treachery to the loyal government. They have but to cross the rebel lines to be hailed by the traitors as countrymen, clansmen, kinsmen, and brothers beloved in a common conspiracy. But, fellow-citizens, I have far less solicitude about the position and the influence of this party than I have about that of the great loyal party of the country. We have much less to fear from the bold and shameless wickedness of the one than from the timid and short-sighted policy of the other.

I know we have recently gained a great political victory; but it remains to be seen whether we shall wisely avail ourselves of its manifest advantages. There is danger that, like some of our Generals in the field, who, after soundly whipping the foe, generously allow him time to retreat in order, reorganize his forces, and intrench himself in a new and stronger position, where it will require more power and skill to dislodge him than was required to vanquish him in the first instance. The game is now in our hands. We can put an end to this disloyal party by putting an end to Slavery. While the Democratic party is in existence as an organization, we are in danger of a slaveholding peace, and of Rebel rule. There is but one way to avert this calamity, and that is destroy Slavery and enfranchise the black man while we have the power. While there is a vestige of Slavery remaining, it will unite the South with itself, and carry with it the Democracy of the North. The South united and the North divided, we shall be hereafter as heretofore, firmly held under the heels of Slavery.

Here is a part of the platform of principles upon which it seems to me every loyal man should take his stand at this hour:

First: That this war, which we are compelled to wage against slaveholding rebels and traitors, at untold cost of blood and treasure, shall be, and of right ought to be, an Abolition war.

Secondly: That we, the loyal people of the North and of the whole country, while determined to make this a short and final war, will offer no peace, accept no peace, consent to no peace, which shall not be to all intents and purposes an Abolition peace.

Thirdly: That we regard the whole colored population of the country, in the loyal as well as in the disloyal states, as our countrymen—valuable in peace as laborers, valuable in war as soldiers—entitled to all the rights, protection, and opportunities for achieving distinction enjoyed by any other class of our countrymen.

Fourthly: Believing that the white race has nothing to fear from fair competition with the black race, and that the freedom and elevation of one race are not to be purchased or in any manner rightfully subserved by the disfranchisement of another, we shall favor immediate and unconditional emancipation in all the states, invest the black man everywhere with the right to vote and to be voted for, and remove all discriminations against his rights on account of his color, whether as a citizen or as a soldier.

Ladies and gentlemen, there was a time when I hoped that events unaided by discussion would couple this rebellion and slavery in a common grave. But, as I have before intimated, the facts do still fall short of our hopes. The question as to what shall be done with slavery—and especially what shall be done with the Negro—threaten to remain open questions for some time yet.

It is true we have the Proclamation of January 1863. It was a vast and glorious step in the right direction. But unhappily, excellent as that paper is—and much as it has accomplished temporarily—it settles nothing. It is still open to decision by courts, canons and Congresses. I have applauded that paper and do now applaud it, as a wide measure—while I detest the motive and principle upon which it is based. By it the holding and flogging of Negroes is the exclusive luxury of loyal men.

Our chief danger lies in the absence of all moral feeling in the utterances of our rulers. In his letter to Mr. Greeley the President told the country virtually that the abolition or non-abolition of slavery was a matter of indifference to him. He would save the Union with slavery or without slavery. In his last Message he shows the same moral indifference, by saying as he does say that he had hoped that the rebellion could be put down without the abolition of slavery.

When the late Stephen A. Douglas uttered the sentiment that he did not care whether slavery were voted up or voted down in the territories, we thought him lost to all genuine feeling on the subject, and no man more than Mr. Lincoln denounced that sentiment as unworthy of the lips of any American statesman. But today, after nearly three years of a slaveholding rebellion, Douglas wanted popular sovereignty; Mr. Lincoln wants the Union. Now did a warm heart and a high moral feeling control the utterance of the President, he would welcome, with joy unspeakable and full of glory, the opportunity afforded by the rebellion to free the country form the matchless crime and infamy. But policy, policy, everlasting policy, has robbed our statesmanship of all soul-moving utterances.

The great misfortune is and has been during all the progress of this war, that the government and loyal people have not understood and accepted its true mission. Hence we have been floundering in the depths of dead issues. Endeavoring to impose old and worn-out condition upon new relations—putting new wines into old bottles, new cloth into old garments and thus making the rent worse then before.

Had we been wise we should have recognized the war at the outset as at once the signal and the necessity for a new order of social and political relations among the whole people. We could, like the ancients, discern the face of the sky, but not the signs of the times. Hence we have been talking of the importance of carrying on the war within the limits of a Constitution broken down by the very people in whose behalf the Constitution is pleaded! Hence we have from the first been deluding ourselves with the miserable dream that the old Union can be revived in the states where it has been abolished.

Now, we of the North have seen many strange things and may see many more; but that old Union, whose canonized bones we saw hearse in death and inurned under the frowning battlements of Sumter, we shall never see again while the world standeth. The issue before us is a living issue. We are not fighting for the dead past, but for the living present and the glorious future. We are not fighting for the old Union, nor for anything like it, but for that which is ten thousand times more important; and that thing, crisply rendered, is national unity. Both sections have tried union. It has failed.

The lesson for the statesmen at his hour is to discover and apply some principle of government which shall produce unity of sentiment, unity of idea, unity of object. Union without unity is, as we have seen, body without soul, marriage without love, a barrel without hoops, which falls at the first touch.

The statesmen of the South understood this matter earlier and better than the statesmen of the North. The dissolution of the Union on the old bases of compromise was plainly foreseen and predicted thirty years ago. Mr. Calhoun, and not Mr. Seward, is the original author of the doctrine of the irrepressible conflict. The South is logical and consistent. Under the teachings of their great leader they admit into their form of government no disturbing force. They have based their confederacy squarely on their cornerstone. Their two great all-commanding ideas are, first, that slavery is right, and second, that the slaveholders are a superior order or class. Around these two ideas their manners, morals, politics, religion and laws revolve. Slavery being right, all that is inconsistent with its entire security is necessarily wrong, and of course ought to be put down. There is no flaw in their logic.

They first endeavored to make the federal government stand upon their accursed cornerstone; and we but barely escaped, as well you know, that calamity. Fugitive-slave laws, slavery-extension laws, and Dred Scott decisions were among the steps to get the nation squarely upon the cornerstone now chosen by the Confederate states. The loyal North is less definite in regard to the necessity of principles of national unity. Yet, unconsciously to ourselves, and against our own protestations, we are in reality, like the South, fighting for national unity—a unity of which the great principles of liberty and equality, and not slavery and class superiority, are the cornerstone.

Long before this rude and terrible war came to tell us of a broken Constitution and a dead Union, the better portion of the loyal people had outlived and outgrown what they had been taught to believe were the requirements of the old Union. We had come to detest the principle by which slavery had a strong representation in Congress. We had come to abhor the idea of being called upon to suppress slave insurrections. We had come to be ashamed of slave hunting, and being made the watchdogs of slaveholders, who were too proud to scent out and hunt down their slaves for themselves. We had so far outlived the old Union four years ago that we thought the little finger of the hero of Harpers Ferry of more value to the world struggling for liberty than all the first families of old Virginia put together.

What business, then, have we to be pouring out our treasure and shedding our best blood like water for that old worn-out, dead and buried Union, which had already become a calamity and a curse? The fact is, we are not fighting for any such thing, and we ought to come out under our own true colors, and let the South and the whole world know that we don't want and will not have anything analogous to the old Union.

What we now want is a country—a free country—a country not saddened by the footprints of a single slave—and nowhere cursed by the presence of a slaveholder. We want a country which shall not brand the Declaration of Independence as a lie. We want a country whose fundamental institutions we can proudly defend before the highest intelligence and civilization of the age. Hitherto we have opposed European scorn of our slavery with a blush of shame as our best defense. We now want a country in which the obligations of patriotism shall not conflict with fidelity to justice and liberty. We want a country, and are fighting for a country, which shall be free from sectional political parties—free from sectional religious dominations—free from sectional benevolent associations—free from every kind and description of sect, party, and combination of a sectional character. We want a country where men may assemble from any part of it, without prejudice to their interests or peril to their persons. We are in fact, and from absolute necessity, transplanting the whole South with the higher civilization of the North. The New England schoolhouse is bound to take the place of the Southern whipping post. Not because we love the Negro, but the nation; not because we prefer to do this, because we must or give up the contest and give up the country. WE want a country, and are fighting for a country, where social intercourse and commercial relations shall neither be embarrassed nor embittered by the imperious exactions of an insolent slaveholding oligarchy which required Northern merchants to sell their souls as a condition precedent to selling their goods. We want a country, and are fighting for a country, through the length and breadth of which the literature and learning of any section of it may float to its extremities unimpaired, and thus become the common property of all the people—a country in which no man shall be fined for reading a book, or imprisoned for selling a book—a country where no man may be imprisoned or flogged or sold for learning to read, or teaching a fellow mortal how to read. We want a country, and are fighting for a country, in any part of which to be called an American citizen shall mean as much as it did to be called a Roman citizen in the palmist days of the Roman empire.

We have heard much in other days of manifest destiny. I don't go all the lengths to which such theories are pressed, but I do believe that it is the manifest destiny of this war to unify and reorganize the institutions of the country, and that herein is the secret of the strength, the fortitude, the persistent energy—in a word, the sacred significance—of this war. Strike out the high ends and aims thus indicated, and the war would appear to the impartial eye of an onlooking world like little better than a gigantic enterprise for shedding human blood.

A most interesting and gratifying confirmation of this theory of its mission is furnished in the varying fortunes of the struggle itself. Just in proportion to the progress made in taking upon itself the character I have ascribed to it has the war prospered and the rebellion lost ground.

Justice and humanity are often overpowered, but they are persistent and eternal forces, and fearful to contend against. Let but our rulers place the government fully within these trade winds of omnipotence, and the hand of death is upon the Confederate rebels. A war waged as ours seemed to be at first, merely for power and empire, repels sympathy though supported by legitimacy. If Ireland should strike for independence tomorrow, the sympathy of this country would be with her, and I doubt if American statesmen would be more discreet in the expression of their opinions of the merits of the contest than British statesmen have been concerning the merits of ours. When we were merely fighting for the old Union the world looked coldly upon our government. But now the world begins to see something more than legitimacy, something more than national pride. It sees national wisdom aiming at national unity, and national justice breaking the chains of a long-enslaved people. It is this new complexion of our cause which warms our hearts and strengthens our hands at home, disarms our enemies and increases our friends abroad. It is this more than all else which has carried consternation in to the bloodstained halls of the South. It has sealed the fiery and scornful lips of the Roebucks and Lindsays of England, and caused even the eloquent Mr. Gladstone to restrain the expression of his admiration for Jeff Davis and his rebel nation. It has placed the broad arrow of British suspicion on the prows of the rebel rams in the Mersey and performed a like service in France. It has driven Mason, the shameless man hunter, from London, where he never should have been allowed to stay for an hour, except as a bloodhound is tolerated in Regent Park for exhibition. We have had, from the first, warm friends in England. We owe a debt of respect and gratitude to William Edward Forster, John Bright, Richard Cobden, and other British Statesmen, in that they outran us in comprehending the high character of our struggle. They saw that his must be a war for human nature, and walked by faith to its defense while all was darkness about us—while we were yet conducting it in profound reverence for slavery.

I know we are not to be praised for this changed character of the war. We did our very best to prevent it. WE had but one object at the beginning, and that was, as I have said, the restoration of the old Union; and for the first two years the war was kept to that object strictly, and you know full well and bitterly with what results. I will not stop here to blame and denounce the past; but I will say that the most of the blunders and disasters of the earlier part of the war might have been avoided had our armies and generals not repelled the only true friends the Union cause had in the rebel states. The Army of the Potomac took up an anti-Negro position from the first and has not entirely renounced it yet. The colored people told me a few days ago in Washington that they were the victims of the most brutal treatment by these Northern soldiers when they first came there. But let that pass. Few men, however great their wisdom, are permitted to see the end from the beginning. Events are mightier than our rulers, and these divine forces, with overpowering logic, have fixed upon this war, against the wishes of our government, the comprehensive character and mission I have ascribed to it. The collecting of revenue in the rebel ports, the repossession of a few forts and arsenals and other public property stolen by the rebels, have almost disappeared from the recollection of the people. The war has been a growing war in every sense of the word. It began weak and has risen strong. It began low and has risen high. It began narrow and has become broad. It began with few and now, behold, the country is full of armed men, ready, with courage and fortitude, to make the wisest and best idea of American statesmanship the law of the land.

Let, then, the war proceed in its strong, high and broad course till the rebellion is put down and our country is saved beyond the necessity of being saved again!

I have already hinted at our danger. Let me be a little more direct and pronounced.

The Democratic party, though defeated in the elections last fall, is still a power. It is the ready organized nucleus of a powerful proslavery and pro-rebel reaction. Though it has lost in members, it retains all the elements of its former power and malevolence.

That party has five very strong points in its favor, and its public men and journals know well how to take advantage of them.

First: There is the absence of any deep moral felling among the loyal people against slavery itself, their feeling against it being on account of its rebellion against the government, and not because it is a stupendous crime against human nature.

Secondly: The vast expense of the war and the heavy taxes in money as well as men which the war requires for its prosecution. Loyalty has a strong back, but taxation has often broken it.

Thirdly: The earnest desire for peace which is shared by all classes except government contractors who are making money out of the war; a feeling which may be kindled to a flame by any serious reverses to our arms. It is silent in victory but vehement and dangerous in defeat.

Fourthly: And superior to all others, is the national prejudice and hatred toward all colored people of the country, a feeling which has done more to encourage the hopes of the rebels than all other powers beside.

Fifthly: An Abolitionist is an object of popular dislike. The guilty rebel who with broad blades and bloody hands seeks the life of the nation, is at this hour more acceptable to the Northern Democracy than an Abolitionist guilty of no crime. Whatever may be a man's abilities, virtue or service, the fact that he is an Abolitionist makes him an object of popular hate.

Upon these five strings the Democrats still have hopes of playing themselves into power, and not without reason. While our government has the meanness to ask Northern colored men to give up the comfort of home, endure untold hardships, peril health, limbs and life itself, in its defense, and then degrades them in the eyes of other soldiers, by offering them the paltry sum of seven dollars power month, and refuses to reward their valor with even the hope of promotion—the Democratic party may well enough presume upon the strength of popular prejudice for support.

While our Republican government at Washington makes color and not character the criterion of promotion in the Army and degrades colored commissioned officers at New Orleans below the rank to which even the rebel government had elevated them, I think we are in danger of a compromise with slavery.

Our hopeful Republican friends tell me this is impossible—that the day of compromise with slavery is past. This may do for some men, but will not do for me.

The Northern people have always been remarkably confident of their own virtue. They are hopeful to the last. Twenty years ago we hoped that Texas could not be annexed; but if that could not be prevented we hoped that she would come in a free state. Thirteen years ago we were quite sure that no such abomination as the Fugitive Slave Bill could get itself on our national statute book; but when it got there we were equally sure that it never could be enforced. Four years ago we were sure that the slave states would not rebel, but if they did we were sure it would be a very short rebellion. I know that times have changed very rapidly, and that we have changed them. Nevertheless, I know also we are the same old American people, and that what we have done once we may possibly do again. The leaven of compromise is among us. I repeat, while we have a Democratic party at the North trimming its sails to catch the Southern breeze in the next Presidential election, we are in danger of compromise. Tell me not of amnesties and oaths of allegiance. They are valueless in the presence of twenty hundred millions invested in human flesh. Let but the little finger of slavery get back into this Union, and in one year you shall see its whole body again upon our backs.

While a respectable colored man or woman can be kicked out of the commonest streetcar in New York where any white ruffian may ride unquestioned, we are in danger of a compromise with slavery. While the North is full of such papers as the New York World, Express and Herald, firing the nation's heart with hatred to Negroes and Abolitionists, we are in danger of a slaveholding peace. While the major part of antislavery profession is based upon devotion to the Union rather than hostility to slavery, there is danger of a slaveholding peace. Until we shall see the election of November next, and that it has resulted in the election of a sound antislavery man as President, we shall be in danger of a slaveholding compromise. Indeed, as long as slavery has any life in it anywhere in the country, we are in danger of such a compromise.

Then there is the danger arising from the impatience of the people on account of the prolongation of the war. I know the American people. They are an impulsive people, impatient of delay, clamorous for change, and often look for results out of all proportion to the means employed in attaining them.

You and I know that the mission of this war is national regeneration. We know and consider that a nation is not born in a day. We know that large bodies move slowly—and often seem to move thus when, could we perceive their actual velocity, we should be astonished at its greatness. A great battle lost or won is easily described, understood and appreciated, but the moral growth of a great nation requires reflection, as well as observation, to appreciate it. There are vast numbers of voters, who make no account of the moral growth of a great nation and who only look at the war as a calamity to be endured only so long as they have no power to arrest it. Now, this is just the sort of people whose votes may turn the scale against us in the last event.

Thoughts of this kind tell me that there never was a time when antislavery work was more needed than now. The day that shall see the rebels at our feet, their weapons flung away, will be the day of trial. We have need to prepare for that trial. We have long been saved a proslavery peace by the stubborn, unbending persistence of the rebels. Let them bend as they will bend, there will come the test of our sternest virtues.

I have now given, very briefly, some of the grounds of danger. A word as to the ground of hope. The best that can be offered is that we have made progress—vast and striking progress—within the last two years.

President Lincoln introduced his administration to the country as one which would faithfully catch, hold and return runaway slaves to their masters. He avowed his determination to protect and defend the slaveholder's right to plunder the black laborer of his hard earnings. Europe was assured by Mr. Seward that no slave should gain his freedom by this war. Both the President and the Secretary of State have made progress since then.

Our generals, at the beginning of the war, were horribly proslavery. They took to slave catching and slave killing like ducks to water. They are now very generally and very earnestly in favor of putting an end to slavery. Some of them, like Hunter and Butler, because they hate slavery on its own account, and others, because slavery is in arms against the government.

The rebellion has been a rapid educator. Congress was the first to respond to the instinctive judgment of the people, and fixed the broad brand of its reprobation upon slave hunting in shoulder straps. Then came very temperate talk about confiscation, which soon came to be pretty radical talk. Then came propositions for Border State, gradual, compensated, colonized emancipation. Then came the threat of a proclamation, and then came the Proclamation. Meanwhile the Negro had passed along from a loyal spade and pickax to a Springfield rifle.

Haiti and Liberia are recognized. Slavery is humbled in Maryland, threatened in Tennessee, stunned nearly to death in western Kentucky, and gradually melting away before our arms in the rebellious states.

The hour is one of hope as well as danger. But whatever may come to pass, onething is clear: The principles involved in the contest, the necessities of both sections of the country, the obvious requirements of the age, and every suggestion of enlightened policy demand the utter extirpation of slavery from every foot of American soil, and the enfranchisement of the entire colored population of the country. Elsewhere we may find peace, but it will be a hollow and deceitful peace. Elsewhere we may find prosperity, but it will be a transient prosperity. Elsewhere we may find greatness and renown, but if these are based upon anything less substantial than justice they will vanish, for righteousness alone can permanently exalt a nation.

I end where I began—no war but an Abolition war; no peace but an Abolition peace; liberty for all, chains for none; the black man a soldier in war, a laborer in peace; a voter at the South as well as at the North; America his permanent home, and all Americans his fellow countrymen. Such, fellow citizens, is my idea of the mission of the war. If accomplished, our glory as a nation will be complete, our peace will flow like a river, and our foundation will be the everlasting rocks.

What Do Black Men Want

I came here, as I come always to the meetings in New England, as a listener, and not as a speaker; and one of the reasons why I have not been more frequently to the meetings of this society, has been because of the disposition on the part of some of my friends to call me out upon the platform, even when they knew that there was some difference of opinion and of feeling between those who rightfully belong to this platform and myself; and for fear of being misconstrued, as desiring to interrupt or disturb the proceedings of these meetings, I have usually kept away, and have thus been deprived of that educating influence, which I am always free to confess is of the highest order, descending from this platform. I have felt, since I have lived out West (Douglass means west of Boston, in Rochester, NY), that in going there I parted from a great deal that was valuable; and I feel, every time I come to these meetings, that I have lost a great deal by making my home west of Boston, west of Massachusetts; for, if anywhere in the country there is to be found the highest sense of justice, or the truest demands for my race, I look for it in the East, I look for it here. The ablest discussions of the whole question of our rights occur here, and to be deprived of the privilege of listening to those discussions is a great deprivation.

I do not know, from what has been said, that there is any difference of opinion as to the duty of abolitionists, at the present moment. How can we get up any difference at this point, or any point, where we are so united, so agreed? I went especially, however, with that word of Mr. Phillips, which is the criticism of Gen. Banks and Gen. Banks' policy. (Gen. Banks instituted a labor policy in Louisiana that was discriminatory of blacks, claiming that it was to help prepare them to better handle freedom. Wendell Phillips countered by saying, "If there is anything patent in the whole history of our thirty years' struggle, it is that the Negro no more needs to be prepared for liberty than the white man.") I hold that that policy is our chief danger at the present moment; that it practically enslaves the Negro, and makes the Proclamation (the Emancipation Proclamation) of 1863 a mockery and delusion. What is freedom? It is the right to choose one's own employment. Certainly it means that, if it means anything; and when any individual or combination of individuals undertakes to decide for any man when he shall work, where he shall work, at what he shall work, and for what he shall work, he or they practically reduce him to slavery. (Applause.) He is a slave. That I understand Gen. Banks to do—to determine for the so-called freedman, when, and where, and at what, and for how much he shall work, when he shall be punished, and by whom punished. It is absolute slavery. It defeats the beneficent intention of the Government, if it has beneficent intentions, in regards to the freedom of our people.

I have had but one idea for the last three years to present to the American people, and the phraseology in which I clothe it is the old abolition phraseology. I am for the "immediate, unconditional, and universal" enfranchisement of the black man, in every State in the Union. (Loud applause.) Without this, his liberty is a mockery; without this, you might as well almost retain the old name of slavery for his condition; for in fact, if he is not the slave of the individual master, he is the slave of society, and holds his liberty as a privilege, not as a right. He is at the mercy of the mob, and has no means of protecting himself.

It may be objected, however, that this pressing of the Negro's right to suffrage is premature. Let us have slavery abolished, it may be said, let us have labor organized, and then, in the natural course of events, the right of suffrage will be extended to the Negro. I do not agree with this. The constitution of the human mind is such, that if it once disregards the conviction forced upon it by a revelation of truth, it requires the exercise of a higher power to produce the same conviction afterwards. The American people are now in tears. The Shenandoah has run blood—the best blood of the North. All around Richmond, the blood of New England and of the North has been shed—of your sons, your brothers and your fathers. We all feel, in the existence of this Rebellion, that judgments terrible, wide-spread, far-reaching, overwhelming, are abroad in the land; and we feel, in view of these judgments, just now, a disposition to learn righteousness. This is the hour. Our streets are in mourning, tears are falling at every fireside, and under the chastisement of this Rebellion we have almost come up to the point of conceding this great, this all-important right of suffrage. I fear that if we fail to do it now, if abolitionists fail to press it now, we may not see, for centuries to come, the same disposition that exists at this moment. (Applause.) Hence, I say, now is the time to press this right.

It may be asked, "Why do you want it? Some men have got along very well without it. Women have not this right." Shall we justify one wrong by another? This is the sufficient answer. Shall we at this moment justify the deprivation of the Negro of the right to vote, because some one else is deprived of that privilege? I hold that women, as well as men, have the right to vote (Applause), and my heart and voice go with the movement to extend suffrage to woman; but that question rests upon another basis than which our right rests. We may be asked, I say, why we want it. I will tell you why we want it. We want it because it is our right, first of all. No class of men can, without insulting their own nature, be content with any deprivation of their rights. We want it again, as a means for educating our race. Men are so constituted that they derive their conviction of their own possibilities largely by the estimate formed of them by others. If nothing is expected of a people, that people will find it difficult to contradict that expectation. By depriving us of suffrage, you affirm our incapacity to form an intelligent judgment respecting public men and public measures; you declare before the world that we are unfit to exercise the elective franchise, and by this means lead us to undervalue ourselves, to put a low estimate upon ourselves, and to feel that we have no possibilities like other men. Again, I want the elective franchise, for one, as a colored man, because ours is a peculiar government, based upon a peculiar idea, and that idea is universal suffrage. If I were in a monarchial government, or an autocratic or aristocratic government, where the few bore rule and the many were subject, there would be no special stigma resting upon me, because I did not exercise the elective franchise. It would do me no great violence. Mingling with the mass I should partake of the strength of the mass; I should be supported by the mass, and I should have the same incentives to endeavor with the mass of my fellow-men; it would be no particular burden, no particular deprivation; but here where universal suffrage is the rule, where that is the fundamental idea of the Government, to rule us out is to make us an exception, to brand us with the stigma of inferiority, and to invite to our heads the missiles of those about us; therefore, I want the franchise for the black man.

There are, however, other reasons, not derived from any consideration merely of our rights, but arising out of the conditions of the South, and of the country—considerations which have already been referred to by Mr. Phillips—considerations which must arrest the attention of statesmen. I believe that when the tall heads of this Rebellion shall have been swept down, as they will be swept down, when the Davises and Toombses and Stephenses, and others who are leading this Rebellion shall have been blotted out, there will be this rank undergrowth of treason, to which reference has been made, growing up there, and interfering with, and thwarting the quiet operation of the Federal Government in those states. You will see those traitors, handing down, from sire to son, the same malignant spirit which they have manifested and which they are now exhibiting, with malicious hearts, broad blades, and bloody hands in the field, against our sons and brothers. That spirit will still remain; and whoever sees the Federal Government extended over those Southern States will see that Government in a strange land, and not only in a strange land, but in an enemy's land. A post-master of the United States in the South will find himself surrounded by a hostile spirit; a collector in a Southern port will find himself surrounded by a hostile spirit; a United States marshal or United States judge will be surrounded there by a hostile element. That enmity will not die out in a year, will not die out in an age. The Federal Government will be looked upon in those States precisely as the Governments of Austria and France are looked upon in Italy at the present moment. They will endeavor to circumvent, they will endeavor to destroy, the peaceful operation of this Government. Now, where will you find the strength to counterbalance this spirit, if you do not find it in the Negroes of the South? They are your friends, and have always been your friends. They were your friends even when the Government did not regard them as such. They comprehended the genius of this war before you did. It is a significant fact, it is a marvellous fact, it seems almost to imply a direct interposition of Providence, that this war, which began in the interest of slavery on both sides, bids fair to end in the interest of liberty on both sides. (Applause.) It was begun, I say, in the interest of slavery on both sides. The South was fighting to take slavery out of the Union, and the North was fighting to keep it in the Union; the South fighting to get it beyond the limits of the United States Constitution, and the North fighting to retain it within those limits; the South fighting for new guarantees, and the North fighting for the old guarantees;— both despising the Negro, both insulting the Negro. Yet, the Negro, apparently endowed with wisdom from on high, saw more clearly the end from the beginning than we did. When Seward said the status of no man in the country would be changed by the war, the Negro did not believe him. (Applause.) When our generals sent their underlings in shoulder-straps to hunt the flying Negro back from our lines into the jaws of slavery, from which he had escaped, the Negroes thought that a mistake had been made, and that the intentions of the Government had not been rightly understood by our officers in shoulder-straps, and they continued to come into our lines, threading their way through bogs and fens, over briers and thorns, fording streams, swimming rivers, bringing us tidings as to the safe path to march, and pointing out the dangers that threatened us. They are our only friends in the South, and we should be true to them in this their trial hour, and see to it that they have the elective franchise.

I know that we are inferior to you in some things—virtually inferior. We walk about you like dwarfs among giants. Our heads are scarcely seen above the great sea of humanity. The Germans are superior to us; the Irish are superior to us; the Yankees are superior to us (Laughter); they can do what we cannot, that is, what we have not hitherto been allowed to do. But while I make this admission, I utterly deny, that we are originally, or naturally, or practically, or in any way, or in any important sense, inferior to anybody on this globe. (Loud applause.) This charge of inferiority is an old dodge. It has been made available for oppression on many occasions. It is only about six centuries since the blue-eyed and fair-haired Anglo-Saxons were considered inferior by the haughty Normans, who once trampled upon them. If you read the history of the Norman Conquest, you will find that this proud Anglo-Saxon was once looked upon as of coarser clay than his Norman master, and might be found in the highways and byways of Old England laboring with a brass collar on his neck, and the name of his master marked upon it. You were down then! (Laughter and applause.) You are up now. I am glad you are up, and I want you to be glad to help us up also. (Applause.)

The story of our inferiority is an old dodge, as I have said; for wherever men oppress their fellows, wherever they enslave them, they will endeavor to find the needed apology for such enslavement and oppression in the character of the people oppressed and enslaved. When we wanted, a few years ago, a slice of Mexico, it was hinted that the Mexicans were an inferior race, that the old Castilian blood had become so weak that it would scarcely run down hill, and that Mexico needed the long, strong and beneficent arm of the Anglo-Saxon care extended over it. We said that it was necessary to its salvation, and a part of the "manifest destiny" of this Republic, to extend our arm over that dilapidated government. So, too, when Russia wanted to take possession of a part of the Ottoman Empire, the Turks were an "inferior race." So, too, when England wants to set the heel of her power more firmly in the quivering heart of old Ireland, the Celts are an "inferior race." So, too, the Negro, when he is to be robbed of any right which is justly his, is an "inferior man." It is said that we are ignorant; I admit it. But if we know enough to be hung, we know enough to vote. If the Negro knows enough to pay taxes to support the government, he knows enough to vote; taxation and representation should go together. If he knows enough to shoulder a musket and fight for the flag, fight for the government, he knows enough to vote. If he knows as much when he is sober as an Irishman knows when drunk, he knows enough to vote, on good American principles. (Laughter and applause.)

But I was saying that you needed a counterpoise in the persons of the slaves to the enmity that would exist at the South after the Rebellion is put down. I hold that the American people are bound, not only in self-defence, to extend this right to the freedmen of the South, but they are bound by their love of country, and by all their regard for the future safety of those Southern States, to do this—to do it as a measure essential to the preservation of peace there. But I will not dwell upon this. I put it to the American sense of honor. The honor of a nation is an important thing. It is said in the Scriptures, "What doth it profit a man if he gain the whole world, and lose his own soul?" It may be said, also, What doth it profit a nation if it gain the whole world, but lose its honor? I hold that the American government has taken upon itself a solemn obligation of honor, to see that this war—let it be long or short, let it cost much or let it cost little—that this war shall not cease until every freedman at the South has the right to vote. (Applause.) It has bound itself to it. What have you asked the black men of the South, the black men of the whole country to do? Why, you have asked them to incure the enmity of their masters, in order to befriend you and to befriend this Government. You have asked us to call down, not only upon ourselves, but upon our children's children, the deadly hate of the entire Southern people. You have called upon us to turn our backs upon our masters, to abandon their cause and espouse yours; to turn against the South and in favor of the North; to shoot down the Confederacy and uphold the flag—the American flag. You have called upon us to expose ourselves to all the subtle machinations of their malignity for all time. And now, what do you propose to do when you come to make peace? To reward your enemies, and trample in the dust your friends? Do you intend to sacrifice the very men who have come to the rescue of your banner in the South, and incurred the lasting displeasure of their masters thereby? Do you intend to sacrifice them and reward your enemies? Do you mean to give your enemies the right to vote, and take it away from your friends? Is that wise policy? Is that honorable? Could American honor withstand such a blow? I do not believe you will do it. I think you will see to it that we have the right to vote. There is something too mean in looking upon the Negro, when you are in trouble, as a citizen, and when you are free from trouble, as an alien. When this nation was in trouble, in its early struggles, it looked upon the Negro as a citizen. In 1776 he was a citizen. At the time of the formation of the Constitution the Negro had the right to vote in eleven States out of the old thirteen. In your trouble you have made us citizens. In 1812 Gen. Jackson addressed us as citizens—"fellow-citizens." He wanted us to fight. We were citizens then! And now, when you come to frame a conscription bill, the Negro is a citizen again. He has been a citizen just three times in the history of this government, and it has always been in time of trouble. In time of trouble we are citizens. Shall we be citizens in war, and aliens in peace? Would that be just?

I ask my friends who are apologizing for not insisting upon this right, where can the black man look, in this country, for the assertion of his right, if he may not look to the Massachusetts Anti-Slavery Society? Where under the whole heavens can he look for sympathy, in asserting this right, if he may not look to this platform? Have you lifted us up to a certain height to see that we are men, and then are any disposed to leave us there, without seeing that we are put in possession of all our rights? We look naturally to this platform for the assertion of all our rights, and for this one especially. I understand the anti-slavery societies of this country to be based on two principles,—first, the freedom of the blacks of this country; and, second, the elevation of them. Let me not be misunderstood here. I am not asking for sympathy at the hands of abolitionists, sympathy at the hands of any. I think the American people are disposed often to be generous rather than just. I look over this country at the present time, and I see Educational Societies, Sanitary Commissions, Freedmen's Associations, and the like,—all very good: but in regard to the colored people there is always more that is benevolent, I perceive, than just, manifested towards us. What I ask for the Negro is not benevolence, not pity, not sympathy, but simply justice. (Applause.) The American people have always been anxious to know what they shall do with us. Gen. Banks was distressed with solicitude as to what he should do with the Negro. Everybody has asked the question, and they learned to ask it early of the abolitionists, "What shall we do with the Negro?" I have had but one answer from the beginning. Do nothing with us! Your doing with us has already played the mischief with us. Do nothing with us! If the apples will not remain on the tree of their own strength, if they are worm eaten at the core, if they are early ripe and disposed to fall, let them fall! I am not for tying or fastening them on the tree in any way, except by nature's plan, and if they will not stay there, let them fall. And if the Negro cannot stand on his own legs, let him fall also. All I ask is, give him a chance to stand on his own legs! Let him alone! If you see him on his way to school, let him alone, don't disturb him! If you see him going to the dinner table at a hotel, let him go! If you see him going to the ballot-box, let him alone, don't disturb him! (Applause.) If you see him going into a work-shop, just let him alone,—your interference is doing him a positive injury. Gen. Banks' "preparation" is of a piece with this attempt to prop up the Negro. Let him fall if he cannot stand alone! If the Negro cannot live by the line of eternal justice, so beautifully pictured to you in the illustration used by Mr. Phillips, the fault will not be yours, it will be his who made the Negro, and established that line for his government. (Applause.) Let him live or die by that. If you will only untie his hands, and give him a chance, I think he will live. He will work as readily for himself as the white man. A great many delusions have been swept away by this war. One was, that the Negro would not work; he has proved his ability to work. Another was, that the Negro would not fight; that he possessed only the most sheepish attributes of humanity; was a perfect lamb, or an "Uncle Tom;" disposed to take off his coat whenever required, fold his hands, and be whipped by anybody who wanted to whip him. But the war has proved that there is a great deal of human nature in the Negro, and that "he will fight," as Mr. Quincy, our President, said, in earlier days than these, "when there is reasonable probability of his whipping anybody."

We Are All Bound Up Together

I feel I am something of a novice upon this platform. Born of a race whose inheritance has been outrage and wrong, most of my life had been spent in battling against those wrongs. But I did not feel as keenly as others, that I had these rights, in common with other women, which are now demanded. About two years ago, I stood within the shadows of my home. A great sorrow had fallen upon my life. My husband had died suddenly, leaving me a widow, with four children, one my own, and the others stepchildren. I tried to keep my children together. But my husband died in debt; and before he had been in his grave three months, the administrator had swept the very milk-crocks and wash tubs from my hands. I was a farmer's wife and made butter for the Columbus market; but what could I do, when they had swept all away? They left me one thing—and that was a looking glass! Had I died instead of my husband, how different would have been the result! By this time he would have had another wife, it is likely; and no administrator would have gone into his house, broken up his home, and sold his bed, and taken away his means of support.

I took my children in my arms, and went out to seek my living. While I was gone, a neighbor to whom I had once lent five dollars, went before a magistrate and Swore that he believed I was a non-resident, and laid an attachment on my very bed. And I went back to Ohio with my orphan children in my arms, without a single feather bed in this wide world, that was not in the custody of the law. I say, then, that justice is not fulfilled so long as woman is unequal before the law.

We are all bound up together in one great bundle of humanity, and society cannot trample on the weakest and feeblest of its members without receiving the curse in its own soul. You tried that in the case of the Negro. You pressed him down for two centuries; and in so doing you crippled the moral strength and paralyzed the spiritual energies of the white men of the country. When the hands of the black were fettered, white men were deprived of the liberty of speech and the freedom of the press. Society cannot afford to neglect the enlightenment of any class of its members. At the South, the legislation of the country was in behalf of the rich slaveholders, while the poor white man was neglected. What is the consequence today? From that very class of neglected poor white men, comes the man who stands today, with his hand upon the helm of the nation. He fails to catch the watchword of the hour, and throws himself, the incarnation of meanness, across the pathway of the nation. My objection to Andrew Johnson is not that he has been a poor white man; my objection is that he keeps "poor whits" all the way through. That is the trouble with him.

This grand and glorious revolution which has commenced, will fail to reach its climax of success, until throughout the length and brea(d)th of the American Republic, the nation shall be so color-blind, as to know no man by the color of his skin or the curl of his hair. It will then have no privileged class, trampling upon and outraging the unprivileged classes, but will be then one great privileged nation, whose privilege will be to produce the loftiest manhood and womanhood that humanity can attain.

I do not believe that giving the woman the ballot is immediately going to cure all the ills of life. I do not believe that white women are dew-drops just exhaled from the skies. I think that like men they may be divided into three classes, the good, the bad, and the indifferent. The good would vote according to their convictions and principles; the bad, as dictated by preju(d)ice or malice; and the indifferent will vote on the strongest side of the question, with the winning party.

You white women speak here of rights. I speak of wrongs. I, as a colored woman, have had in this country an education which has made me feel as if I were in the situation of Ishmael, my hand against every man, and every man's hand against me. Let me go tomorrow morning and take my seat in one of your street cars—I do not know that they will do it in New York, but they will in Philadelphia—and the conductor will put up his hand and stop the car rather than let me ride.

Going from Washington to Baltimore this Spring, they put me in the smoking car. Aye, in the capital of the nation, where the black man consecrated himself to the nation's defence, faithful when the white man was faithless, they put me in the smoking car! They did it once; but the next time they tried it, they failed; for I would not go in. I felt the fight in me; but I don't want to have to fight all the time. Today I am puzzled where to make my home. I would like to make it in Philadelphia, near my own friends and relations. But if I want to ride in the streets of Philadelphia, they send me to ride on the platform with the driver. Have women nothing to do with this? Not long since, a colored woman took her seat in an Eleventh Street car in Philadelphia, and the conductor stopped the car, and told the rest of the passengers to get out, and left the car with her in it alone, when they took it back to the station. One day I took my seat in a car, and the conductor came to me and told me to take another seat. I just screamed "murder." The man said if I was black I ought to behave myself. I knew that if he was white he was not behaving himself. Are there not wrongs to be righted?

In advocating the cause of the colored man, since the Dred Scott decision, I have sometimes said I thought the nation had touched bottom. But let me tell you there is a depth of infamy lower than that. It is when the nation, standing upon the threshold of a great peril, reached out its hands to a feebler race, and asked that race to help it, and when the peril was over, said, You are good enough for soldiers, but not good enough for citizens. . .

We have a woman in our country who has received the name of "Moses," not by lying about it, but by acting it out—a woman who has gone down into the Egypt of slavery and brought out hundreds of our people into liberty. The last time I saw that woman, her hands were swollen. That woman who had led one of Montgomery's most successful expeditions, who was brave enough and secretive enough to act as a scout for the American army, had her hands all swollen from a conflict with a brutal conductor, who undertook to eject her from her place. That woman, whose courage and bravery won a recognition from our army and from every black man in the land, is excluded from every thoroughfare of travel. Talk of giving women the ballot-box? Go on. It is a normal school, and the white women of this country need it. While there exists this brutal element in society which tramples upon the feeble and treads down the weak, I tell you that if there is any class of people who need to be lifted out of their airy nothings and selfishness, it is the white women of America.

Appeal to Congress for
Impartial Suffrage

A very limited statement of the argument for impartial suffrage, and for including the negro in the body politic, would require more space than can be reasonably asked here. It is supported by reasons as broad as the nature of man, and as numerous as the wants of society. Man is the only government-making animal in the world. His right to a participation in the production and operation of government is an inference from his nature, as direct and self-evident as is his right to acquire property or education. It is no less a crime against the manhood of a man, to declare that he shall not share in the making and directing of the government under which he lives, than to say that he shall not acquire property and education. The fundamental and unanswerable argument in favor of the enfranchisement of the negro is found in the undisputed fact of his manhood. He is a man, and by every fact and argument by which any man can sustain his right to vote, the negro can sustain his right equally. It is plain that, if the right belongs to any, it belongs to all. The doctrine that some men have no rights that others are bound to respect, is a doctrine which we must banish as we have banished slavery, from which it emanated. If black men have no rights in the eyes of white men, of course the whites can have none in the eyes of the blacks. The result is a war of races, and the annihilation of all proper human relations.

But suffrage for the negro, while easily sustained upon abstract principles, demands consideration upon what are recognized as the urgent necessities of the case. It is a measure of relief,—a shield to break the force of a blow already descending with violence, and render it harmless. The work of destruction has already been set in motion all over the South. Peace to the country has literally meant war to the loyal men of the South, white and black; and negro suffrage is the measure to arrest and put an end to that dreadful strife.

Something then, not by way of argument, (for that has been done by Charles Sumner, Thaddeus Stevens, Wendell Phillips, Gerrit Smith, and other able men,) but rather of statement and appeal.

For better or for worse, (as in some of the old marriage ceremonies,) the negroes are evidently a permanent part of the American population. They are too numerous and useful to be colonized, and too enduring and self-perpetuating to disappear by natural causes. Here they are, four millions of them, and, for weal or for woe, here they must remain. Their history is parallel to that of the country; but while the history of the latter has been cheerful and bright with blessings, theirs has been heavy and dark with agonies and curses. What O'Connell said of the history of Ireland may with greater truth be said of the negro's. It may be "traced like a wounded man through a crowd, by the blood." Yet the negroes have marvellously survived all the exterminating forces of slavery, and have emerged at the end of two hundred and fifty years of bondage, not morose, misanthropic, and revengeful, but cheerful, hopeful, and forgiving. They now stand before Congress and the country, not complaining of the past, but simply asking for a better future. The spectacle of these dusky millions thus imploring, not demanding, is touching; and if American statesmen could be moved by a simple appeal to the nobler elements of human nature, if they had not fallen, seemingly, into the incurable habit of weighing and measuring every proposition of reform by some standard of profit and loss, doing wrong from choice, and right only from necessity or some urgent demand of human selfishness, it would be enough to plead for the negroes on the score of past services and sufferings. But no such appeal shall be relied on here. Hardships, services, sufferings, and sacrifices are all waived. It is true that they came to the relief of the country at the hour of its extremest need. It is true that, in many of the rebellious States, they were almost the only reliable friends the nation had throughout the whole tremendous war. It is true that, notwithstanding their alleged ignorance, they were wiser than their masters, and knew enough to be loyal, while those masters only knew enough to be rebels and traitors. It is true that they fought side by side in the loyal cause with our gallant and patriotic white soldiers, and that, but for their help,—divided as the loyal States were,—the Rebels might have succeeded in breaking up the Union, thereby entailing border wars and troubles of unknown duration and incalculable calamity. All this and more is true of these loyal negroes. Many daring exploits will be told to their credit. Impartial history will paint them as men who deserved well of their country. It will tell how they forded and swam rivers, with what consummate address they evaded the sharp-eyed Rebel pickets, how they toiled in the darkness of night through the tangled marshes of briers and thorns, barefooted and weary, running the risk of losing their lives, to warn our generals of Rebel schemes to surprise and destroy our loyal army. It will tell how these poor people, whose rights we still despised, behaved to our wounded soldiers, when found cold, hungry, and bleeding on the deserted battle-field; how they assisted our escaping prisoners from Andersonville, Belle Isle, Castle Thunder, and elsewhere, sharing with them their wretched crusts, and otherwise affording them aid and comfort; how they promptly responded to the trumpet call for their services, fighting against a foe that denied them the rights of civilized warfare, and for a government which was without the courage to assert those rights and avenge their violation in their behalf; with what gallantry they flung themselves upon Rebel fortifications, meeting death as fearlessly as any other troops in the service. But upon none of these things is reliance placed. These facts speak to the better dispositions of the human heart; but they seem of little weight with the opponents of impartial suffrage.

It is true that a strong plea for equal suffrage might be addressed to the national sense of honor. Something, too, might be said of national gratitude. A nation might well hesitate before the temptation to betray its allies. There is something immeasurably mean, to say nothing of the cruelty, in placing the loyal negroes of the South under the political power of their Rebel masters. To make peace with our enemies is all well enough; but to prefer our enemies and sacrifice our friends,—to exalt our enemies and cast down our friends,—to clothe our enemies, who sought the destruction of the government, with all political power, and leave our friends powerless in their hands,—is an act which need not be characterized here. We asked the negroes to espouse our cause, to be our friends, to fight for us, and against their masters; and now, after they have done all that we asked them to do,—helped us to conquer their masters, and thereby directed toward themselves the furious hate of the vanquished,—it is proposed in some quarters to turn them over to the political control of the common enemy of the government and of the negro. But of this let nothing be said in this place. Waiving humanity, national honor, the claims of gratitude, the precious satisfaction arising from deeds of charity and justice to the weak and defenceless,—the appeal for impartial suffrage addresses itself with great pertinency to the darkest, coldest, and flintiest side of the human heart, and would wring righteousness from the unfeeling calculations of human selfishness.

For in respect to this grand measure it is the good fortune of the negro that enlightened selfishness, not less than justice, fights on his side. National interest and national duty, if elsewhere separated, are firmly united here. The American people can, perhaps, afford to brave the censure of surrounding nations for the manifest injustice and meanness of excluding its faithful black soldiers from the ballot-box, but it cannot afford to allow the moral and mental energies of rapidly increasing millions to be consigned to hopeless degradation.

Strong as we are, we need the energy that slumbers in the black man's arm to make us stronger. We want no longer any heavy-footed, melancholy service from the negro. We want the cheerful activity of the quickened manhood of these sable millions. Nor can we afford to endure the moral blight which the existence of a degraded and hated class must necessarily inflict upon any people among whom such a class may exist. Exclude the negroes as a class from political rights,—teach them that the high and manly privilege of suffrage is to be enjoyed by white citizens only,—that they may bear the burdens of the state, but that they are to have no part in its direction or its honors,—and you at once deprive them of one of the main incentives to manly character and patriotic devotion to the interests of the government; in a word, you stamp them as a degraded caste,—you teach them to despise themselves, and all others to despise them. Men are so constituted that they largely derive their ideas of their abilities and their possibilities from the settled judgments of their fellow-men, and especially from such as they read in the institutions under which they live. If these bless them, they are blest indeed; but if these blast them, they are blasted indeed. Give the negro the elective franchise, and you give him at once a powerful motive for all noble exertion, and make him a man among men. A character is demanded of him, and here as elsewhere demand favors supply. It is nothing against this reasoning that all men who vote are not good men or good citizens. It is enough that the possession and exercise of the elective franchise is in itself an appeal to the nobler elements of manhood, and imposes education as essential to the safety of society.

To appreciate the full force of this argument, it must be observed, that disfranchisement in a republican government based upon the idea of human equality and universal suffrage, is a very different thing from disfranchisement in governments based upon the idea of the divine right of kings, or the entire subjugation of the masses. Masses of men can take care of themselves. Besides, the disabilities imposed upon all are necessarily without that bitter and stinging element of invidiousness which attaches to disfranchisement in a republic. What is common to all works no special sense of degradation to any. But in a country like ours, where men of all nations, kindred, and tongues are freely enfranchised, and allowed to vote, to say to the negro, You shall not vote, is to deal his manhood a staggering blow, and to burn into his soul a bitter and goading sense of wrong, or else work in him a stupid indifference to all the elements of a manly character. As a nation, we cannot afford to have amongst us either this indifference and stupidity, or that burning sense of wrong. These sable millions are too powerful to be allowed to remain either indifferent or discontented. Enfranchise them, and they become self-respecting and country-loving citizens. Disfranchise them, and the mark of Cain is set upon them less mercifully than upon the first murderer, for no man was to hurt him. But this mark of inferiority—all the more palpable because of a difference of color—not only dooms the negro to be a vagabond, but makes him the prey of insult and outrage everywhere. While nothing may be urged here as to the past services of the negro, it is quite within the line of this appeal to remind the nation of the possibility that a time may come when the services of the negro may be a second time required. History is said to repeat itself, and, if so, having wanted the negro once, we may want him again. Can that statesmanship be wise which would leave the negro good ground to hesitate, when the exigencies of the country required his prompt assistance? Can that be sound statesmanship which leaves millions of men in gloomy discontent, and possibly in a state of alienation in the day of national trouble? Was not the nation stronger when two hundred thousand sable soldiers were hurled against the Rebel fortifications, than it would have been without them?

Arming the negro was an urgent military necessity three years ago,—are we sure that another quite as pressing may not await us? Casting aside all thought of justice and magnanimity, is it wise to impose upon the negro all the burdens involved in sustaining government against foes within and foes without, to make him equal sharer in all sacrifices for the public good, to tax him in peace and conscript him in war, and then coldly exclude him from the ballot-box?

Look across the sea. Is Ireland, in her present condition, fretful, discontented, compelled to support an establishment in which she does not believe, and which the vast majority of her people abhor, a source of power or of weakness to Great Britain? Is not Austria wise in removing all ground of complaint against her on the part of Hungary? And does not the Emperor of Russia act wisely, as well as generously, when he not only breaks up the bondage of the serf, but extends him all the advantages of Russian citizenship? Is the present movement in

England in favor of manhood suffrage—for the purpose of bringing four millions of British subjects into full sympathy and co-operation with the British government—a wise and humane movement, or otherwise? Is the existence of a rebellious element in our borders—which New Orleans, Memphis, and Texas show to be only disarmed, but at heart as malignant as ever, only waiting for an opportunity to reassert itself with fire and sword—a reason for leaving four millions of the nation's truest friends with just cause of complaint against the Federal government? If the doctrine that taxation should go hand in hand with representation can be appealed to in behalf of recent traitors and rebels, may it not properly be asserted in behalf of a people who have ever been loyal and faithful to the government? The answers to these questions are too obvious to require statement. Disguise it as we may, we are still a divided nation. The Rebel States have still an anti-national policy. Massachusetts and South Carolina may draw tears from the eyes of our tender-hearted President by walking arm in arm into his Philadelphia Convention, but a citizen of Massachusetts is still an alien in the Palmetto State.

There is that, all over the South, which frightens Yankee industry, capital, and skill from its borders. We have crushed the Rebellion, but not its hopes or its malign purposes. The South fought for perfect and permanent control over the Southern laborer. It was a war of the rich against the poor. They who waged it had no objection to the government, while they could use it as a means of confirming their power over the laborer. They fought the government, not because they hated the government as such, but because they found it, as they thought, in the way between them and their one grand purpose of rendering permanent and indestructible their authority and power over the Southern laborer. Though the battle is for the present lost, the hope of gaining this object still exists, and pervades the whole South with a feverish excitement. We have thus far only gained a Union without unity, marriage without love, victory without peace. The hope of gaining by politics what they lost by the sword, is the secret of all this Southern unrest; and that hope must be extinguished before national ideas and objects can take full possession of the Southern mind. There is but one safe and constitutional way to banish that mischievous hope from the South, and that is by lifting the laborer beyond the unfriendly political designs of his former master. Give the negro the elective franchise, and you at once destroy the purely sectional policy, and wheel the Southern States into line with national interests and national objects.

The last and shrewdest turn of Southern politics is a recognition of the necessity of getting into Congress immediately, and at any price. The South will comply with any conditions but suffrage for the negro. It will swallow all the unconstitutional test oaths, repeal all the ordinances of Secession, repudiate the Rebel debt, promise to pay the debt incurred in conquering its people, pass all the constitutional amendments, if only it can have the negro left under its political control. The proposition is as modest as that made on the mountain: "All these things will I give unto thee if thou wilt fall down and worship me."

But why are the Southerners so willing to make these sacrifices? The answer plainly is, they see in this policy the only hope of saving something of their old sectional peculiarities and power. Once firmly seated in Congress, their alliance with Northern Democrats re-established, their States restored to their former position inside the Union, they can easily find means of keeping the Federal government entirely too busy with other important matters to pay much attention to the local affairs of the Southern States. Under the potent shield of State Rights, the game would be in their own hands. Does any sane man doubt for a moment that the men who followed Jefferson Davis through the late terrible Rebellion, often marching barefooted and hungry, naked and penniless, and who now only profess an enforced loyalty, would plunge this country into a foreign war today, if they could thereby gain their coveted independence, and their still more coveted mastery over the negroes? Plainly enough, the peace not less than the prosperity of this country is involved in the great measure of impartial suffrage. King Cotton is deposed, but only deposed, and is ready today to reassert all his ancient pretensions upon the first favorable opportunity. Foreign countries abound with his agents. They are able, vigilant, devoted. The young men of the South burn with the desire to regain what they call the lost cause; the women are noisily malignant towards the Federal government. In fact, all the elements of treason and rebellion are there under the thinnest disguise which necessity can impose.

What, then, is the work before Congress? It is to save the people of the South from themselves, and the nation from detriment on their account. Congress must supplant the evident sectional tendencies of the South by national dispositions and tendencies. It must cause national ideas and objects to take the lead and control the politics of those States. It must cease to recognize the old slave-masters as the only competent persons to rule the South. In a word, it must enfranchise the negro, and by means of the loyal negroes and the loyal white men of the South build up a national party there, and in time bridge the chasm between North and South, so that our country may have a common liberty and a common civilization. The new wine must be put into new bottles. The lamb may not be trusted with the wolf. Loyalty is hardly safe with traitors.

Statesmen of America! beware what you do. The ploughshare of rebellion has gone through the land beam-deep. The soil is in readiness, and the seed-time has come. Nations, not less than individuals, reap as they sow. The dreadful calamities of the past few years came not by accident, nor unbidden, from the ground. You shudder today at the harvest of blood sown in the spring-time of the Republic by your patriot fathers. The principle of slavery, which they tolerated under the erroneous impression that it would soon die out, became at last the dominant principle and power at the South. It early mastered the Constitution, became superior to the Union, and enthroned itself above the law.

Freedom of speech and of the press it slowly but successfully banished from the South, dictated its own code of honor and manners to the nation, brandished the bludgeon and the bowie-knife over Congressional debate, sapped the foundations of loyalty, dried up the springs of patriotism, blotted out the testimonies of the fathers against oppression, padlocked the pulpit, expelled liberty from its literature, invented nonsensical theories about master-races and slave-races of men, and in due season produced a Rebellion fierce, foul, and bloody.

This evil principle again seeks admission into our body politic. It comes now in shape of a denial of political rights to four million loyal colored people. The South does not now ask for slavery. It only asks for a large degraded caste, which shall have no political rights. This ends the case. Statesmen, beware what you do. The destiny of unborn and unnumbered generations is in your hands. Will you repeat the mistake of your fathers, who sinned ignorantly? or will you profit by the blood-bought wisdom all round you, and forever expel every vestige of the old abomination from our national borders? As you members of the Thirty-ninth Congress decide, will the country be peaceful, united, and happy, or troubled, divided, and miserable.

I Claim the Rights of a Man

Mr. Speaker: Before proceeding to argue this question upon its intrinsic merits, I wish the members of this House to understand the position that I take. I hold that I am a member of this body. Therefore, sir, I shall neither fawn nor cringe before any party, nor stoop to beg them for my rights. Some of my colored fellow members, in the course of their remarks, took occasion to appeal to the sympathies of members on the opposite side, and to eulogize their character for magnanimity. It reminds me very much, sir, of slaves begging under the lash. I am here to demand my rights and to hurl thunderbolts at the men who would dare to cross the threshold of my manhood. There is an old aphorism which says, "fight the devil with fire," and if I should observe the rule in this instance, I wish gentlemen to understand that it is but fighting them with their own weapon.

The scene presented in this House, today, is one unparalleled in the history of the world. From this day, back to the day when God breathed the breath of life into Adam, no analogy for it can be found. Never, in the history of the world, has a man been arraigned before a body clothed with legislative, judicial or executive functions, charged with the offense of being a darker hue than his fellow men. I know that questions have been before the courts of this country, and of other countries, involving topics not altogether dissimilar to that which is being discussed here today. But, sir, never in the history of the great nations of this world never before has a man been arraigned, charged with an offense committed by the God of Heaven Himself. Cases may be found where men have been deprived of their rights for crimes and misdemeanors; but it has remained for the state of Georgia, in the very heart of the nineteenth century, to call a man before the bar, and there charge him with an act for which he is no more responsible than for the head which he carries upon his shoulders. The Anglo Saxon race, sir, is a most surprising one. No man has ever been more deceived in that race than I have been for the last three weeks. I was not aware that there was in the character of that race so much cowardice or so much pusillanimity. The treachery which has been exhibited in it by gentlemen belonging to that race has shaken my confidence in it more than anything that has come under my observation from the day of my birth.

What is the question at issue? Why, sir, this Assembly, today, is discussing and deliberating on a judgment; there is not a Cherub that sits around God's eternal throne today that would not tremble even were an order issued by the Supreme God Himself to come down here and sit in judgment on my manhood. Gentlemen may look at this question in whatever light they choose, and with just as much indifference as they may think proper to assume, but I tell you, sir, that this is a question which will not die today. This event shall be remembered by posterity for ages yet to come, and while the sun shall continue to climb the hills of heaven.

Whose legislature is this? Is it a white man's legislature, or is it a black man's legislature? Who voted for a constitutional convention, in obedience to the mandate of the Congress of the United States? Who first rallied around the standard of Reconstruction? Who set the ball of loyalty rolling in the state of Georgia? And whose voice was heard on the hills and in the valleys of this state? It was the voice of the brawny armed Negro, with the few humanitarian hearted white men who came to our assistance. I claim the honor, sir, of having been the instrument of convincing hundreds yea, thousands of white men, that to reconstruct under the measures of the United States Congress was the safest and the best course for the interest of the state.

Let us look at some facts in connection with this matter. Did half the white men of Georgia vote for this legislature? Did not the great bulk of them fight, with all their strength, the Constitution under which we are acting? And did they not fight against the organization of this legislature? And further, sir, did they not vote against it? Yes, sir! And there are persons in this legislature today who are ready to spit their poison in my face, while they themselves opposed, with all their power, the ratification of this Constitution. They question my right to a seat in this body, to represent the people whose legal votes elected me. This objection, sir, is an unheard of monopoly of power. No analogy can be found for it, except it be the case of a man who should go into my house, take possession of my wife and children, and then tell me to walk out. I stand very much in the position of a criminal before your bar, because I dare to be the exponent of the views of those who sent me here. Or, in other words, we are told that if black men want to speak, they must speak through white trumpets; if black men want their sentiments expressed, they must be adulterated and sent through white messengers, who will quibble and equivocate and evade as rapidly as the pendulum of a clock. If this be not done, then the black men have committed an outrage, and their representatives must be denied the right to represent their constituents.

The great question, sir, is this: Am I a man? If I am such, I claim the rights of a man. Am I not a man because I happen to be of a darker hue than honorable gentlemen around me? Let me see whether I am or not. I want to convince the House today that I am entitled to my seat here. A certain gentleman has argued that the Negro was a mere development similar to the orangoutang or chimpanzee, but it so happens that, when a Negro is examined, physiologically, phrenologically and anatomically, and I may say, physiognomically, he is found to be the same as persons of different color. I would like to ask any gentleman on this floor, where is the analogy? Do you find me a quadruped, or do you find me a man? Do you find three bones less in my back than in that of the white man? Do you find fewer organs in the brain? If you know nothing of this, I do; for I have helped to dissect fifty men, black and white, and I assert that by the time you take off the mucous pigment the color of the skin you cannot, to save your life, distinguish between the black man and the white. Am I a man? Have I a soul to save, as you have? Am I susceptible of eternal development, as you are? Can I learn all the arts and sciences that you can? Has it ever been demonstrated in the history of the world? Have black men ever exhibited bravery as white men have done? Have they ever been in the professions? Have they not as good articulative organs as you? Some people argue that there is a very close similarity between the larynx of the Negro and that of the orangoutang. Why, sir, there is not so much similarity between them as there is between the larynx of the man and that of the dog, and this fact I dare any member of this House to dispute. God saw fit to vary everything in nature. There are no two men alike no two voices alike no two trees alike. God has weaved and tissued variety and versatility throughout the boundless space of His creation. Because God saw fit to make some red, and some white, and some black, and some brown, are we to sit here in judgment upon what God has seen fit to do? As well might one play with the thunderbolts of heaven as with that creature that bears God's image God's photograph.

The question is asked, "What is it that the Negro race has done?" Well, Mr. Speaker, all I have to say upon the subject is this: If we are the class of people that we are generally represented to be, I hold that we are a very great people. It is generally considered that we are the children of Canaan, and the curse of a father rests upon our heads, and has rested, all through history. Sir, I deny that the curse of Noah had anything to do with the Negro. We are not the Children of Canaan; and if we are, sir, where should we stand? Let us look a little into history. Melchizedek was a Canaanite; all the Phoenicians all those inventors of the arts and sciences were the posterity of Canaan; but, sir, the Negro is not. We are the children of Cush, and Canaan's curse has nothing whatever to do with the Negro. If we belong to that race, Ham belonged to it, under whose instructions Napoleon Bonaparte studied military tactics. If we belong to that race, Saint Augustine belonged to it. Who was it that laid the foundation of the great Reformation? Martin Luther, who lit the light of gospel truth alight that will never go out until the sun shall rise to set no more; and, long ere then, Democratic principles will have found their level in the regions of Pluto and of Prosperpine. . .

The honorable gentleman from Whitfield (Mr. Shumate), when arguing this question, a day or two ago, put forth the proposition that to be a representative was not to be an officer "it was a privilege that citizens had a right to enjoy." These are his words. It was not an office; it was a "privilege." Every gentleman here knows that he denied that to be a representative was to be an officer. Now, he is recognized as a leader of the Democratic party in this House, and generally cooks victuals for them to eat; makes that remarkable declaration, and how are you, gentlemen on the other side of the House, because I am an officer, when one of your great lights says that I am not an officer? If you deny my right the right of my constituents to have representation here because it is a "privilege," then, sir, I will show you that I have as many privileges as the whitest man on this floor. If I am not permitted to occupy a seat here, for the purpose of representing my constituents, I want to know how white men can be permitted to do so. How can a white man represent a colored constituency, if a colored man cannot do it? The great argument is: "Oh, we have inherited" this, that and the other. Now, I want gentlemen to come down to cool, common sense. Is the created greater than the Creator? Is man greater than God? It is very strange, if a white man can occupy on this floor a seat created by colored votes, and a black man cannot do it. Why, gentlemen, it is the most shortsighted reasoning in the world. A man can see better than that with half an eye; and even if he had no eye at all, he could forge one, as the Cyclops did, or punch one with his finger, which would enable him to see through that.

It is said that Congress never gave us the right to hold office. I want to know, sir, if the Reconstruction measures did not base their action on the ground that no distinction should be made on account of race, color or previous condition? Was not that the grand fulcrum on which they rested? And did not every reconstructed state have to reconstruct on the idea that no discrimination, in any sense of the term, should be made? There is not a man here who will dare say No. If Congress has simply given me a merely sufficient civil and political rights to make me a mere political slave for Democrats, or anybody else giving them the opportunity of jumping on my back in order to leap into political power I do not thank Congress for it. Never, so help me God, shall I be a political slave. I am not now speaking for those colored men who sit with me in this House, nor do I say that they endorse my sentiments, but assisting Mr. Lincoln to take me out of servile slavery did not intend to put me and my race into political slavery. If they did, let them take away my ballot I do not want it, and shall not have it. I don't want to be a mere tool of that sort. I have been a slave long enough already.

I tell you what I would be willing to do: I am willing that the question should be submitted to Congress for an explanation as to what was meant in the passage of their Reconstruction measures, and of the Constitutional Amendment. Let the Democratic Party in this House pass a resolution giving this subject that direction, and I shall be content. I dare you, gentlemen, to do it. Come up to the question openly, whether it meant that the Negro might hold office, or whether it meant that he should merely have the right to vote. If you are honest men, you will do it. If, however, you will not do that, I would make another proposition: Call together, again, the convention that framed the constitution under which we are acting; let them take a vote upon the subject, and I am willing to abide by their decision. . .

These colored men, who are unable to express themselves with all the clearness and dignity and force of rhetorical eloquence, are laughed at in derision by the Democracy of the country. It reminds me very much of the man who looked at himself in a mirror and, imagining that he was addressing another person, exclaimed: "My God, how ugly you are!" These gentlemen do not consider for a moment the dreadful hardships which these people have endured, and especially those who in any way endeavored to acquire an education. For myself, sir, I was raised in the cotton field of South Carolina, and in order to prepare myself for usefulness, as well to myself as to my race, I determined to devote my spare hours to study. When the overseer retired at night to his comfortable couch, I sat and read and thought and studied, until I heard him blow his horn in the morning. He frequently told me, with an oath, that if he discovered me attempting to learn, that he would whip me to death, and I have no doubt he would have done so, if he had found an opportunity. I prayed to Almighty God to assist me, and He did, and I thank Him with my whole heart and soul...

So far as I am personally concerned, no man in Georgia has been more conservative than I "Anything to please the white folks" has been my motto; and so closely have I adhered to that course, that many among my own party have classed me as a Democrat. One of the leaders of the Republican party in Georgia has not been at all favorable to me for some time back, because he believed that I was too "conservative" for a Republican. I can assure you, however, Mr. Speaker, that I have had quite enough, and to spare, of such "conservatism" . . .

But, Mr. Speaker, I do not regard this movement as a thrust at me. It is a thrust at the Bible a thrust at the God of the Universe, for making a man and not finishing him; it is simply calling the Great Jehovah a fool. Why, sir, though we are not white, we have accomplished much. We have pioneered civilization here; we have built up your country; we have worked in your fields and garnered your harvests for two hundred and fifty years! And what do we ask of you in return? Do we ask you for compensation for the sweat our fathers bore for you for the tears you have caused, and the hearts you have broken, and the lives you have curtailed, and the blood you have spilled? Do we ask retaliation? We ask it not. We are willing to let the dead past bury its dead; but we ask you, now for our rights. You have all the elements of superiority upon your side; you have our money and your own; you have our education and your own; and you have our land and your own too. We, who number hundreds of thousands in Georgia, including our wives and families, with not a foot of land to call our own strangers in the land of our birth; without money, without education, without aid, without a roof to cover us while we live, nor sufficient clay to cover us when we die! It is extraordinary that a race such as yours, professing gallantry and chivalry and education and superiority, living in a land where ringing chimes call child and sire to the church of God a land where Bibles are read and Gospel truths are spoken, and where courts of justice are presumed to exist; it is extraordinary that, with all these advantages on your side, you can make war upon the poor defenseless black man. You know we have no money, no railroads, no telegraphs, no advantages of any sort, and yet all manner of injustice is placed upon us. You know that the black people of this country acknowledge you as their superiors, by virtue of your education and advantages...

You may expel us, gentlemen, but I firmly believe that you will some day repent it. The black man cannot protect a country, if the country doesn't protect him; and if, tomorrow, a war should arise, I would not raise a musket to defend a country where my manhood is denied. The fashionable way in Georgia, when hard work is to be done, is for the white man to sit at his ease while the black man does the work; but, sir, I will say this much to the colored men of Georgia, as, if I should be killed in this campaign, I may have no opportunity of telling them at any other time: Never lift a finger nor raise a hand in defense of Georgia, until Georgia acknowledges that you are men and invests you with the rights pertaining to manhood. Pay your taxes, however, obey all orders from your employers, take good counsel from friends, work faithfully, earn an honest living, and show, by your conduct, that you can be good citizens.

Go on with your oppressions. Babylon fell. Where is Greece? Where is Nineveh? And where is Rome, the Mistress Empire of the world? Why is it that she stands, today, in broken fragments throughout Europe? Because oppression killed her. Every act that we commit is like a bounding ball. If you curse a man, that curse rebounds upon you; and when you bless a man, the blessing returns to you; and when you oppress a man, the oppression also will rebound. Where have you ever heard of four millions of freemen being governed by laws, and yet have no hand in their making? Search the records of the world, and you will find no example. "Governments derive their just powers from the consent of the governed." How dare you to make laws by which to try me and my wife and children, and deny me a voice in the making of these laws? I know you can establish a monarchy, an autocracy, an oligarchy, or any other kind of ocracy that you please; and that you can declare whom you please to be sovereign; but tell me, sir, how you can clothe me with more power than another, where all are sovereigns alike? How can you say you have a republican form of government, when you make such distinction and enact such proscriptive laws?

Gentlemen talk a good deal about the Negroes "building no monuments." I can tell the gentlemen onething: that is, that we could have built monuments of fire while the war was in progress. We could have fired your woods, your barns and fences, and called you home. Did we do it? No, sir! And God grant that the Negro may never do it, or do anything else that would destroy the good opinion of his friends. No epithet is sufficiently opprobrious for us now. I saw, sir, that we have built a monument of docility, of obedience, of respect, and of self control, that will endure longer than the Pyramids of Egypt.

We are a persecuted people. Luther was persecuted; Galileo was persecuted; good men in all nations have been persecuted; but the persecutors have been handed down to posterity with shame and ignominy. If you pass this bill, you will never get Congress to pardon or enfranchise another rebel in your lives. You are going to fix an everlasting disfranchisement upon Mr. Toombs and the other leading men of Georgia. You may think you are doing yourselves honor by expelling us from this House; but when we go, we will do as Wickliffe and as Latimer did. We will light a torch of truth that will never be extinguished the impression that will run through the country, as people picture in their mind's eye these poor black men, in all parts of this Southern country, pleading for their rights. When you expel us, you make us forever your political foes, and you will never find a black man to vote a Democratic ticket again; for, so help me God, I will go through all the length and breadth of the land, where a man of my race is to be found, and advise him to beware of the Democratic party. Justice is the great doctrine taught in the Bible. God's Eternal justice is founded upon Truth, and the man who steps from justice steps from Ruth, and cannot make his principles to prevail.

I have now, Mr. Speaker, said all that my physical condition will allow me to say. Weak and ill, though I am, I could not sit passively here and see the sacred rights of my race destroyed at one blow. We are in a position somewhat similar to that of the famous "Light Brigade," of which Tennyson says, they had.

Cannon to right of them, Cannon to left of them, Cannon in front of them, Volleyed and thundered.

I hope that our poor, downtrodden race may act well and wisely through this period of trial, and that they will exercise patience and discretion under all circumstances.

You may expel us, gentlemen, by your votes, today; but, while you do it, remember that there is a just God in Heaven, whose All-Seeing Eye beholds alike the acts of the oppressor and the oppressed, and who, despite the machinations of the wicked, never fails to vindicate the cause of Justice, and the sanctity of His own handiwork.

Race Unity

Mr. Chairman and Gentlemen of the Conference: The subject assigned me is one of great importance. The axioms which teach us of the strength in unity and the certain destruction following close upon the heels of strife and dissension, need not be here repeated. Race elevation can be attained only through race unity. Pious precepts, business integrity, and moral stamina of the most exalted stamp, may win the admiration for a noble few, but unless the moral code, by the grandeur of its teachings, actuates every individual and incites us as a race to nobler aspirations and quickens us to the realization of our moral shortcomings, the distinction accorded to the few will avail us nothing. The wealth of the Indies may crown the efforts of fortune's few favored ones. They may receive all the homage wealth invariably brings, but unless we as a race check the spirit of pomp and display, and by patiently practicing the most rigid economy, secure homes for ourselves and children, the preferment won by a few wealthy ones will prove short lived and unsatisfactory. We may have our educational lights here and there, and by the brilliancy of their achievements they may be living witness to the falsity of the doctrine of our inherited inferiority, but this alone will not suffice. It is a general enlightenment of the race which must engage our noblest powers. One vicious, ignorant Negro is readily conceded to be a type of all the rest, but a Negro educated and refined is said to be an exception. We must labor to reverse this rule; education and moral excellence must become general and characteristic, with ignorance and depravity for the exception.

Seeing, then, the necessity of united action and universal worth rather than individual brilliancy, we sorrowfully admit that race unity with us is a blessing not yet enjoyed, but to be possessed. We are united only in the conditions which degrade, and actions which paralyze the efforts of the worthy, who labor for the benefit of the multitude. We are a race of leaders, everyone presuming that his neighbor and not himself was decreed to be a follower. Today, if any one of you should go home and announce yourself candidate for a certain position, the following day would find a dozen men in the field, each well prepared to prove that he alone is capable of obtaining and filling the position. Failing to convince the people, he would drop out (of) the race entirely or do all in his power to jeopardize the interest of a more successful brother.

Why this non fraternal feeling? Why such a spirit of dissension? We attribute it, first, to lessons taught in by gone days by those whose security rested in our disunion. If the same spirit of race unity had actuated the Negro which has always characterized the Indian, this Government would have trembled under the blow of that immortal hero, John Brown, and the first drop of fratricidal blood would have been shed, not at Fort Sumter, but at Harper's Ferry. Another cause may be found in our partial enlightenment. The ignorant man is always narrow minded in politics, business or religion. Unfold to him a plan, and if he cannot see some interest resulting to self, however great the resulting good to the multitude, it meets only his partial approbation and fails entirely to secure his active co operation. A third reason applies, not to the unlearned, but to the learned. Too many of our learned men are afflicted with a mental and moral aberration, termed in common parlance "big headed." Having reached a commendable degree of eminence, they seem to stand and say, "Lord, we thank Thee we are not as other men are." They view with perfect unconcern the struggles of a worthy brother; they proffer him no aid, but deem it presumption in him to expect it. They may see a needed step but fail to take it. Others may see the necessity, take steps to meet it, and call them to aid. But, no; they did not lead; they will not follow, and half of their influence for good is sacrificed by an insane jealousy that is a consuming fire in every bosom wherein it finds lodgment.

A few of the prominent causes which retard race unity having been noticed, let us look for the remedy. First, our natural jealousy must be overcome. The task is no easy one. We must look for fruits of our labor in the next generation. With us our faults are confirmed. An old slave once lay dying, friends and relatives were gathered around. The minister sat at the bedside endeavoring to prepare the soul for the great change. The old man was willing to forgive every one except a certain particularly obstreperous African who had caused him much injury. But being over persuaded he yielded and said: "Well, if I dies I forgives him, but if I lives dat darkey better take care." It is much the same with us; when we die our natures will change, but while we live our neighbors must take care. Upon the young generation our instruction may be effective. They must be taught that in helping one another they help themselves; and that in the race of life, when a favored one excels and leads the rest, their powers must be employed, not in retarding his progress, but in urging him on and inciting others to emulate his example.

We must dissipate the gloom of ignorance which hangs like a pall over us. In former days we were trained in ignorance, and many of my distinguished hearers will remember when they dare not be caught cultivating an intimate acquaintance with the spelling book. But the time is passed when the seeker after knowledge is reviled and persecuted. Throughout the country the public school system largely obtains; books without number and papers without price lend their enlightenment; while high schools, colleges and universities all over our broad domain throw open their inviting doors and say, "Whosoever will may come."

We must not fail to notice any dereliction of our educated people. They must learn that their duty is to elevate their less favored brethren, and this cannot be done while pride and conceit prevent them from entering heartily into the work. A spirit of missionary zeal must actuate them to go down among the lowly, and by word and action say: "Come with me and I will do you good."

We must help one another. Our industries must be patronized, and our laborers encouraged. There seems to be a natural disinclination on our part to patronize our own workmen. We are easily pleased with the labor of the white hands, but when the same is known to be the product of our own skill and energy, we become extremely exacting and hard to please. From colored men we expect better work, we pay them less, and usually take our own good time for payment. We will patronize a colored merchant as long as he will credit us, but when, on the verge of bankruptcy he is obliged to stop the credit system, we pass by him and pay our money to the white rival. For these reasons our industries are rarely remunerative. We must lay aside these "besetting sins" and become united in our appreciation and practical encouragement of our own laborers.

Our societies should wield their influence to secure colored apprentices and mechanics. By a judicious disposition of their custom, they might place colored apprentices in vocations at present entirely unpracticed by us. Our labor is generally menial. We have hitherto had a monopoly of America's menial occupations, but thanks to a progressive Caucasian element, we no longer suffer from that monopoly. The white man enters the vocations hitherto exclusively ours, and we must enter and become proficient in professions hitherto exclusively practiced by him.

Our communities must be united. By concerted action great results can be accomplished. We must not only act upon the defensive, but when necessary we should take the offensive. We should jealously guard our every interest, public and private. Let us here speak of our schools. They furnish the surest and swiftest means in our power of obtaining knowledge, confidence and respect. There is no satisfactory reason why all children who seek instruction should not have full and equal privileges, but law has been so perverted in many places, North and South, that sanction is given to separate schools; a pernicious system of discrimination which invariably operates to the disadvantage of the colored race. If we are separate, let it be from "turret to foundation stone." It is unjust to draw the color line in schools, and our communities should resent the added insult of forcing the colored pupils to receive instructions from the refuse material of white educational institutions. White teachers take colored schools from necessity, not from choice. We except of course those who act from a missionary spirit.

White teachers in colored schools are nearly always mentally, morally, or financially bankrupts, and no colored community should tolerate the imposition. High schools and colleges are sending learned colored teachers in the field constantly, and it is manifestly unjust to make them stand idle and see their people taught by those whose only interest lies in securing their monthly compensation in dollars and cents. Again, colored schools thrive better under colored teachers. The St. Louis schools furnish an excellent example. According to the report of Superintendent Harris, during the past two years the schools have increased under colored teachers more than fifty per cent, and similar results always follow the introduction of colored teachers. In case of mixed schools our teachers should be eligible to positions. They invariably prove equal to their requirements. In Detroit and Chicago they have been admitted and proved themselves unquestionably capable. In Chicago their white pupils outnumber the colored ten to one, and yet they have met with decided success. Such gratifying results must be won by energetic, united action on the part of the interested communities. White people grant us few privileges voluntarily. We must wage continued warfare for our rights, or they will be disregarded and abridged.

Mr. President, we might begin to enumerate the rich results of race unity at sunrise and continue to sunset and half would not be told. In behalf of the people we are here to represent, we ask for some intelligent action of this Conference; some organized movement whereby concerted action may be had by our race all over the land. Let us decide upon some intelligent, united system of operation, and go home and engage the time and talent of our constituents in prosperous labor. We are laboring for race elevation, and race unity is the all important factor in the work. It must be secured at whatever cost. Individual action, however insignificant, becomes powerful when united and exerted in a common channel. Many thousand years ago, a tiny coral began a reef upon the ocean's bed. Years passed and others came. Their fortunes were united and the structure grew. Generations came and went, and corals by the million came, lived, and died, each adding his mite to the work, till at last the waters of the grand old ocean broke in ripples around their ireless heads, and now, as the traveler gazes upon the reef, hundreds of miles in extent, he can faintly realize what great results will follow united action. So we must labor, with the full assurance that we will reap our reward in due season. Though deeply submerged by the wave of popular opinion, which deems natural inferiority inseparably associated with a black skin, though weighted down by an accursed prejudice that seeks every opportunity to crush us, still we must labor and despair not patiently, ceaselessly, and unitedly. The time will come when our heads will rise above the troubled waters. Though generations come and go, the result of our labors will yet be manifest, and an impartial world will accord us that rank among other races which all may aspire to, but only the worthy can win.

I Am An Anarchist

I am an anarchist. I suppose you came here, the most of you, to see what Ia real, live anarchist looked like. I suppose some of you expected to see me with a bomb in one hand and a flaming torch in the other, but are disappointed in seeing neither. If such has been your ideas regarding an anarchist, you deserved to be disappointed. Anarchists are peaceable, law abiding people. What do anarchists mean when they speak of anarchy? Webster gives the term two definitions chaos and the state of being without political rule. We cling to the latter definition. Our enemies hold that we believe only in the former.

Do you wonder why there are anarchists in this country, in this great land of liberty, as you love to call it? Go to New York. Go through the byways and alleys of that great city. Count the myriads starving; count the multiplied thousands who are homeless; number those who work harder than slaves and live on less and have fewer comforts than the meanest slaves. You will be dumbfounded by your discoveries, you who have paid no attention to these poor, save as objects of charity and commiseration. They are not objects of charity, they are the victims of the rank injustice that permeates the system of government, and of political economy that holds sway from the Atlantic to the Pacific. Its oppression, the misery it causes, the wretchedness it gives birth to, are found to a greater extent in New York than elsewhere. In New York, where not many days ago two governments united in unveiling a statue of liberty, where a hundred bands played that hymn of liberty, "The Marseillaise." But almost its equal is found among the miners of the West, who dwell in squalor and wear rags, that the capitalists, who control the earth that should be free to all, may add still further to their millions! Oh, there are plenty of reasons for the existence of anarchists.

But in Chicago they do not think anarchists have any right to exist at all. They want to hang them there, lawfully or unlawfully. You have heard of a certain Haymarket meeting. You have heard of a bomb. You have heard of arrests and of succeeding arrests effected by detectives. Those detectives! There is a set of men nay, beasts for you! Pinkerton detectives! They would do anything. I feel sure capitalists wanted a man to throw that bomb at the Haymarket meeting and have the anarchists blamed for it. Pinkerton could have accomplished it for him. You have heard a great deal about bombs. You have heard that the anarchists said lots about dynamite. You have been told that Lingg made bombs. He violated no law. Dynamite bombs can kill, can murder, so can Gatling guns. Suppose that bomb had been thrown by an anarchist. The constitution says there are certain inalienable rights, among which are a free press, free speech and free assemblage. The citizens of this great land are given by the constitution the right to repel the unlawful invasion of those rights. The meeting at Haymarket square was a peaceable meeting. Suppose, when an anarchist saw the police arrive on the scene, with murder in their eyes, determined to break up that meeting, suppose he had thrown that bomb; he would have violated no law. That will be the verdict of your children. Had I been there, had I seen those murderous police approach, had I heard that insolent command to disperse, had I heard Fielden say, "Captain, this is a peaceable meeting," had I seen the liberties of my countrymen trodden under foot, I would have flung the bomb myself. I would have violated no law, but would have upheld the constitution.

If the anarchists had planned to destroy the city of Chicago and to massacre the police, why was it they had only two or three bombs in hand? Such was not their intention. It was a peaceable meeting. Carter Harrison, the mayor of Chicago, was there. He said it was a quiet meeting. He told Bonfield (Captain John Bonfield, Commander of Desplaines Police Station) to send the police to their different beats. I do not stand here to gloat over the murder of those policemen. I despise murder. But when a ball from the revolver of a policeman kills it is as much murder as when death results from a bomb.

The police rushed upon that meeting as it was about to disperse. Mr. Simonson talked to Bonfield about the meeting. Bonfield said he wanted to do the anarchists up. Parsons went to the meeting. He took his wife, two ladies and his two children along. Toward the close of the meeting, he said, "I believe it is going to rain. Let us adjourn to Zeph's hall." Fielden said he was about through with his speech and would close it at once. The people were beginning to scatter about, a thousand of the more enthusiastic still lingered in spite of the rain. Parsons, and those who accompanied him started for home. They had gone as far as the Desplaine's street police station when they saw the police start at a double quick. Parsons stopped to see what was the trouble. Those 200 policemen rushed on to do the anarchists up. Then we went on. I was in Zeph's hall when I heard that terrible detonation. It was heard around the world. Tyrants trembled and felt there was something wrong.

The discovery of dynamite and its use by anarchists is a repetition of history. When gun powder was discovered, the feudal system was at the height of its power. Its discovery and use made the middle classes. Its first discharge sounded the death knell of the feudal system. The bomb at Chicago sounded the downfall of the wage system of the nineteenth century. Why? Because I know no intelligent people will submit to despotism. The first means the diffusion of power. I tell no man to use it. But it was the achievement of science, not of anarchy, and would do for the masses. I suppose the press will say I belched forth treason. If I have violated any law, arrest me, give me a trial, and the proper punishment, but let the next anarchist that comes along ventilate his views without hindrance.

Well, the bomb exploded, the arrests were made and then came that great judicial farce, beginning on June 21. The jury was impaneled. Is there a Knight of Labor here? Then know that a Knight of Labor was not considered competent enough to serve on that jury. "Are you a Knight of Labor?" "Have you any sympathy with labor organizations?" were the questions asked each talisman. If an affirmative answer was given, the talisman was bounced. It was not are you a Mason, a Knight Templar? O, no! (Great applause.) I see you read the signs of the times by that expression. Hangman Gary, miscalled judge, ruled that if a man was prejudiced against the defendants, it did not incapacitate him for serving on the jury. For such a man, said Hangman Gary, would pay closer attention to the law and evidence and would be more apt to render a verdict for the defense. Is there a lawyer here? If there is he knows such a ruling is without precedent and contrary to all law, reason or common sense.

In the heat of patriotism the American citizen sometimes drops a tear for the nihilist of Russia. They say the nihilist can't get justice, that he is condemned without trial. How much more should he weep for his next door neighbor, the anarchist, who is given the form of trial under such a ruling.

There were "squealers" introduced as witnesses for the prosecution. There were three of them. Each and every one was compelled to admit they had been purchased and intimidated by the prosecution. Yet Hangman Gary held their evidence as competent. It came out in the trial that the Haymarket meeting was the result of no plot, but was caused in this wise. The day before the wage slaves in McCormick's factory had struck for eight hours labor, McCormick, from his luxurious office, with one stroke of the pen by his idle, be ringed fingers, turned 4,000 men out of employment. Some gathered and stoned the factory. Therefore they were anarchists, said the press. But anarchists are not fools; only fools stone buildings. The police were sent out and they killed six wage slaves. You didn't know that. The capitalistic press kept it quiet, but it made a great fuss over the killing of some policemen. Then these crazy anarchists, as they are called, thought a meeting ought to be held to consider the killing of six brethren and to discuss the eight hour movement. The meeting was held. It was peaceable. When Bonfield ordered the police to charge those peaceable anarchists, he hauled down the American flag and should have been shot on the spot.

While the judicial farce was going on the red and black flags were brought into court, to prove that the anarchists threw the bomb. They were placed on the walls and hung there, awful specters before the jury. What does the black flag mean? When a cable gram says it was carried through the streets of a European city it means that the people are suffering—that the men are out of work, the women starving, the children barefooted. But, you say, that is in Europe. How about America? The Chicago Tribune said there were 30,000 men in that city with nothing to do. Another authority said there were 10,000 barefooted children in mid winter. The police said hundreds had no place to sleep or warm. Then President Cleveland issued his Thanksgiving proclamation and the anarchists formed in procession and carried the black flag to show that these thousands had nothing for which to return thanks. When the Board of Trade, that gambling den, was dedicated by means of a banquet, $30 a plate, again the black flag was carried, to signify that there were thousands who couldn't enjoy a 2 cent meal.

But the red flag, the horrible red flag, what does that mean? Not that the streets should run with gore, but that the same red blood courses through the veins of the whole human race. It meant the brotherhood of man. When the red flag floats over the world the idle shall be called to work. There will be an end of prostitution for women, of slavery for man, of hunger for children.

Liberty has been named anarchy. If this verdict is carried out it will be the death knell of America's liberty. You and your children will be slaves. You will have liberty if you can pay for it. If this verdict is carried out, place the flag of our country at half mast and write on every fold "shame." Let our flag be trailed in the dust. Let the children of workingmen place laurels to the brow of these modern heroes, for they committed no crime. Break the two fold yoke. Bread is freedom and freedom is bread.

Lynch Law in All Its Phases

I am before the American people today through no inclination of my own, but because of a deep seated conviction that the country at large does not know the extent to which lynch law prevails in parts of the Republic nor the conditions which force into exile those who speak the truth. I cannot believe that the apathy and indifference which so largely obtains regarding mob rule is other than the result of ignorance of the true situation. And yet, the observing and thoughtful must know that in one section, at least, of our common country, a government of the people, by the people, and for the people, means a government by the mob; where the land of the free and home of the brave means a land of lawlessness, murder and outrage; and where liberty of speech means the license of might to destroy the business and drive from home those who exercise this privilege contrary to the will of the mob. Repeated attacks on the life, liberty and happiness of any citizen or class of citizens are attacks on distinctive American institutions; such attacks imperiling as they do the foundation of government, law and order, merit the thoughtful consideration of far sighted Americans; not from a standpoint of sentiment, not even so much from a standpoint of justice to a weak race, as from a desire to preserve our institutions.

The race problem or negro question, as it has been called, has been omnipresent and all pervading since long before the Afro American was raised from the degradation of the slave to the dignity of the citizen. It has never been settled because the right methods have not been employed in the solution. It is the Banquo's ghost of politics, religion, and sociology which will not down at the bidding of those who are tormented with its ubiquitous appearance on every occasion. Times without number, since invested with citizenship, the race has been indicted for ignorance, immorality and general worthlessness declared guilty and executed by its self constituted judges. The operations of law do not dispose of negroes fast enough, and lynching bees have become the favorite pastime of the South. As excuse for the same, a new cry, as false as it is foul, is raised in an effort to blast race character, a cry which has proclaimed to the world that virtue and innocence are violated by Afro-Americans who must be killed like wild beasts to protect womanhood and childhood.

Born and reared in the South, I had never expected to live elsewhere. Until this past year I was one among those who believed the condition of masses gave large excuse for the humiliations and proscriptions under which we labored; that when wealth, education and character became more feral among us, the cause being removed the effect would cease, and justice being accorded to all alike. I shared the general belief that good newspapers entering regularly the homes of our people in every state could do more to bring about this result than any agency. Preaching the doctrine of self help, thrift and economy every week, they would be the teachers to those who had been deprived of school advantages, yet were making history everyday and train to think for themselves our mental children of a larger growth. And so, three years ago last June, I became editor and part owner of the Memphis Free Speech. As editor, I had occasion to criticize the city School Board's employment of inefficient teachers and poor school buildings for Afro-American children. I was in the employ of that board at the time, and at the close of that school term one year ago, was not re elected to a position I had held in the city schools for seven years. Accepting the decision of the Board of Education, I set out to make a race newspaper pay a thing which older and wiser heads said could not be done. But there were enough of our people in Memphis and surrounding territory to support a paper, and I believed they would do so. With nine months hard work the circulation increased from 1,500 to 3,500; in twelve months it was on a good paying basis. Throughout the Mississippi Valley in Arkansas, Tennessee and Mississippi on plantations and in towns, the demand for and interest in the paper increased among the masses. The newsboys who would not sell it on the trains, voluntarily testified that they had never known colored people to demand a paper so eagerly.

To make the paper a paying business I became advertising agent, solicitor, as well as editor, and was continually on the go. Wherever I went among the people, I gave them in church, school, public gatherings, and home, the benefit of my honest conviction that maintenance of character, money getting and education would finally solve our problem and that it depended us to say how soon this would be brought about. This sentiment bore good fruit in Memphis. We had nice homes, representatives in almost every branch of business and profession, and refined society. We had learned helping each other helped all, and every well conducted business by Afro-Americans prospered. With all our proscription in theatres, hotels and railroads, we had never had a lynching and did not believe we could have one. There had been lynchings and brutal outrages of all sorts in our state and those adjoining us, but we had confidence and pride in our city and the majesty of its laws. So far in advance of other Southern cities was ours, we were content to endure the evils we had, to labor and to wait.

But there was a rude awakening. On the morning of March 9, the bodies of three of our best young men were found in an old field horribly shot to pieces. These young men had owned and operated the "People's Grocery," situated at what was known as the Curve a suburb made up almost entirely of colored people about a mile from city limits. Thomas Moss, one of the oldest letter carriers in the city, was president of the company, Cal McDowell was manager and Will Stewart was a clerk. There were about ten other stockholders, all colored men. The young men were well known and popular and their business flourished, and that of Barrett, a white grocer who kept store there before the "People's Grocery" was established, went down. One day an officer came to the "People's Grocery" and inquired for a colored man who lived in the neighborhood, and for whom the officer had a warrant. Barrett was with him and when McDowell said he knew nothing as to the whereabouts of the man for whom they were searching, Barrett, not the officer, then accused McDowell of harboring the man, and McDowell gave the lie. Barrett drew his pistol and struck McDowell with it; thereupon McDowell who was a tall, fine looking six footer, took Barrett's pistol from him, knocked him down and gave him a good thrashing, while Will Stewart, the clerk, kept the special officer at bay. Barrett went to town, swore out a warrant for their arrest on a charge of assault and battery. McDowell went before the Criminal Court, immediately gave bond and returned to his store. Barrett then threatened (to use his own words) that he was going to clean out the whole store. Knowing how anxious he was to destroy their business, these young men consulted a lawyer who told them they were justified in defending themselves if attacked, as they were a mile beyond city limits and police protection. They accordingly armed several of their friends not to assail, but to resist the threatened Saturday night attack.

When they saw Barrett enter the front door and a half dozen men at the rear door at 11 o'clock that night, they supposed the attack was on and immediately fired into the crowd, wounding three men. These men, dressed in citizen's clothes, turned out to be deputies who claimed to be hunting for another man for whom they had a warrant, and whom any one of them could have arrested without trouble. When these men found they had fired upon officer of the law, they threw away their firearms and submitted to arrest, confident they should establish their innocence of intent to fire upon officers of the law. The daily papers in flaming headlines roused the evil passions of whites, denounced these poor boys in unmeasured terms, nor permitted a word in their own defense.

The neighborhood of the Curve was searched next day, and about thirty persons were thrown into jail, charged with conspiracy. No communication was to be had with friends any of the three days these men were in jail; bail was refused and Thomas Moss was not allowed to eat the food his wife prepared for him. The judge is reported to have said, "Any one can see them after three days." They were seen after three days, but they were no longer able to respond to the greetings of friends. On Tuesday following the shootings at the grocery, the papers which had made much of the sufferings of the wounded deputies, and promised it would go hard with those who did the shooting, if they died, announced that the officers were all out of danger, and would recover. The friends of the prisoners breathed more easily and relaxed their vigilance. They felt that as the officers would not die, there was no danger that in the heat of passion the prisoners would meet violent death at hands of the mob. Besides, we had such confidence in the law. But the law did not provide capital punishment for shooting which did not kill. So the mob did what the law could not be made to do, as a lesson to the Afro-American that he must not shoot a white man, no matter what the provocation. The same night after the announcement was made in the papers that thee officers would get well, the mob, in obedience to a plan known to every eminent white man in the city, went to the jail between two and three in the morning, dragged out these young men, hatless and shoeless, put them on the yard engine of the railroad which was in waiting just behind the jail, carried them a mile north of the city limits and horribly shot them to death while the locomotive at a given signal let off steam and blew the whistle to deaden the sound of the firing.

"It was done by unknown men," said the jury, yet the Appeal Avalanche which goes to press at 3 A.M., had a two column account of the lynching. The papers also told how McDowell got hold of the guns of the mob and as his grasp could not be loosened, his hand was shattered with a pistol ball and all the lower part of his face was torn away. There were four pools of blood found and only three bodies. It was whispered that he, McDowell killed one of the lynchers with his gun, and it is well known that a police man who was seen on the street a few days previous to the lynching, died very suddenly the next day after. "It was done by unknown parties," said the jury, yet the papers told how Tom Moss begged for his life, for the sake of his wife, his little daughter and his unborn infant. They also told us that his last words were, "If you will kill us, turn our faces to the West."

All this we learn too late to save these men, even if the law had not be in the hands of their murderers. When the colored people realized that the flower of our young manhood had been stolen away at night and murdered there was a rush for firearms to avenge the wrong, but no house would sell a colored man a gun; the armory of the Tennessee Rifles, our only colored military company, and of which McDowell was a member, was broken into by order of the Criminal Court judge, and its guns taken. One hundred men and irresponsible boys from fifteen years and up were armed by order of authorities and rushed out to the Curve, where it was reported that the colored people were massing, and at point of the bayonet dispersed these men who could do nothing but talk. The cigars, wines, etc., of the grocery stock were freely used by the mob, who possessed the place on pretence of dispersing the conspiracy. The money drawer was broken into and contents taken. The trunk of Calvin McDowell, who had a room in the store, was broken open, and his clothing, which was not good enough to take away, was throw out and trampled on the floor.

These men were murdered, their stock was attached by creditors and sold for less than one eighth of its cost to that same man Barrett, who is today running his grocery in the same place. He had indeed kept his word, and by aid of the authorities destroyed the People's Grocery Company root and branch. The relatives of Will Stewart and Calvin McDowell are bereft of their protectors. The baby daughter of Tom Moss, too young to express how she misses her father, toddles to the wardrobe, seizes the legs of the trousers of his letter carrier uniform, hugs and kisses them with evident delight and stretches up her little hands to be taken up into the arms which will nevermore clasp his daughter's form. His wife holds Thomas Moss, Jr., in her arms, upon whose unconscious baby face the tears fall thick and fast when she is thinking of the sad fate of the father he will never see, and of the two helpless children who cling to her for the support she cannot give. Although these men were peaceable, law abiding citizens of this country, we are told there can be no punishment for their murderers nor indemnity for relatives.

I have no power to describe the feeling of horror that possessed every member of the race in Memphis when the truth dawned upon us that the protection of the law which we had so long enjoyed was no longer ours; all had been destroyed in a night, and the barriers of the law had been down, and the guardians of the public peace and confidence scoffed into the shadows, and all authority given into the hands of the mob, and innocent men cut down as if they were brutes the first feeling was one dismay, then intense indignation. Vengeance was whispered from ear to ear, but sober reflection brought the conviction that it would be extreme folly to seek vengeance when such action meant certain death for the men, and horrible slaughter for the women and children, as one of the evening papers took care to remind us. The power of the State, country and city, and civil authorities and the strong arm of the military power were all on the side of the mob and of lawlessness. Few of our men possessed firearms, our only company's guns were confiscated, and the only white man who sell a colored man a gun, was himself jailed, and his store closed. We were helpless in our great strength. It was our first object lesson in the doctrine of white supremacy; an illustration of the South's cardinal principle no matter what the attainments, character or standing of an Afro-American, the laws of the South will not protect him against a white man.

There was only onething we could do, and a great determination seized the people to follow the advice of the martyred Moss, and "turn our faces to the West," whose laws protect all alike. The Free Speech supported ministers and leading business men advised the people to leave a community whose laws did not protect them. Hundreds left on foot to walk four hundred miles between Memphis and Oklahoma. A Baptist minister went to the territory, built a church, and took his entire congregation out in less than a month. Another minister sold his church and took his flock to California, and still another has settled in Kansas. In two months, six thousand persons had left the city and every branch of business began to feel this silent resentment of the outrage, and failure of the authorities to punish lynchers. There were a number of business failures and blocks of houses for rent. The superintendent and treasurer of the street railway company called at the office of the Free Speech, to have us urge the colored people again on the street cars. A real estate dealer said to a colored man who returned some property he had been buying on the installment plan: "I see what you 'niggers' are cutting up about. You got off light. We first intend to kill every one of those thirty one niggers' in jail, but concluded to let all go but the 'leaders.'" They did let all go to the penitentiary. These so-called rioters have since been tried in the Criminal Court for the conspiracy of defending their property, and are now serving terms of three, eight, and fifteen years each in the Tennessee State prison.

To restore the equilibrium and put a stop to the great financial loss, the next move was to get rid of the Free Speech, the disturbing element which kept the waters troubled; which would not let the people forget, and in obedience to whose advice nearly six thousand persons had left the city. In casting about for an excuse, the mob found it in the following editorial which appeared in the Memphis Free Speech, May 21, 1892: "Eight negroes lynched at Little Rock, Ark., where the citizens broke into the penitentiary and got their man; three near Anniston, Ala., and one in New Orleans, all on the same charge, the new alarm of assaulting white women and near Clarksville, Ga., for killing a white man. The same program of hanging then shooting bullets into the lifeless bodies was carried out to the letter. Nobody in this section of the country believes the old threadbare lie that negro men rape white women. If Southern white men are not careful they will overreach themselves, and public sentiment will have a reaction. A conclusion will then be reached which will be very damaging to the moral reputation of their women." Commenting on this, The Daily Commercial of Wednesday following said: "Those negroes who are attempting to make lynching of individuals of their race a means for arousing the worst passions of their kind, are playing with a dangerous sentiment. The negroes well understand that there is no mercy for the negro rapist, and little patience with his defenders. A negro organ printed in this city in a recent issue published the following atrocious paragraph: 'Nobody in this section believes the old threadbare lie that negro men rape white women. If Southern men are not careful they will overreach themselves and public will have a reaction. A conclusion will be reached which will be very damaging to the moral reputation of their women.' The fact that a black scoundrel is allowed to live and utter such loathsome and repulsive calumnies is a volume of evidence as to the wonderful patience of Southern whites. There are some things the Southern white man will not tolerate, and the intimidation of the foregoing has brought the writer to the very uttermost limit of public patience. We hope we have said enough."

The Evening Scimitar of the same day copied this leading editorial and added this comment: "Patience under such circumstances is not a virtue. If the negroes themselves do not apply the remedy without delay, it will be the duty of those he has attacked, to tie the wretch who utters these calumnies to a stake at the intersection of Main and Madison streets, brand him in the forehead with a hot iron and—"

Such open suggestions by the leading daily papers of the progressive city of Memphis were acted upon by the leading citizens and a meeting was held at the Cotton Exchange that evening. The Commercial two days later had the following account of it: ATROCIOUS BLACKGUARDISM.

There will be no Lynching and no Repetition of the Offense.

In its issue of Wednesday The Commercial reproduced and commented upon an editorial which appeared a day or two before a negro organ known as the Free Speech. The article was so insufferably and indecently slanderous that the whole city awoke to a feeling of intense resentment which came within an ace of culminating in one of those occurrences whose details are so eagerly seized and so prominently published by Northern newspapers. Conservative counsels, however, prevailed, and no extreme measures were resorted to. On Wednesday afternoon a meeting of citizens was held. It was not an assemblage of hoodlums or irresponsible fire eaters, but solid, substantial business men who knew exactly what they were doing and who were far more indignant at the villainous insult to the women of the south than they would have been at any injury done themselves. This meeting appointed a committee to seek the author of the infamous editorial and warn him quietly that upon repetition of the offense, he would find some other part of the country a good deal safer and pleasanter place of residence than this. The committee called a negro named Nightingale, but he disclaimed responsibility and convinced the gentlemen that he had really sold out his paper to a woman named Wells. This woman is not in Memphis at present. It was finally learned that one Fleming, a negro who was driven out of Crittenden Co. during the trouble there a few years ago, wrote the paragraph. He had, however, heard of the meeting, and fled from a fate he feared was in store for him, and which he knew he deserved. His whereabouts could not be ascertained, and the committee so reported. Later on, a communication from Fleming to a prominent Republican politician, and that politician's reply were shown to one or two gentlemen. The former was an inquiry as to whether the writer might safely return to Memphis, the latter was an emphatic answer in negative, and Fleming is still in hiding. Nothing further will be done in the matter. There will be no lynching, and it is very certain that there will be will be no repetition of the outrage. If there should be Friday, May 25.

The only reason there was no lynching of Mr. Fleming who was business manager and half owner of the Free Speech, and who did not write the editorials himself because this same white Republican told him the committee was coming and warned him not to trust them, but get out of the way. The committee scoured the city hunting him, and had to be content with Mr. Nightingale who was dragged to the meeting, shamefully abused (although it was known he had sold out his interest in the paper six months before). He was in the face and forced at the pistol's point to sign a letter which was written by them, in which he denied all knowledge of the editorial, denounced it and condemned it as slander on white women. I do not censure Mr. Nightingale for his action because, having never been at the pistol's point myself, I do not feel that I am competent to sit in judgment on him, or say What I would do under such circumstances.

I had written that editorial with other matter for the week's paper before leaving home the Friday previous for the General Conference of the A.M.E. Church in Philadelphia. The conference adjourned Tuesday, and Thursday, May 25, at 3 P.M., I landed in New York City for a few days' stay before returning home, and there learned from the papers that my business manager had been driven away and the paper suspended. Telegraphing for news, I received telegrams and letters in return informing me that the trains were being watched, that I was to be dumped into the river and beaten, if not killed; it had been learned that I wrote the editorial and I was to be hanged in front of the court house and my face bled if I returned, and I was implored by my friends to remain away. The creditors attached the office in the meantime and the outfit was sold without more ado, thus destroying effectually that which it had taken years to build. One prominent insurance agent publicly declares he will make it his business to shoot me down on sight if I return to Memphis in twenty years, while a leading white lady had remarked she was opposed to the lynching of those three men in March, but she wished there was some way by which I could be gotten back and lynched.

I have been censured for writing that editorial, but when I think of five men who were lynched that week for assault on white women and that not a week passes but some poor soul is violently ushered into eternity on this trumped up charge, knowing the many things I do, and part of which tried to tell in the New York Age of June 25, (and in the pamphlets I have with me) seeing that the whole race in the South was injured in the estimation of the world because of these false reports, I could no longer hold my peace, and I feel, yes, I am sure, that if it had to be done over again (provided no one else was the loser save myself) I would do and say the very same again.

The lawlessness here described is not confined to one locality. In the past ten years over a thousand colored men, women and children have been butchered, murdered and burnt in all parts of the South. The details of these terrible outrages seldom reach beyond the narrow world where they occur. Those who commit the murders write the reports, and hence these blots upon the honor of a nation cause but a faint ripple on the outside world. They arouse no great indignation and call forth no adequate demand for justice. The victims were black, and the reports are so written as to make it appear that the helpless creatures deserved the fate which overtook them.

Not so with the Italian lynching of 1891. They were not black men, and three of them were not citizens of the Republic, but subjects of the King of Italy. The chief of police of New Orleans was shot and eleven Italians arrested and charged with the murder; they were tried and the jury disagreed; the good, law abiding citizens of New Orleans thereupon took them from the jail and lynched them at high noon. A feeling of horror ran through the nation at this outrage. All Europe was amazed. The Italian government demanded thorough investigation and redress, and the Federal Government promised to give the matter the consideration which was its due. The diplomatic relations between the two countries became very much strained and for a while war talk was freely indulged. Here was a case where the power of the Federal Government to protect its own citizens and redeem its pledges to a friendly power was put to the test. When our State Department called upon the authorities of Louisiana for investigation of the crime and punishment of the criminals, the United States government was told that the crime was strictly within the authority of the State of Louisiana, and Louisiana would attend to it. After a farcical investigation, the usual verdict in such cases was rendered: "Death at the hand of parties unknown to the jury," the same verdict which had been pronounced over the bodies of over 1,000 colored persons! Our federal government has thus admitted that it has no jurisdiction over the crimes committed at New Orleans upon citizens of the country, nor upon those citizens of a friendly power to whom the general government and not the State government has pledged protection. Not only has our general government made the confession that one of the states is greater than the Union, but the general government has paid $25,000 of the people's money to the King of Italy for the lynching of those three subjects, the evil doing of one State, over which it has no control, but for whose lawlessness the whole country must pay. The principle involved in the treaty power of the government has not yet been settled to the satisfaction of foreign powers; but the principle involved in the right of State jurisdiction in such matters, was settled long ago by the decision of the United States Supreme Court.

I beg your patience while we look at another phase of the lynching mania. We have turned heretofore to the pages of ancient and medieval history, roman tyranny, the Jesuitical Inquisition of Spain for the spectacle of a human being burnt to death. In the past ten years three instances, at least, have been furnished where men have literally been roasted to death to appease the fury of Southern mobs. The Texarkana instance of last year and Paris, Texas, case of this month are the most recent as they are the most shocking and repulsive. Both were charged with crimes from which the laws provide adequate punishment. The Texarkana man, Ed Coy, was charged with assaulting a white woman. A mob pronounced him guilty, strapped him to a tree, chipped the flesh from his body, poured coal oil over him and the woman in the case set fire to him. The country looked on and in many cases applauded, because it was published that this man had violated the honor of the white woman, although he protested his innocence to the last. Judge Tourjee in the Chicago Inter Ocean of recent date says investigation has shown that Ed Coy had supported this woman, (who was known to be a bad character,) and her drunken husband for over a year previous to the burning.

The Paris, Texas, burning of Henry Smith, February 1st, has exceeded the others in its horrible details. The man was drawn through the streets on a float, as the Roman generals used to parade their trophies of war, while scaffold ten feet high, was being built, and irons were heated in the fire. He was bound on it, and red-hot irons began at his feet and slowly branded his body while the mob howled with delight at his shrieks. Red hot irons were run down his throat and cooked his tongue; his eyes were burned out, when he was at last unconscious, cotton seed hulls were placed under him, coal oil poured all over him, and a torch applied to the mass. When the flames burned away the ropes which bound Smith and scorched his flesh he was brought back to sensibility and burned and maimed and as he was, he rolled off the platform and away from the fire. His half-cooked body was seized and trampled and thrown back into the flames while a mob of twenty thousand persons who came from all over the country howled with delight, and gathered up some buttons and ashes after all was over to preserve for relics. The man was charged with outraging and murdering a four year old white child, covering her body with brush, sleeping beside the body through the night, then making his escape. If true, it was the deed of a madman, and should have been clearly proven so. The fact that no time for verification of the newspaper reports was given, is suspicious, especially when I remember that a negro was lynched in Indianola, Sharkey Co., Miss. last summer. The dispatches said it was because he had assaulted the sheriff's eight year old daughter. The girl was more than eighteen years old and was found by her father in this man's room, who was a servant on the place.

These incidents have been made the basis of this terrible story they overshadow all others of a like nature in cruelty and represent the legal phases of the whole question. They could be multiplied without number and each outrival the other in the fiendish cruelty exercised, and the frequent awful lawlessness exhibited. The following table shows the number of men lynched from January 1, 1882, to January 1, 1892: In 1882, 52; 1883, 39; 1884, 53; 1885, 77; 1886, 73; 1887, 70; 1888, 72; 1889, 95; 1890, 100; 1891, 169. Of these 728 black men who were murdered, 269 were charged with rape, 253 with murder, 44 with robbery, 37 with incendiarism, 32 with reasons unstated (it was not necessary to have a reason), 27 with race prejudice, 13 with quarreling with white men, 10 with making threats, 7 with rioting, 5 with miscegenation, 4 with burglary. One of the men lynched in 1891 was Will Lewis, who was lynched because "he was drunk and saucy to white folks." A woman who was one of the 73 victims in 1886, was hung in Jackson, Tenn., because the white woman for whom she cooked, died suddenly of poisoning. An examination showed arsenical poisoning. A search in the cook's room found rat poison. She was thrown into jail, and when the mob had worked itself up to the lynching pitch, she was dragged out, every stitch of clothing torn from her body, and was hung in the public court house square in sight of everybody. That white woman's husband has since died in the insane asylum, a raving maniac, and his ravings have led to the conclusion that he and not the cook, was the poisonier of his wife. A fifteen year old colored girl was lynched last spring, at Rayville, La., on the same charge of poisoning. A woman was also lynched at Hollendale, Miss. last spring, charged with being an accomplice in the murder of her paramour who had abused her. These were only two of the 159 persons lynched in the South from January 1, 1892, to January 1, 1893. Over a dozen black men have been lynched already since this new year set in, not yet two months old.

It will thus be seen that neither age, sex nor decency are spared. Although the impression has gone abroad that most of the lynchings take place because of assaults on white women only one third of the number lynched in the past ten years have been charged with that offense, to say nothing of those who were not guilty of the charge. And according to law none of them until proven so. But the unsupported word of any white person for any cause is sufficient to cause a lynching. So bold have the lynchers become masks are laid aside, the temples of justice and strongholds of law are invaded in broad daylight and prisoners taken out and lynched, while governors of states and officers of law stand by and see the work well done.

And yet this Christian nation, the flower of the nineteenth century civilization says it can do nothing to stop this inhuman slaughter. The general government is willingly powerless to send troops to protect the lives of its black citizens, but the state governments are free to use state troops to shoot them down like cattle, when in desperation the black men attempt to defend themselves, and then tell the world that it was necessary to put down a "race war."

Persons unfamiliar with the condition of affairs in the Southern States do not credit the truth when it is told them. They cannot conceive how such a condition of affairs prevails so near them with steam power, telegraph wires, and printing presses in daily and hourly touch with the localities where such disorder reigns. In a former generation the ancestors of these same people refused to believe that slavery was the "league with death and the covenant with hell." Wm. Lloyd Garrison declared it to be, until he was thrown into a dungeon in Baltimore, until the signal lights of Nat Turners lit the dull skies of Northampton County, and until sturdy old John Brown made his attack on Harper's Ferry. When freedom of speech was martyred in the person of Elijah Lovejoy at Alton, when the liberty of free discussion in Senate in the Nation's Congress was struck down in the person of the fearless Charles Sumner, the Nation was at last convinced that slavery was not only a monster by a tyrant. That same tyrant is at work under a new name and guise. The lawlessness which has been here described is like unto that which prevailed under slavery. The very same forces are at work now as then. The attempt is being made to subject to a condition of civil and industrial independence, those whom the Constitution declares to be free men. The events which have led up to the present wide spread lawlessness in the South can be traced to the very first year Lee's conquered veterans marched from Appomattox to their homes in the Southland. They were conquered in war, but not in spirit. They believed as firmly as ever that it was their right to rule black men and dictate to the National Government. The Knights of White Liners, and the Ku Klux Klans were composed of veterans of the army who were determined to destroy the effect of all the slave had gained by the war. They finally accomplished their purpose in 1876. The right of the Afro American to vote and hold office remains in the Federal Constitution, but is destroyed in the constitution of the Southern states. Having destroyed the citizenship of the man, they are now trying to destroy the manhood of the citizen. All their laws are shaped to this end,—school laws railroad car regulations, those governing labor liens on crops, every device is adopted to make slaves of free men and rob them of their wages. Whenever a malicious law is violated in any of its parts, any farmer, any railroad conductor, or merchant can call together a posse of his neighbors and punish even with death the black man who resists and the legal authorities sanction what is done by failing to prosecute and punish the murders. The Repeal of the Civil Rights Law removed their last barrier and the black man's last bulwark and refuge. The rule of the mob is absolute.

Those who know this recital to be true, say there is nothing they can do they cannot interfere and vainly hope by further concession to placate the imperious and dominating part of our country in which this lawlessness prevails. Because this country has been almost rent in twain by internal dissension, the other sections seem virtually to have agreed that the best way to heal the breach is to permit the taking away of civil, political, and even human rights, to stand by in silence and utter indifference while the South continues to wreak fiendish vengeance on the irresponsible cause. They pretend to believe that with all the machinery of law and government in its hands; with the jails and penitentiaries and convict farms filled with pretty race criminals; with the well-known fact that no negro has ever been known to escape conviction and punishment for any crime in the South—still there are those who try to justify and condone the lynching of over a thousand black men in less than ten years an average of one hundred a year. The public sentiment of the country, by its silence in press, pulpit and in public meetings has encouraged this state of affairs, and public sentiment is stronger than law. With all this country's disposition to condone and temporize with the South and its methods; with its many instances of sacrificing principles to prejudice for the sake of making friends and healing the breach made by the late war; of going into the lawless country with capital to build up its waste places and remaining silent in the presence of outrage and wrong, the South is as vindictive and bitter as ever. She is willing to make friends as long as she is permitted to pursue unmolested and uncensored, her course of proscription, injustice, outrage and vituperation. The malignant misrepresentation of General Butler, the uniformly indecent and abusive assault of this dead man whose only crime was a defence of his country, is a recent proof that the South has lost none of its bitterness. The Nashville American, one of the leading papers of one of the leading southern cities, gleefully announced editorially that "'The Beast is dead.' Early yesterday morning, acting under the devil's orders, the angel of Death took Ben Butler and landed him in the lowest depths of hell, and we pity even the devil the possession has secured." The men who wrote these editorials are without exception young men who know nothing of slavery and scarcely anything of the war. The bitterness and hatred have been instilled in and taught them by their parents, and they are men who make and reflect the sentiment of their section. The South spares nobody else's feelings, and it seems a queer logic that when it comes to a question of right, involving lives of citizens and the honor of the government, the South's feelings must be respected and spared.

Do you ask the remedy? A public sentiment strong against lawlessness must be aroused. Every individual can contribute to this awakening. When a sentiment against lynch law as strong, deep and mighty as that roused by slavery prevails, I have no fear of the result. It should be already established as a fact and not as a theory, that every human being must have a fair trial for his life and liberty, no matter what the charge against him. When a demand goes up from fearless and persistent reformers from press and pulpit, from industrial and moral associations that this shall be so from Maine to Texas and from ocean to ocean, a way will be found to make it so.

In deference to the few words of condemnation uttered at the M.E. General conference last year, and by other organizations, Governors Hogg of Texas, Northern of Georgia, and Tillman of South Carolina, have issued proclamations offering rewards for the apprehension of lynchers. These rewards have never been claimed, and these governors knew they would not be when offered. In many cases they knew the ringleaders of the mobs. The prosecuting attorney of Shelby County, Tenn., wrote Governor Buchanan to offer a reward for the arrest of the lynchers of three young men murdered in Memphis. Everybody in that city and state knew well that the letter was written for the sake of effect and the governor did not even offer the reward. But the country at large deluded itself with the belief that the officials of the South and the leading citizens condemned lynching. The lynchings go on in spite of offered rewards, and in face of Governor Hogg's vigorous talk, the second man was burnt alive in his state with the utmost deliberation and publicity. Since he sent a message to the legislature the mob found and hung Henry Smith's stepson, because he refused to tell where Smith was when they were hunting for him. Public sentiment which shall denounce these crimes in season and out; public sentiment which turns capital and immigration from a section given over to lawlessness; public sentiment which insists on the punishment of criminals and lynchers by law must be aroused.

It is no wonder in my mind that the party which stood for their years as the champion of human liberty and human rights, the part of great moral ideas should suffer overwhelming defeat when it has proven recreant to its professions and abandoned a position it created; when although its followers were being outraged in every sense, it was afraid to stand for the right, and appeal to the American people to sustain them in it. It put aside the question of a free ballot and fair count of every citizen and give its voice and influence for the protection of the coat instead of the man who wore it, for the product of labor instead of the laborer; for the seal of citizenship rather than the citizen, and insisted upon the evils of free trade instead of the sacredness of speech. I am no politician but I believe if the Republican party had met issues squarely for human rights instead of the tariff it would have occupied a different position today. The voice of the people is the voice of God, I long with all the intensity of my soul for the Garrison, Douglass, Sumner, Whittier, and Phillips who shall rouse this nation to a demand that from Greenland's icy mountains to the coral reefs of the Southern seas, mob rule shall be put down and equal and exact justice be accorded to every citizen of whatever race, who finds a home within the borders of the land of the free and the home of the brave.

Then no longer will our national hymn be sounding brass and a tinkling cymbal, but every member of this great composite nation will be a living, harmonious illustration of the words, and all can honestly and gladly join in singing:

My country! 'tis of thee,
Sweet land of liberty
Of thee I sing.
Land where our fathers died,
Land of the Pilgrim's pride,
From every mountain side
Freedom does ring.

WOMEN'S CAUSE IS ONE AND UNIVERSAL

The higher fruits of civilization can not be extemporized, neither can they be developed normally, in the brief space of thirty years. It requires the long and painful growth of generations. Yet all through the darkest period of the colored women's oppression in this country her yet unwritten history is full of heroic struggle, a struggle against fearful and overwhelming odds, that often ended in a horrible death, to maintain and protect that which woman holds dearer than life. The painful, patient, and silent toil of mothers to gain a free simple title to the bodies of their daughters, the despairing fight, as of an entrapped tigress, to keep hallowed their own persons, would furnish material for epics. That more went down under the flood than stemmed the current is not extraordinary. The majority of our women are not heroines but I do not know that a majority of any race of women are heroines. It is enough for me to know that while in the eyes of the highest tribunal in America she was deemed no more than a chattel, an irresponsible thing, a dull block, to be drawn hither or thither at the volition of an owner, the Afro American woman maintained ideals of womanhood unshamed by any ever conceived. Resting or fermenting in untutored minds, such ideals could not claim a hearing at the bar of the nation. The white woman could least plead for her own emancipation; the black woman, doubly enslaved, could but suffer and struggle and be silent. I speak for the colored women of the South, because it is there that the millions of blacks in this country have watered the soil with blood and tears, and it is there too that the colored woman of America has made her characteristic history, and there her destiny evolving. Since emancipation the movement has been at times confused and stormy, so that we could not always tell whether we were going forward or groping in a circle. We hardly knew what we ought to emphasize, whether education or wealth, or civil freedom and recognition. We were utterly destitute. Possessing no homes nor the knowledge of how to make them, no money nor the habit of acquiring it, no education, no political status, no influence, what could we do? But as Frederick Douglass had said in darker days than those, "One with God is a majority," and our ignorance had hedged us in from the fine spun theories of agnostics. We had remaining at least a simple faith that a just God is on the throne of the universe, and that somehow—we could not see, nor did we bother our heads to try to tell how—he would in his own good time make all right that seemed most wrong.

Schools were established, not merely public day schools, but home training and industrial schools, at Hampton, at Fisk, Atlanta, Raleigh, and other stations, and later, through the energy of the colored people themselves, such schools as the Wilberforce, the Livingstone, the Allen, and the Paul Quinn were opened. These schools were almost without exception co-educational. Funds were too limited to be divided on sex lines, even had it been ideally desirable; but our girls as well as our boys flocked in and battled for an education. Not even then was that patient, untrumpeted heroine, the slave-mother, released from self-sacrifice, and many an unbuttered crust was t in silent content that she might eke out enough from her poverty to send her young folks off to school. She "never had the chance," she would tell you, with tears on her withered cheek, so she wanted them to get all they could. The work in these schools, and in such as these, has been like the little leaven hid in the measure of meal, permeating life throughout the length and breadth of the Southland, lifting up ideals of home and of womanhood; diffusing a contagious longing for higher living and purer thinking, inspiring woman herself with a new sense of her dignity in the eternal purposes of nature. Today there are twenty five thousand five hundred and thirty colored schools in the United States with one million three hundred and fifty-three thousand three hundred and fifty two pupils of both sexes. This is not quite the thirtieth year since their emancipation, and the color people hold in landed property for churches and schools twenty five million dollars. Two and one half million colored children have learned to read a write, and twenty two thousand nine hundred and fifty six colored men a women (mostly women) are teaching in these schools. According to Doctor Rankin, President of Howard University, there are two hundred and for seven colored students (a large percentage of whom are women) now preparing themselves in the universities of Europe. Of other colleges which give the B.A. course to women, and are broad enough not to erect barriers against colored applicants, Oberlin, the first to open its doors to both woman and the negro, has given classical degrees to six colored women, one of whom, the first and most eminent, Fannie Jackson Coppin, we shall listen to tonight. Ann Arbor and Wellesley have each graduated three of our women; Cornell University one, who is now professor of sciences in a Washington high school. A former pupil of my own from the Washington High School who was snubbed by Vassar, has since carried off honors in a competitive examination in Chicago University. The medical and law colleges of country are likewise bombarded by colored women, and every year some sister of the darker race claims their professional award of "well done." Eminent in their profession are Doctor Dillon and Doctor James, and there sailed to Africa last month a demure little brown woman who had just outstripped a whole class of men in a medical college in Tennessee.

In organized efforts for self help and benevolence also our women been active. The Colored Women's League, of which I am at present corresponding secretary, has active, energetic branches in the South and West. The branch in Kansas City, with a membership of upward of one hundred and fifty, already has begun under their vigorous president, Mrs. Yates, the erection of a building for friendless girls. Mrs. Coppin will, I hope, herself tell you something of her own magnificent creation of an industrial society in Philadelphia. The women of the Washington branch of the league have subscribed to a fund of about five thousand dollars to erect a woman's building for educational and industrial work, which is also to serve as headquarters for gathering and disseminating general information relating to the efforts of our women. This is just a glimpse of what we are doing.

Now, I think if I could crystallize the sentiment of my constituency, and deliver it as a message to this congress of women, it would be something like this: Let woman's claim be as broad in the concrete as in the abstract. We take our stand on the solidarity of humanity, the oneness of life, and the unnaturalness and injustice of all special favoritisms, whether of sex, race, country, or condition. If one link of the chain be broken, the chain is broken. A bridge is no stronger than its weakest part, and a cause is not worthier an its weakest element. Least of all can woman's cause afford to decry the weak. We want, then, as toilers for the universal triumph of justice and human rights, to go to our homes from this Congress, demanding an entrance not through a gateway for ourselves, our race, our sex, or our sect, but a grand highway for humanity. The colored woman feels that woman's cause is one and universal; and that not till the image of God, whether in parian or ebony, is sacred and inviolable; not till race, color, sex, and condition are seen as the accidents, and not the substance of life; not till the universal title of humanity to life, liberty, and the pursuit of happiness is conceded to be inalienable to all; not till then is woman's lesson taught and woman's cause won—not the white woman's, nor the black woman's, not the red woman's, but the cause of every man and of every woman who has writhed silently under a mighty wrong. Woman's wrongs are thus indissolubly linked with undefended woe, and the acquirement of her "rights" will mean the final triumph of all right over might, the supremacy of the moral forces of reason, and justice, and love in the government of the nations of earth.

Woman's Political Future

If before sin had cast its deepest shadows or sorrow had distilled its bitterest tears, it was true that it was not good for man to be alone, it is no less true, since the shadows have deepened and life's sorrows have increased, that the world has need of all the spiritual aid that woman can give for the social advancement and moral development of the human race. The tendency of the present age, with its restlessness, religious upheavals, failures, blunders, and crimes, is toward broader freedom, an increase of knowledge, the emancipation of thought, and a recognition of the brotherhood of man; in this movement woman, as the companion of man, must be a sharer. So close is the bond between man and woman that you cannot raise one without lifting the other. The world cannot move without woman's sharing in the movement, and to help give a right impetus to that movement is woman's highest privilege.

If the fifteenth century discovered America to the Old World, the nineteenth is discovering woman to herself. Little did Columbus imagine, when the New World broke upon his vision like a lovely gem in the coronet of the universe, the glorious possibilities of a land where the sun should be our engraver, the winged lightning our messenger, and steam our beast of burden. But as mind is more than matter, and the highest ideal always the true real, so to woman comes the opportunity to strive for richer and grander discoveries than ever gladdened the eye of the Genoese mariner.

Not the opportunity of discovering new worlds, but that of filling this old world with fairer and higher aims than the greed of gold and the lust of power, is hers. Through weary, wasting years men have destroyed, dashed in pieces, and overthrown, but today we stand on the threshold of woman's era, and woman's work is grandly constructive. In her hand are possibilities whose use or abuse must tell upon the political life of the nation, and send their influence for good or evil across the track of unborn ages.

As the saffron tints and crimson flushes of morn herald the coming day, so the social and political advancement which woman has already gained bears the promise of the rising of the full-orbed sun of emancipation. The result will be not to make home less happy, but society more holy; yet I do not think the mere extension of the ballot a panacea for all the ills of our national life. What we need today is not simply more voters, but better voters. Today there are red-handed men in our republic, who walk unwhipped of justice, who richly deserve to exchange the ballot of the freeman for the wristlets of the felon; brutal and cowardly men, who torture, burn, and lynch their fellow-men, men whose defenselessness should be their best defense and their weakness an ensign of protection. More than the changing of institutions we need the development of a national conscience, and the upbuilding of national character. Men may boast of the aristocracy of blood, may glory in the aristocracy of talent, and be proud of the aristocracy of wealth, but there is one aristocracy which must ever outrank them all, and that is the aristocracy of character; and it is the women of a country who help to mold its character, and to influence if not determine its destiny; and in the political future of our nation woman will not have done what she could if she does not endeavor to have our republic stand foremost among the nations of the earth, wearing sobriety as a crown and righteousness as a garment and a girdle. In coming into her political estate woman will find a mass of illiteracy to be dispelled. If knowledge is power, ignorance is also power. The power that educates wickedness may manipulate and dash against the pillars of any state when they are undermined and honeycombed by injustice.

I envy neither the heart nor the head of any legislator who has been born to an inheritance of privileges, who has behind him ages of education, dominion, civilization, and Christianity, if he stands opposed to the passage of a national education bill, whose purpose is to secure education to the children of those who were born under the shadow of institutions which made it a crime to read.

Today women hold in their hands influence and opportunity, and with these they have already opened doors which have been closed to others. By opening doors of labor woman has become a rival claimant for at least some of the wealth monopolized by her stronger brother. In the home she is the priestess, in society the queen, in literature she is a power, in legislative halls law-makers have responded to her appeals, and for her sake have humanized and liberalized their laws. The press has felt the impress of her hand. In the pews of the church she constitutes the majority; the pulpit has welcomed her, and in the school, she has the blessed privilege of teaching children and youth. To her is apparently coming the added responsibility of political power; and what she now possesses should only be the means of preparing her to use the coming power for the glory of God and the good of mankind; for power without righteousness is one of the most dangerous forces in the world.

Political life in our country has plowed in muddy channels, and needs the infusion of clearer and cleaner waters. I am not sure that women are naturally so much better than men that they will clear the stream by the virtue of their womanhood; it is not through sex but through character that the best influence of women upon the life of the nation must be exerted.

I do not believe in unrestricted and universal suffrage for either men or women. I believe in moral and educational tests. I do not believe that the most ignorant and brutal man is better prepared to add value to the strength and durability of the government than the most cultured, upright, and intelligent woman. I do not think that willful ignorance should swamp earnest intelligence at the ballot-box, nor that educated wickedness, violence, and fraud should cancel the votes of honest men. The unsteady hands of a drunkard cannot cast the ballot of a freeman. The hands of lynchers are too red with blood to determine the political character of the government for even four short years. The ballot in the hands of woman means power added to influence. How well she will use that power I cannot foretell. Great evils stare us in the face that need to be throttled by the combined power of an upright manhood and an enlightened womanhood; and I know that no nation can gain its full measure of enlightenment and happiness if one-half of it is free and the other half is fettered. China compressed the feet of her women and thereby retarded the steps of her men. The elements of a nation's weakness must ever be found at the hearthstone.

More than the increase of wealth, the power of armies, and the strength of fleets is the need of good homes, of good fathers, and good mothers.

The life of a Roman citizen was in danger in ancient Palestine, and men had bound themselves with a vow that they would eat nothing until they had killed the Apostle Paul. Pagan Rome threw around that imperiled life a bulwark of living clay consisting of four hundred and seventy human hearts, and Paul was saved. Surely the life of the humblest American citizen should be as well protected in America as that of a Roman citizen was in heathen Rome. A wrong done to the weak should be an insult to the strong. Woman coming into her kingdom will find enthroned three great evils, for whose overthrow she should be as strong in a love of justice and humanity as the warrior is in his might. She will find intemperance sending its flood of shame, and death, and sorrow to the homes of men, a fretting leprosy in our politics, and a blighting curse in our social life; the social evil sending to our streets women whose laughter is sadder than their tears, who slide from the paths of sin and shame to the friendly shelter of the grave; and lawlessness enacting in our republic deeds over which angels might weep, if heaven knows sympathy.

How can any woman send petitions to Russia against the horrors of Siberian prisons if, ages after the Inquisition has ceased to devise its tortures, she has not done all she could by influence, tongue, and pen to keep men from making bonfires of the bodies of real or supposed criminals?

O women of America! into your hands God has pressed one of the sublimest opportunities that ever came into the hands of the women of any race or people. It is yours to create a healthy public sentiment; to demand justice, simple justice, as the right of every race; to brand with everlasting infamy the lawless and brutal cowardice that lynches, burns, and tortures your own countrymen.

To grapple with the evils which threaten to undermine the strength of the nation and to lay magazines of powder under the cribs of future generations is no child's play.

Let the hearts of the women of the world respond to the song of the herald angels of peace on earth and good will to men. Let them throb as one heart unified by the grand and holy purpose of uplifting the human race, and humanity will breathe freer, and the world grow brighter. With such a purpose Eden would spring up in our path, and Paradise be around our way.

Address to the First National Conference of Colored Women

It is with especial joy and pride that I welcome you all to this, our first conference. It is only recently that women have waked up to the importance of meeting in council, and great as has been the advantage to women generally, and important as it is and has been that they should confer, the necessity has not been nearly so great, matters at stake not nearly so vital, as that we, bearing peculiar blunders, suffering under especial hardships, enduring peculiar privations, should meet for a "good talk" among ourselves. Although rather hastily called, you as well as I can testify how long and how earnestly a conference has been thought of and hoped for and even prepared for.

These women's clubs, which have sprung up all over the country, build and run upon broad and strong lines, have all been a preparation, small conferences in themselves, and their spontaneous birth and enthusiastic support have been little less than inspiration on the part of our women and a general preparation for a large union such as it is hoped this conference will lead to. Five years ago we had no colored women's club outside of those formed for the special work; today, with little over a month's notice, we are able to call representatives from more than twenty clubs. It is a good showing, it stands for much, it shows that we are truly American women, with all the adaptability, readiness to seize and possess our opportunities, willingness to do our part for good as other American women.

The reasons why we should confer are so apparent that it would seem hardly necessary to enumerate them, and yet there is none of them but demand our serious consideration. In the first place we need to feel the cheer and inspiration of meeting each other; we need to gain the courage and fresh life that comes from the mingling of congenial souls, of those working for the same ends. Next we need to talk over not only those things which are of vital importance to us as women, but also the things that are of special interest to us as colored women, the training of our children, openings for boys and girls, how they can be prepared for occupations and occupations may be found or opened for them, what we especially can do in the moral education of the race with which we are identified, our mental elevation and physical development, the home training it is necessary to give our children in order to prepare them to meet the peculiar conditions in which they shall find themselves, how to make the most of our own, to some extent, limited opportunities, these are some of our own peculiar questions to be discussed. Besides these are the general questions of the day, which we cannot afford to be indifferent to: temperance, morality, the higher education, hygiene and domestic questions. If these things need the serious consideration of women more advantageously placed by reason of all the aid to right thinking and living with which they are surrounded, surely we, with everything to pull us back, to hinder us in developing, need to take every opportunity and means for the thoughtful consideration which shall lead to wise action.

I have left the strongest reason for our conferring together until the last. All over America there is to be found a large and growing class of earnest, intelligent, progressive colored women, women who, if not leading full useful lives, are only waiting for the opportunity to do so, many of them warped and cramped for lack of opportunity, not only to do more but to be more; and yet, if an estimate of the colored women of American is called for, the inevitable reply, glibly given is: "For the most past ignorant and immoral, some exceptions, of course, but these don't count." Now for the sake of the thousands of self-sacrificing young women teaching and preaching in lonely southern backwoods for the noble army of mothers who has given birth to these girls, mothers whose intelligence is only limited by their opportunity to get at books, for the sake of the fine cultured women who have carried off the honors in school here and often abroad, for the sake of our own dignity, the dignity of our race and the future good name of our children, it is "mete, right and our bounded duty" to stand forth and declare ourselves and principles, to teach an ignorant and suspicious world that our aims and interests are identical with those of all good aspiring women.

Too long have we been silent under unjust and unholy charges; we cannot expect to have them removed until we disprove them through ourselves. It is not enough to try and disprove unjust charges through individual effort that never goes any further. Year after year southern women have protested against the admission of colored women into any national organization on the ground of eh immorality of these women, and because all refutation has only been tried by individual work the charge has never been crushed, as it could and should have been at the first. Now with an army of organized women standing for purity and mental worth, we in ourselves deny the charge and open the eyes of the world to a state of affairs to which they have been blind, often willfully so, and the very fact that the charges, audaciously and flippantly made, as they often are, are of so humiliating and delicate a nature, serves to protect the accuser by driving the helpless accused into mortified silence. It is to break this silence, not by noisy protestations of what we are not, but by a dignified showing of what we are and hope to become that we are impelled to take this step, to make of this gathering an object lesson to the world.

For many and apparent reasons it is especially fitting that the women of the race take the lead in this movement, but for all this we recognize the necessity of the sympathy of our husbands, brothers and fathers. Our women's movement is woman's movement in that it is led and directed by women for the good of women and men, for the benefit of all humanity, which is more than any one branch or section of it. We want, we ask the active interest of our men, and, too, we are not drawing the color line; we are women, American women, as intensely interested in all that pertains to us as such as all other American women: we are not alienating or withdrawing, we are only coming to the front, willing to join any others in the same work and cordially inviting and welcoming any others to join us. If there is any onething I would especially enjoin upon this conference it is union and earnestness. The questions that are to come before us are of too much import to be weakened by any trivialities or personalities. If any differences arise, let them be quickly settled, with the feeling that we are all workers to the same end, to elevate and dignify colored American womanhood.

This conference will not be what I expect if it does not show the wisdom, indeed the absolute necessity of a national organization of our women. Every year new questions coming up will prove it to us. This hurried, almost informal convention does not begin to meet our needs, it is only a beginning, made here in dear old Boston, where the scales of justice and generosity hang evenly balanced, and where the people "dare be true" to their best instincts and stand ready to lend aid and sympathy to worthy strugglers. It is hoped and believed that from this will spring an organization that will in truth bring in a new era to the colored women of America.

Democracy and Education

Mr. Chairman, Ladies and Gentlemen

It is said that the strongest chain is no stronger than its weakest link. In the Southern part of our country there are twenty-two millions of your brethren who are bound to you by ties which you cannot tear asunder if you would. The most intelligent man in your community has his intelligence darkened by the ignorance of a fellow citizen in the Mississippi bottoms. The most wealthy in your city would be more wealthy but for the poverty of a fellow being in the Carolina rice swamps. The most moral and religious among you has his religion and morality modified by the degradation of the man in the South whose religion is a mere matter of form or emotionalism.

The vote in your state that is cast for the highest and purest form of government is largely neutralized by the vote of the man in Louisiana whose ballot is stolen or cast in ignorance. When the South is poor, you are poor; when the South commits crime, you commit crime. My friends, there is no mistake; you must help us to raise the character of our civilization or yours will be lowered. . .

Can you make your intelligence affect us in the same ratio that our ignorance affects you? Let us put a not improbable case, one that involves peace or war, the honor or dishonor of our nation—yea, the very existence of the government. The North and West are divided. There are five million votes to be cast in the South, and of this number one half are ignorant. Not only are one half the voters ignorant, but, because of this ignorant vote, corruption, dishonesty in a dozen forms have crept into the exercise of the political franchise. . . The time may not be far off when to this kind of jury we shall have to look for the verdict that is to decide the course of our democratic institutions.

When a great national calamity stares us in the face, we are, I fear, too much given to depending on a short campaign of education to do on the hustings what should have been accomplished in the schoolroom. With this preliminary survey, let us examine with more care the work to be done in the South before all classes will be fit for the highest duties of citizenship.

In reference to my own race I am confronted with some embarrassment at the outset because of the various and conflicting opinions as to what is to be its final place in our economic and political life. Within the last thirty years—and, I might add, within the last three months—it has been proven by eminent authority that the Negro is increasing in numbers so fast that it is only a question of a few years before he will far outnumber the white race in the South, and it has also been proven that the Negro is fast dying out and it is only a question of a few years before he will have completely disappeared. It has also been proven that crime among us is on the increase and that crime is on the decrease; that education helps the Negro, that education also hurts him; that he is fast leaving the South and taking up his residence in the North and West, and that the tendency of the Negro is to drift to the lowlands of the Mississippi bottoms. It has been proven that as a slave laborer he produced less cotton than a free man. It has been proven that education unfits the Negro for work. . .

In the midst of this confusion there are a few things of which I feel certain that furnish a basis for thought and action. I know. . . that, whether in slavery or freedom, we have always been loyal to the Stars and Stripes, that no schoolhouse has been opened for us that has not been filled; that 1,500,000 ballots that we have the right to cast are as potent for weal and woe as the ballot cast by the whitest and most influential man in your commonwealth. . .

I fear that the wisest and most interested have not fully comprehended the task which American slavery has laid at the doors of the Republic. Few, I fear, realize what is to be done before the seven million of my people in the South can be made a safe, helpful, progressive part of our institutions. The South, in proportion to its ability, has done well, but this does not change facts. Let me illustrate what I mean by a single example. In spite of all that has been done, I was in a county in Alabama a few days ago where there are some thirty thousand colored people and about seven thousand whites; in this county not a single public school for Negroes has been open this year longer than three months, not a single colored teacher has been paid more than fifteen dollars a month for his teaching. Not one of these schools was taught in a building worthy of the name of schoolhouse. In this county the state or public authorities do not own a dollar's worth of school property—not a schoolhouse, a blackboard, or a piece of crayon.

Each colored child had spent on him this year for his education about fifty cents, while one of your children had spent on him this year for education not far from twenty dollars. And yet each citizen of this county is expected to share the burdens and privileges of our democratic form of government just as intelligently and conscientiously as the citizens of your beloved Kings County. A vote in this county means as much to the nation as a vote in the city of Boston. . .

I have referred to industrial education as a means of fitting the millions of my people in the South for the duties of citizenship. Until there is industrial independence it is hardly possible to have a pure ballot. In the country districts of the Gulf states it is safe to say that not more than one black man in twenty owns the land he cultivates. Where so large a proportion of the people are dependent, live in other people's houses, eat other people's food, and wear clothes they have not paid for, it is a pretty hard thing to tell how they are going to vote.

My remarks thus far have referred mainly to my own race. But there is another side. The longer I live and the more I study the question, the more I am convinced that it is not so much a problem as to what you will do with the Negro as what the Negro will do with you and your civilization. . . The educators, the statesmen, the philanthropists have never comprehended their duty toward the millions of poor whites in the South who were buffeted for two hundred years between slavery and freedom, between civilization and degredation, who were disregarded by both master and slave. It needs no prophet to tell the character of our future civilization when the poor white boy in the country districts of the South receives one dollar's worth of education and your boy twenty dollars' worth, when one never enters a library or reading room and the other has libraries and reading rooms in every ward and town. When one hears lectures and sermons once in two months and the other can hear a lecture or sermon everyday in the year. When you help the South you help yourselves. . .

Some years ago a bright young man of my race succeeded in passing a competitive examination for a cadetship at the United States Naval Academy at Annapolis. Says the young man, Mr. Henry Baker, in describing his stay at this institution: "I was several times attacked with stones and was forced finally to appeal to the officers, when a marine was detailed to accompany me across the campus and from the mess hall at meal times. My books were mutilated, my clothes were cut and in some instances destroyed, and all the petty annoyances which ingenuity could devise were inflicted upon me daily, and during seamanship practice aboard the Dale attempts were often made to do me personal injury while I would be aloft in the rigging. No one ever addressed me by name. I was called the Moke usually, the Nigger for variety. I was shunned as if I were a veritable leper, and received curses and blows as the only method my persecutors had of relieving the monotony."

Not once during the two years, with one exception, did any one of the more than four hundred cadets enrolled ever come to him with a word of advice, counsel, sympathy, or information. . . The one exception was in the case of a Pennsylvania boy, who stealthily brought him a piece of his birthday cake at twelve o'clock one night. The act so surprised Baker that his suspicions were aroused, but these were dispelled by the donor, who read to him a letter which he had received from his mother, from whom the cake came, in which she requested that a slice be given to the colored cadet who was without friends.

I recite this incident not for the purpose merely of condemning the wrong done a member of my race; no, no, not that. I mention the case, not for the one cadet, but for the sake of the four hundred cadets, for the sake of the four hundred American families, the four hundred American communities whose civilization and Christianity these cadets represented. Here were four hundred and more young men representing the flower of our country, who had passed through our common schools and were preparing themselves at public expense to defend the honor of our country. And yet, with grammar, reading, and arithmetic in the public schools, and with lessons in the arts of war, the principles of physical courage at Annapolis, both systems seemed to have utterly failed to prepare a single one of these young men for real life, that he could be brave enough, Christian enough, American enough, to take this poor defenseless black boy by the hand in open daylight and let the world know that he was his friend. Education, whether of black man or white man, that gives one physical courage to stand in front of the cannon and fails to give him moral courage to stand up in defense of right and justice is a failure.

. . . My friends, we are one in this country. The question of the highest citizenship and the complete education of all concerns nearly ten million of my own people and over sixty million of yours. We rise as you rise; when we fall you fall. When you are strong we are strong; when we are weak you are weak. There is no power than can separate our destiny. The Negro can afford to be wronged; the white man cannot afford to wrong him. . . If a white man steals a Negro's ballot it is the white man who is permanently injured. Physical death comes to the one Negro lynched in a county, but death of the morals—death of the soul—comes to the thousands responsible for the lynching.

We are a patient, humble people. We can afford to work and wait. There is plenty in this country for us to do. Away up in the atmosphere of goodness, forbearance, patience, long-suffering, and forgiveness the workers are not many or overcrowded. If others would be little we can be great. If others would be mean we can be good. If others would push us down we can help push them up. Character, not circumstances, makes the man. . .

During the next half-century and more my race must continue passing through the severe American crucible. We are to be tested in our patience, in our forbearance, our power to endure wrong, to withstand temptation, to succeed, to acquire and use skill, our ability to compete, to succeed in commerce; to disregard the superficial for the real, the appearance for the substance; to be great and yet the servant of all. This, this is the passport to all that is best in the life of our republic, and the Negro must possess it or be debarred. In working out our destiny, while the main burden and center of activity must be with us, we shall need in a large measure the help, the encouragement, the guidance that the strong can give the weak. Thus helped, we of both races in the South shall soon throw off the shackles of racial and sectional prejudice and rise above the clouds of ignorance, narrowness, and selfishness into that atmosphere, that pure sunshine, where it will be our highest ambition to serve man, our brother, regardless of race or past conditions.

In Union There is Strength

In Union there is strength is a truism that has been acted upon by Jew and Gentile, by Greek and Barbarian, by all classes and conditions alike from the creation of the universe to the present day. It did not take long for men to learn that by combining their strength, a greater amount of work could be accomplished with less effort in a shorter time. Upon this principle of union, governments have been founded and states built. Our own republic teaches the same lesson. Force a single one of the states of the United States to stand alone, and it becomes insignificant, feeble, and a prey to the rapacity of every petty power seeking to enlarge its territory and increase its wealth. But form a republic of United States, and it becomes one of the great nations of the earth, strong in its might. Acting upon this principle of concentration and union have the colored women of the United States banded themselves together to fulfill a mission to which they feel peculiarly adapted and especially called. We have become National, because from the Atlantic to the Pacific, from Maine to the Gulf, we wish to set in motion influences that shall stop the ravages made by practices that sap our strength and preclude the possibility of advancement which under other circumstances could easily be made.

We call ourselves an Association to signify that we have joined hands one with the other to work together in a common cause. We proclaim to the world that the women of our race have become partners in the great firm of progress and reform. We denominate ourselves colored, not because we are narrow, and wish to lay special emphasis on the color of the skin, for which no one is responsible, which of itself is no proof of an individual's virtue nor of his vice, which neither is a stamp, neither of one's intelligence nor of ignorance, but we refer to the fact that this is an association of colored women, because our peculiar status in this country at the present time seems to demand that we stand by ourselves in the special work for which we have organized. For this reason it was thought best to invite the attention of the world to the fact that colored women feel their responsibility as a unit, and together have clasped hands to assume it. Special stress has been laid upon the fact that our association is composed of women, not because we wish to deny rights and privileges to out brothers in imitation of the example they have set for us so many years, but because the work which we hope to accomplish can be done better, by the mothers, wives, daughters, and sisters of our race than by the fathers, husbands, brothers, and sons. The crying need of our organization of colored women is questioned by no one conversant with our peculiar trials and perplexities, and acquainted with the almost insurmountable obstacles in our path to those attainments and acquisitions to which it is the right and privilege of every member of every race to aspire. It is not because we are discouraged at the progress made by our people that we have uttered the cry of alarm which has called together this band of earnest women assembled here tonight.

In the unprecedented advancement made by the Negro since his emancipation, we take great pride and extract therefore both courage and hope. From a condition of dense ignorance. But thirty years ago, we have advanced so far in the realm of knowledge and letters as to have produced scholars and authors of repute. Though penniless as a race a short while ago, we have among us today a few men of wealth and multitudes who own their homes and make comfortable livings. We therefore challenge any other race to present a record more creditable and show a progress more wonderful than that made by the ex slaves of the United States and that too in the face of prejudice, proscription, and persecution against which no other people has ever had to contend in the history of the world. And yet while rejoicing in our steady march, onward and upward, to the best and highest things of life, we are nevertheless painfully mindful of our weaknesses and defects (in) which we know the Negro is no worse than other races equally poor, equally ignorant, and equally oppressed, we would nevertheless see him lay aside the sins that do so easily beset him, and come forth clothed in all these attributes of mind and grace of character that claims the real man. To accomplish this end through the simplest, swiftest, surest methods, the colored women have organized themselves into this Association, whose power for good, let us hope, will be as enduring as it is unlimited.

Believing that it is only through the home that a people can become really good and truly great, the N.A.C.W. shall enter that sacred domain to inculcate right principles of living and correct false views of life. Homes, more homes, purer homes, better homes, is the text upon which our sermons to the masses must be preached. So long s the majority of people call that place home in which the air is foul, the manners bad, and the morals worse, just so long is this so called home a menace to health, a breeder of vice, and the abode of crime. Not alone upon the inmates of these hovels are the awful consequences of their filth and immorality visited, but upon the heads of those who sit calmly by and make no effort to stem the tide of disease and vice will vengeance as surely fall.

The colored youth is vicious we are told, and statistics showing the multitudes of our boys and girls who fill the penitentiaries and crowd the jails appall and discourage us. Side by side with these facts and figures of crime, I would have presented and pictured the miserable hovels from which these youthful criminals come. Crowded into alleys, many of them the haunts of vice, few if any of them in a proper sanitary condition, most of them fatal to mental and moral growth, and destructive of healthful physical development as well, thousands of our children have a wretched heritage indeed. It is, therefore, into the home, sisters of the Association, that we must go, filled with all the zeal and charity which such a mission demands.

To the children of the race we owe, as women, a debt which can never be paid, until Herculean efforts are made to rescue them from evil and shame for which they are in no way responsible. Listen to the cry of the children, my sisters. Upon you they depend for the light of knowledge, and the blessing of a good example. As an organization of women, surely nothing can be nearer our hearts than the children, many of whose lives so sad and dark we might brighten and bless. It is kindergartens we need. Free kindergartens in every city and hamlet of this broad land we must have, if the children are to receive from us what it is our duty to give. The more unfavorable the environments of children, the more necessary is it that steps be taken to counteract the hateful influences upon innocent victims. How imperative is it then that we inculcate correct principles, and set good examples for our own youth whose little feet will have so many thorny paths of prejudice, temptations, and injustice to tread. Make a visit to the settlements of colored people who in many cities are relegated to the most noisome sections permitted by the municipal government, and behold the miles of inhumanity that infest them. Here are our little ones, the future representatives of the race, fairly drinking in the permissible example of their elders, coming in contact with nothing but ignorance and vice, till at the age of six evil habits are formed that no amount of civilizing and Christianizing can ever completely break. As long as the evil nature alone is encouraged to develop, while the higher, nobler qualities in little ones are dwarfed and deadened by the very atmosphere which they breathe, the negligent, pitiless public is responsible for the results and is partner of their crimes.

Let the women of the National Association see to it that the little strays of the alleys come in contact with intelligence and virtue, at least a few times a week, that the noble aspirations with which they are born may not be entirely throttled by the evil influences which these poor little ones are powerless to escape. The establishment of free kindergartens! You exclaim! Where is the money coming from? How can we do it? This charity you advocate though beautiful in theory is nevertheless impossible of attainment. Let the women of the race once be thoroughly aroused to their duty to the children, let them be consumed with desire to save them from lives of degradation and shame, and the establishment of free kindergartens for the poor will become a living, breathing, saving reality at no distant day. What movement looking toward the reformation and regeneration of mankind was ever proposed that did not instantly assume formidable portions to the fainthearted. But how soon obstacles that have once appeared insuperable dwindle into nothingness, after the shoulder is put to the wheel and united effort determines to remove them! In every organization of the Association let committees be appointed whose special mission it will be to do for the little strays of the alleys what is not done by their mothers, who in many instances fall far short of their duty, not because they are vicious and depraved, but because they are ignorant and poor.

Through mother meetings which have been in the past year and will be in the future a special feature of the Association, much useful informatics in everything pertaining to the home will be disseminated. Object lessons in the best way to sweep, to dust, to cook and to wash should be given by women who have made a special study of the art and science of housekeep. How to clothe children neatly, how to make, and especially how to mend garments, how to manage their households economically, what food is the most nutritious and best for the money, how to ventilate as thoroughly as possible the dingy stuffy quarters which the majority are forced to inhabit. . . all these are subjects on which the women of the masses need more knowledge. Let us teach mothers of families how to save wisely. Let us have heart to heart talks with our women that we may strike at the root of evil. If the women of the dominant race with all the centuries of education. refinement, and culture back of them, with all their wealth of opportunity ever present with them, if these women felt a responsibility to call a Mother's Congress that they might be ever enlightened as to the best methods of rearing children and conducting their homes, how much more do the women of our race from whom the shackles of slavery have just fallen need information on the same subjects? Let us have Mother Congresses in every community in which our women can be counseled. The necessity of increasing the self respect of our children is important. Let the reckless, ill advised, and oftentimes brutal methods of punishing children be everywhere condemned Let us teach our mothers that by punishing children inhumanely, they destroy their pride, crush their spirit and convert them into hardened culprits whom it will be impossible later on to reach or touch in anyway at all.

More than any other race at present in this country, we should strive to implant feelings of self respect and pride in our children, whose spirits are crushed and whose hearts saddened enough by indignities from which as victims of unreasonable cruel prejudice it is impossible to shield them. Let it be the duty of every friend of the race to teach children who are humiliated on learning that they are descendants of slaves that the majority of races on the earth have at some time in their history been subjects to another. This knowledge of humiliation will be important when we are victims of racism. Let us not only preach, but practice race unity, race pride, reverence and sect for those capable of leading and advising us. Let the youth of the race impressed about the dignity of labor and inspired with a desire to work. Let us do nothing to handicap children in the desperate struggle for existence in which their unfortunate condition in this country forces them to engage. Let us purify the atmosphere of our homes till it becomes so sweet that those who dwell in them carry on a great work of reform. That we have no money to help the needy and poor, I reply, that having hearts, generous natures, willing feet, and helpful hands can without the token of a single penny work miracles in the name of humanity and right.

Money we need, money we must have to accomplish much which we ape to effect. But it is not by powerful armies and the outlays of vast fortunes that the greatest revolutions are wrought and the most enduring reforms inaugurated. It is by the silent, though powerful force of individual influences thrown on the side of right, it is by arduous persistence and effort keep those with whom we come in daily contact, to enlighten the heathen our door, to create wholesome public sentiment in the communities in hick we live, that the heaviest blows are struck for virtue and right. Let us not only preach, but practice race unity, race pride, reverence, and respect for those capable of leading and advising us. Let the youth of the race Be impressed about the dignity of labor and inspired with a desire to work. Let us do nothing to handicap children in the desperate struggle for existence in which their unfortunate condition in this country forces them to engage. Let us purify the atmosphere of our homes till it become so sweet it those who dwell in them will have a heritage more precious than silver or gold.

The Attitude of the American Mind Toward the Negro Intellect

For the first time in the history of this nation the colored people of America have undertaken the difficult task, of stimulating and fostering the genius of their race as a distinct and definite purpose. Other and many gatherings have been made, during our own two and a half centuries' residence on this continent, for educational purposes; but ours is the first which endeavors to rise up to the plane of culture. For my own part I have no misgivings either with respect to the legitimacy, the timeliness, or the prospective success of our venture.

The race in the brief period of a generation, has been so fruitful in intellectual product, that the time has come for a coalescence of powers, and for reciprocity alike in effort and appreciation. I congratulate you, therefore, on this your first anniversary. To me it is, I confess, a matter of rejoicing that we have, as a people, reached a point where we have a class of men who will come together for purposes, so pure, so elevating, so beneficent, as the cultivation of mind, with the view of meeting the uses and the needs of our benighted people. I feel that if this meeting were the end of this Academy; if I could see that it would die this very day, I would nevertheless, cry out "All hail!" even if I had to join in with the salutation "farewell forever!"

For, first of all, you have done, during the year, that which was never done so completely before, a work which has already told upon the American mind; and next you have awakened in the Race an ambition which, in some form, is sure to reproduce both mental and artistic organization in the future. The cultured classes of our country have never interested themselves to stimulate the desires or aspirations of the mind of our race. They have left us terribly alone. Such stimulation, must, therefore, in the very nature of things, come from ourselves. Let us state here a simple, personal incident, which will well serve to illustrate a history. I entered, sometime ago, the parlor of a distinguished southern clergyman. A kinsman was standing at his mantel, writing. The clergyman spoke to his relative "Cousin, let me introduce to you the Rev. C., a clergyman of our Church." His cousin turned and looked down at me; but as soon as he saw my black face, he turned away with disgust, and paid no more attention to me than if I were a dog. Now, this porcine gentleman, would have been perfectly courteous, if I had gone into this parlor as a cook, or a waiter, or a bootblack. But my profession, as a clergyman, suggested the idea of letters and cultivation; and the contemptible snob at once forgot his manners, and put aside the common decency of his class.

Now, in this, you can see the attitude of the American mind toward the Negro intellect. A reference to this attitude seems necessary, if we would take in, properly, the present condition of Negro culture. It presents a most singular phenomenon. Here was a people laden with the spoils of the centuries, bringing with them into this new land the culture of great empires; and, withal, claiming the exalted name and grand heritage of Christians. By their own voluntary act they placed right beside them a large population of another race of people, seized as captives, and brought to their plantations from a distant continent. This other race was an unlettered, unenlightened, and a pagan people. What was the attitude taken by this master race toward their benighted bondsmen? It was not simply that of indifference or neglect. There was nothing negative about it. They began, at the first, a systematic ignoring of the fact of intellect in this abased people. They undertook the process of darkening their minds. "Put out the light, and then, put out the light!" was their cry for centuries. Paganizing themselves, they sought a deeper paganizing of their serfs than the original paganism that these had brought from Africa. There was no legal artifice conceivable which was not resorted to, to blindfold their souls from the light of letters; and the church, in not a few cases, was the prime offender.

Then the legislatures of the several states enacted laws and Statutes, closing the pages of every book printed to the eyes of Negroes; barring the doors of every school room against them! And this was the systematized method of the intellect of the South, to stamp out the brains of the Negro! It was done, too, with the knowledge that the Negro had brain power. There was then, no denial that the Negro had intellect. That denial was an after thought. Besides, legislatures never pass laws forbidding the education of pigs, dogs, and horses. They pass such laws against the intellect of men. However, there was then, at the very beginning of the slave trade, everywhere, in Europe, the glintings forth of talent in great Negro geniuses, in Spain, and Portugal, in France and Holland and England; and Phillis Wheatley and Banneker and Chavis and Peters, were in evidence on American soil. It is manifest, therefore, that the objective point in all this legislation was INTELLECT, the intellect of the Negro! It was an effort to becloud and stamp out the intellect of the Negro!

The first phase of this attitude reached over from about 1700 to 1820: and as the result, almost Egyptian darkness fell upon the mind of the race, throughout the whole land. Following came a more infamous policy. It was the denial of intellectuality in the Negro; the assertion that he was not a human being, that he did not belong to the human race. This covered the period from 1820 to 1835, when Gliddon and Nott and others, published their so called physiological work, to prove that the Negro was of a different species from the white man. A distinguished illustration of this ignoble sentiment can be given. In the year 1833 or 4 the speaker was an errand boy in the Anti-slavery office in New York City. On a certain occasion he heard a conversation between the Secretary and two eminent lawyers from Boston, Samuel E. Sewell and David Lee Child. They had been to Washington on some legal business. While at the Capitol they happened to dine in the company of the great John C. Calhoun, then senator from South Carolina. It was a period of great ferment upon the question of Slavery, States' Rights, and Nullification; and consequently the Negro was the topic of conversation at the table. One of the utterances of Mr. Calhoun was to this effect "That if he could find a Negro who knew the Greek syntax, he would then believe that the Negro was a human being and should be treated as a man." Just think of the crude asininity of even a great man! Mr. Calhoun went to "Yale" to study the Greek Syntax, and graduated there. His son went to Yale to study the Greek syntax, and graduated there. His grandson, in recent years, went to Yale, to learn the Greek Syntax, and graduated there. School and Colleges were necessary for the Calhouns, and all other white men to learn the Greek syntax. And yet this great man knew that there was not a school, nor a college in which a black boy could learn his A, B, C's. He knew that the law in all the Southern States forbade Negro instruction under the severest penalties. How then was the Negro to learn the Greek Syntax? How then was he to evidence to Mr. Calhoun his human nature? Why, it is manifest that Mr. Calhoun expected the Greek syntax to grow in Negro brains, by spontaneous generation! Mr. Calhoun was then, as much as any other American, an exponent of the nation's mind upon his point.

Antagonistic as they were upon other subjects, upon the, rejection of the Negro intellect they were a unit. And this, measurably, is the attitude of the American mind today: measurably, I say, for thanks to the Almighty, it is not universally so. There has always been a school of philanthropists in this land who have always recognized mind in the

Negro; and while recognizing the limitations which individual capacity demanded, claimed that for the RACE, there was no such thing possible for its elevation save the widest, largest, highest, improvement. Such were our friends and patrons in New England in New York, Pennsylvania, a few among the Scotch Presbyterians and the "Friends" in grand old North Carolina; a great company among the Congregationalists of the East, nobly represented down to the present, by the "American Missionary Society," which tolerates no stint for the Negro intellect in its grand solicitudes. But these were exceptional. Down to the year 1825, I know of no Academy or College which would open its doors to a Negro. In the South it was a matter of absolute legal disability. In the North, it was the ostracism of universal caste sentiment. The theological schools of the land, and of all names, shut their doors against the black man. An eminent friend of mine, the noble, fervent, gentlemanly Rev. Theodore S. Wright, then a Presbyterian licentiate, was taking private lessons in theology, at Princeton; and for this offense was kicked out of one of its halls. In the year 1832 Miss Prudence Crandall opened a private school for the education of colored girls; and it set the whole State of Connecticut in a flame. Miss Crandall was mobbed, and the school was broken up. The year following, the trustees of Canaan Academy in New Hampshire opened its doors to Negro youths; and this act set the people of that state on fire. The farmers of the region assembled with 90 yoke of oxen, dragged the Academy into a swamp, and a few weeks afterward drove the black youths from the town. These instances will suffice. They evidence the general statement, i.e. that the American mind has refused to foster and to cultivate the Negro intellect. Join to this a kindred fact, of which there is the fullest evidence. Impelled, at times, by pity, a modicum of schooling and training has been given the Negro; but even this, almost universally, with reluctance, with cold criticism, with microscopic scrutiny, with icy reservation, and at times, with ludicrous limitations.

Cheapness characterizes almost all the dominations of the American people to the Negro: Cheapness, in all the past, has been the regimen provided for the Negro in every line of his intellectual, as well as his lower life. And so, cheapness is to be the rule in the future, as well for his higher, as for his lower life: cheap wages and cheap food, cheap and rotten huts; cheap and dilapidated schools; cheap and stinted weeks of schooling; cheap meeting houses for worship; cheap and ignorant ministers; cheap theological training; and now, cheap learning, culture and civilization! Noble exceptions are found in the grand literary circles in which Mr. Howells moves manifest in his generous editing of our own Paul Dunbar's poems. But this generosity is not general, even in the world of American letters. You can easily see this in the attempt, now a days, to side track the Negro intellect, and to place it under limitations never laid upon any other class. The elevation of the Negro has been a moot question for a generation past. But even today what do we find the general reliance of the American mind in determining this question? Almost universally the resort is to material agencies! The ordinary, and sometimes the extraordinary American is unable to see that the struggle of a degraded people for elevation is, in its very nature, a warfare, and that its main weapon is the cultivated and scientific mind.

Ask the great men of the land how this Negro problem is to be solved, and then listen to the answers that come from divers classes of our white fellow citizens. The merchants and traders of our great cities tell us "The Negro must be taught to work;" and they will pour out their moneys by thousands to train him to toil. The clergy in large numbers, cry out "Industrialism is the only hope of the Negro;" for this is the bed rock, in their opinion, of Negro evangelization! "Send him to Manual Labor Schools," cries out another set of philanthropists. "Hic haec, hoc," is going to prove the ruin of the Negro" says the Rev. Steele, an erudite Southern Savan. "You must begin at the bottom with the Negro," says another eminent author reached the bottom. Says the Honorable George T. Barnes, of Georgia "The kind of education the Negro should receive should not be very refined nor classical, but adapted to his present condition:" As though there is to be no future for the Negro. And so you see that even now, late in the 19th century, in this land of learning and science, the creed is "Thus far and no farther," i.e. for the American black man. One would suppose from the universal demand for the mere industrialism for this race of ours, that the Negro had been going daily to dinner parties, eating terrapin and indulging in champagne; and returning home at night, sleeping on beds of eiderdown; breakfasting in the morning in his bed, and then having his valet to clothe him daily in purple and fine linen all these 250 years of his sojourn in this land. And then, just now, the American people, tired of all this Negro luxury, was calling him, for the first time, to blister his hands with the hoe, and to learn to supply his needs by sweatful toil in the cotton fields.

Listen a moment, to the wisdom of a great theologian, and withal as great philanthropist, the Rev. Dr. Wayland, of Philadelphia. Speaking, not long since, of the "Higher Education" of the colored people of the South, he said "that this subject concerned about 8,000,000 of our fellow citizens, among whom are probably 1,500,000 voters. The education suited to these people is that which should be suited to white people under the same circumstances. These people are bearing the impress which was left on them by two centuries of slavery and several centuries of barbarism. This education must begin at the bottom. It must first of all produce the power of self support to assist them to better their condition. It should teach them good citizenship and should build them up morally. It should be, first, a good English education. They should be imbued with the knowledge of the Bible. They should have an industrial education. An industrial education leads to self support and to the elevation of their condition. Industry is itself largely an education, intellectually and morally, and, above all, an education of character. Thus we should make these people self dependent. This education will do away with pupils being taught Latin and Greek, while they do not know the rudiments of English."

Just notice the cautious, restrictive, limiting nature of this advice! Observe the lack of largeness, freedom and generosity in it. Dr. Wayland, I am sure, has never specialized just such a regimen for the poor Italians, Hungarians or Irish, who swarm, in lowly degradation, in immigrant ships to our shores. No! for them he wants, all Americans want, the widest, largest culture of the land; the instant opening, not simply of the common schools; and then an easy passage to the bar, the legislature, and even the judgeships of the nation. And they oft times get there. But how different the policy with the Negro. He must have "an education which begins at the bottom." "He should have an industrial education," &c. His education must, first of all, produce the power of self support, &c. Now, all this thought of Dr. Wayland is all true. But, my friends, it is all false, too; and for the simple reason that it is only half truth. Dr. Wayland seems unable to rise above the plane of burden bearing for the Negro. He seems unable to gauge the idea of the Negro becoming a thinker. He seems to forget that a race of thoughtless toilers are destined to be forever a race of senseless boys; for only beings who think are men. How pitiable it is to see a great good man be fuddled by a half truth. For to allege "Industrialism" to be the grand agency in the elevation of a race of already degraded laborers, is as much a mere platitude as to say, "they must eat and drink and sleep;" for man cannot live without these habits. But they never civilize man; and civilization is the objective point in the movement for Negro elevation. Labor, just like eating and drinking, is one of the inevitabilities of life; one of its positive necessities. And the Negro has had it for centuries; but it has never given him manhood. It does not now, in wide areas of population, lift him up to moral and social elevation. Hence the need of a new factor in his life. The Negro needs light: light thrown in upon all the circumstances of his life. The light of civilization.

Dr. Wayland fails to see two or three important things in this Negro problem: (a) That the Negro has no need to go to a manual labor school. He has been for two hundred years and more, the greatest laborer in the land. He is a laborer now: and he must always be a laborer, or he must die. But: (b) Unfortunately for the Negro, he has been so wretchedly ignorant that he has never known the value of his sweat and toil. He has been forced into being an unthinking labor machine. And this he is, to a large degree, today under freedom. (c) Now the great need of the Negro, in our day and time, is intelligent impatience at the exploitation of his labor, on the one hand; on the other hand courage to demand a larger share of the wealth which his toil creates for others. It is not a mere negative proposition that settles this question.

It is not that the Negro does not need the hoe, the plane, the plough, and the anvil. It is the positive affirmation that the negro needs the light of cultivation; needs it to be thrown in upon all his toil, upon his whole life and its environments. What he needs is CIVILIZATION. He needs the increase of his higher wants, of his mental and spiritual needs. This, mere animal labor has never given him, and never can give him. But it will come to him, as an individual, and as a class, just in proportion as the higher culture comes to his leaders and teachers, and so gets into his schools, academies and colleges; and then enters his pulpits; and so filters down into his families and his homes; and the Negro learns that he is no longer to be a serf, but that he is to bare his strong brawny arm as a laborer; not to make the white man a Croesus, but to make himself a man. He is always to be a laborer; but now, in these days of freedom and the schools, he is to be a laborer with intelligence, enlightenment and manly ambitions. But, when his culture fits him for something more than a field hand or a mechanic, he is to have an open door set wide before him! And that culture, according to his capacity, he must claim as his rightful heritage, as a man: not stinted training, not a caste education, not a Negro curriculum. The Negro Race in this land must repudiate this absurd notion which is stealing on the American mind. The Race must declare that it is not to be put into a single groove; and for the simple reason (1) that man was made by his Maker to traverse the whole circle of existence, above as well as below; and that universality is the kernel of all true civilization, of all race elevation. And (2) that the Negro mind, imprisoned for nigh three hundred years' needs breadth and freedom, largeness, altitude, and elasticity; not stint nor rigidity, nor contractedness. But the "Gradgrinds" are in evidence on all sides, telling us that the colleges and scholarships given us since emancipation, are all a mistake; and that the whole system must be reversed.

The conviction is widespread that the Negro has no business in the higher walks of scholarship; that, for instance, Prof. Scarborough has no right to labor in philology; Professor Kelly Miller in mathematics; Professor Du Bois, in history; Dr. Bowen, in theology; Professor Turner, in science; nor Mr. Tanner in art. There is no repugnance to the Negro buffoon, and the Negro scullion; but so soon as the Negro stands forth as an intellectual being, this toad of American prejudice, as at the touch of Ithuriel's spear, starts up a devil! It is this attitude, this repellant, this forbidding attitude of the American mind, which forces the Negro in this land, to both recognize and to foster the talent and capacity of his own race, and to strive to put that capacity and talent to use for the race. I have detailed the dark and dreadful attempt to stamp that intellect out of existence. It is not only a past, it is also, modified indeed, a present fact; and out of it springs the need of just such an organization as the Negro Academy.

Now, gentlemen and friends, seeing that the American mind in the general, revolts from Negro genius, the Negro himself is duty bound to see to the cultivation and the fostering of his own race capacity. This is the chief purpose of this Academy. Our special mission is the encouragement of the genius and talent in our own race. Wherever we see great Negro ability it is our office to light upon it not tardily, not hesitatingly; but warmly, ungrudgingly, enthusiastically, for the honor of our race, and for the stimulating self-sacrifice in upbuilding the race. Fortunately for us, as a people, this year has given us more than ordinary opportunity for such recognition. Never before, in American history, has there been such a large discovery of talent and genius among us.

Early in the year there was published by one of our members, a volume of papers and addresses, of more than usual excellence. You know gentlemen, that, not seldom, we have books and pamphlets from the press which, like most of our newspapers, are beneath the dignity of criticism. In language, in style, in grammar and in thought they are often crude and ignorant and vulgar. Not so with "Talks for the Times" by Prof. Crogman, of Clark University. It is a book with largess of high and noble common sense; pure and classical in style; with a large fund of devoted racialism; and replete everywhere with elevated thoughts. Almost simultaneously with the publication of Professor Crogman's book, came the thoughtful and spicy narrative of Rev. Matthew Anderson of Philadelphia. The title of this volume is "Presbyterianism: its relation to the Negro: but the title cannot serve as a revelation of the racy and spirited story of events in the career of its author. The book abounds with stirring incidents, strong remonstrance, clear and lucid argument, powerful reasonings, the keenest satire; while, withal, it sets forth the wide needs of the Race, and gives one of the strongest vindications of its character and its capacity.

Soon after this came the first publication of our Academy. And you all know the deep interest excited by the two papers, the first issue of this Society. They have attracted interest and inquiry where the mere declamatory effusions, or, the so called eloquent harangues of aimless talkers and political wire pullers would fall like snowflakes upon the waters. The papers of Prof. Kelly Miller and Prof. Du Bois have reached the circles of scholars and thinkers in this country. So consummate was the handling of Hoffman's "Race Traits and Tendencies" by Prof. Miller, that we may say that it was the most scientific defense of the Negro ever made in this country by a man of our own blood: accurate, pointed, painstaking, and I claim conclusive. The treatise of Prof. Du Bois upon the "Conservation of Race," separated itself, in tone and coloring, from the ordinary effusions of literary work in this land. It rose to the dignity of philosophical insight and deep historical inference. He gave us, in a most lucid and original method, and in a condensed form, the long settled conclusions of Ethnologists and Anthropologists upon the question of Race. This treatise moreover, furnished but a limited measure of our indebtedness to his pen and brain.

Only a brief time before our assembly last year, Prof. Du Bois had given a large contribution to the literature of the nation as well as to the genius of the race. At that time he had published a work which will, without doubt, stand permanently, as authority upon its special theme. "The Suppression of the Slave Trade" is, without doubt, the one unique and special authority upon that subject, in print. It is difficult to conceive the possible creation of a similar work, so accurate and painstaking, so full of research, so orderly in historical statement, so rational in its conclusions. h is the simple truth, and at the same time the highest praise, the statement of one Review, that "Prof. Du Bois has exhausted his subject." This work is a step forward in the literature of the Race, and a stimulant to studious and aspiring minds among us.

One further reference, that is, to the realm of Art. The year '97 will henceforth be worthy of note in our history. As a race, we have, this year, reached a high point in intellectual growth and expression. In poetry and painting, as well as in letters and thought, the Negro has made, this year, a character. On my return home in October, I met an eminent scientific gentleman; and one of the first remarks he made to me was "Well, Dr. Crummell, we Americans have been well taken down in Paris, this year. Why," he said, "the prize in painting was taken by a colored young man, a Mr. Tanner from America. Do you know him?" The reference was to Mr. Tanner's "Raising of Lazarus," a painting purchased by the French Government, for the famous Luxembourg Gallery. This is an exceptional honor, rarely bestowed upon any American Artist. Well may we all be proud of this, and with this we may join the idea that Tanner, instead of having a hoe in his hand, or digging in a trench, as the faddists on industrialism would fain persuade us, has found his right place at the easel with artists.

Not less distinguished in the world of letters is the brilliant career of our poet friend and co laborer, Mr. Paul Dunbar. It was my great privilege last summer to witness his triumph, on more than one occasion, in that grand metropolis of Letters and Literature, the city of London; as well as to hear of the high value set upon his work, by some of the first scholars and literati of England. Mr. Dunbar has had his poems republished in London by Chapman & Co.; and now has as high a reputation abroad as he has here in America, where his luminous genius has broken down the bars, and with himself, raised the intellectual character of his race in the world's consideration.

These cheering occurrences, these demonstrations of capacity, give us the greatest encouragement in the large work which is before this Academy. Let us enter upon that work, this year, with high hopes, with large purposes, and with calm and earnest persistence. I trust that we shall bear in remembrance that the work we have undertaken is our special function; that it is a work which calls for cool thought, for laborious and tireless painstaking, and for clear discrimination; that it promises nowhere wide popularity, or, exuberant eclat; that very much of its ardent work is to be carried on in the shade; that none of its desired results will spring from spontaneity; that its most prominent features are the demands of duty to a needy people; and that its noblest rewards will be the satisfaction which will spring from having answered a great responsibility, and having met the higher needs of a benighted and struggling Race.

THE NEGRO WILL NEVER ACQUIESCE

Lawlessness is increasing in the South. After thirty three years of freedom our civil and political rights are still denied us; the fourteenth and fifteenth amendments to the Constitution are still a dead letter. The spirit of oppression and injustice is not diminished but increasing. The determination to keep us in a state of civil and political inferiority, and to surround us with such conditions as will tend to crush out of us a manly and self-respecting spirit, is stronger now than it was at the close of the war.

The fixed purpose and determination of the Southern whites is to negative these great amendments, to eliminate entirely the Negro as a political factor. And this purpose is intensifying, is growing stronger and stronger each year. The sentiment everywhere is: This is a white man's government. And that means, not only that the whites shall rule, but that the Negro shall have nothing whatever to do with governmental affairs. If he dares to think otherwise, or aspires to cast a ballot, or to become anything more than a servant, he is regarded as an impudent and dangerous Negro; and according to the most recent declarations of that old slave holding and lawless spirit, all such Negroes are to be driven out of the South, or compelled by force, by what is known as the shot gun policy, to renounce their rights as men and as American citizens.

This is certainly a very discouraging condition of things, but the saddest aspect of it all is that there are members of our race and not the ignorant, unthinking masses, who have had no advantages, and who might be excused for any seeming insensibility to their rights, but the intelligent, the educated who are found condoning such offenses, justifying or excusing such a condition of things on the ground that in view of the great disparity in the condition of the two races, anything different from that could not reasonably be expected. Any Negro who takes that position is a traitor to his race, and shows that he is deficient in manhood, in true self respect.

If the time ever comes when the Negro himself acquiesces in that condition of things, then his fate is sealed and ought to be sealed. Such a race is not fit to be free. But, thank God, the cowardly, ignoble sentiment to which I have just alluded, while it may find lodgment in the breast of a few weak kneed, timeserving Negroes, is not the sentiment of this black race. No, and never will be.

During all these terrible years of suffering and oppression, these years of blood and tears, though he has been shot at, his property destroyed, his family scattered, his home broken up; though he has been forced to fly like the fugitive for his life before the hungry bloodhounds of Southern Democracy; although everything has been done to terrorize him, to keep him from the polls, he still stands up for his rights. In some cases he has stayed away; in others he has gone straightforward in the face of the bullets of the enemy; and has been shot down.

Hundreds of the men of our race have laid their lives down on Southern soil in vindication of their rights as American citizens. And shall we be told, and by black men, too, that the sacred cause for which they poured out their life's blood is to be relinquished; that the white ruffians who shot them down were justified; that in view of all the circumstances it was just what was to have been expected, and therefore that virtually we have no reasonable grounds of complaint? Away with such treasonable utterances; treason to God; treason to man; treason to free institutions, to the spirit of an enlightened and Christian sentiment.

The Negro is an American citizen, and he never will be eliminated as a political factor with his consent. He has been terrorized and kept from the polls by bloody ruffians, but he has never felt that it was right; he has never acquiesced in it, and never will, as long as he lives. As long as there is one manly, self-respecting Negro in this country, the agitation will go on, will never cease until right is triumphant. It is onething to compel the Negro by force to stay away from the polls; it is a very different thing for the Negro himself, freely of his own accord, to relinquish his political rights. The one he may be constrained to do; the other he will not do.

Another discouraging circumstance is to be found in the fact that the pulpits of the land are silent on these great wrongs. The ministers fear to offend those to whom they minister. We hear a great deal from their pulpits about suppressing the liquor traffic, about gambling, about Sabbath desecration, and about the suffering Armenians, and about polygamy in Utah when that question was up, and the Louisiana lottery. They are eloquent in their appeals to wipe out these great wrongs, but when it comes to Southern brutality, to the killing of Negroes and despoiling them of their civil and political rights, they are, to borrow an expression from Isaiah, "dumb dogs that cannot bark." Had the pulpit done its duty, the Southern savages, who have been sinking lower and lower during these years in barbarism, would by this time have become somewhat civilized, and the poor Negro, instead of being hunted down like a wild beast, terrorized by a pack of brutes, would be living amicably by the side of his white fellow citizen, if not in the full enjoyment of all his rights, with a fair prospect, at least of having them all recognized.

This is the charge which I make against the Anglo American pulpit today; its silence has been interpreted as an approval of these horrible outrages. Bad men have been encouraged to continue in their acts of lawlessness and brutality. As long as the pulpits are silent on these wrongs it is in vain to expect the people to do any better than they are doing.

THE PROGRESS OF COLORED WOMEN

When one considers the obstacles encountered by colored women in their effort to educate and cultivate themselves, since they became free, the work they have accomplished and the progress they have made will bear favorable comparison, at least with that of their more fortunate sisters, from whom the opportunity of acquiring knowledge and the means of self-culture have never been entirely withheld. Not only are colored women with ambition and aspiration handicapped on account of their sex, but they are almost everywhere baffled and mocked because of their race. Not only because they are women, but because they are colored women, are discouragement and disappointment meeting them at every turn. But in spite of the obstacles encountered, the progress made by colored women along many lines appears like a veritable miracle of modern times. Forty years ago for the great masses of colored women, there was no such thing as home. Today in each and every section of the country there are hundreds of homes among colored people, the mental and moral tone of which is as high and as pure as can be found among the best people of any land.

To the women of the race may be attributed in large measure the refinement and purity of the colored home. The immorality of colored women is a theme upon which those who know little about them or those who maliciously misrepresent them love to descant. Foul aspersions upon the character of colored women are assiduously circulated by the press of certain sections and especially by the direct descendants of those who in years past were responsible for the moral degradation of their female slaves. And yet, in spite of the fateful heritage of slavery, even though the safeguards usually thrown around maidenly youth and innocence are in some sections entirely withheld from colored girls, statistics compiled by men not inclined to falsify in favor of my race show that immorality among the colored women of the United States is not so great as among women with similar environment and temptations in Italy, Germany, Sweden and France.

Scandals in the best colored society are exceedingly rare, while the progressive game of divorce and remarriage is practically unknown.

The intellectual progress of colored women has been marvelous. So great has been their thirst for knowledge and so Herculean their efforts to acquire it that there are few colleges, universities, high and normal schools in the North, East and West from which colored girls have not graduated with honor. In Wellesley, Vassar, Ann Arbor, Cornell and in Oberlin, my dear alma mater, whose name will always be loved and whose praise will always be sung as the first college in the country broad, just and generous enough to extend a cordial welcome to the Negro and to open its doors to women on an equal footing with the men, colored girls by their splendid records have forever settled the question of their capacity and worth. The instructors in these and other institutions cheerfully bear testimony to their intelligence, their diligence and their success.

As the brains of colored women expanded, their hearts began to grow. No Sooner had the heads of a favored few been filled with knowledge than their hearts yearned to dispense blessings to the less fortunate of their race. With tireless energy and eager zeal, colored women have worked in every conceivable way to elevate their race. Of the colored teachers engaged in instructing our youth it is probably no exaggeration to say that fully eighty percent are women. In the backwoods, remote from the civilization and comforts of the city and town, colored women may be found courageously battling with those evils which such conditions always entail. Many a heroine of whom the world will never hear has thus sacrificed her life to her race amid surroundings and in the face of privations which only martyrs can bear.

Through the medium of their societies in the church, beneficial organizations out of it and clubs of various kinds, colored women are doing a vast amount of good. It is almost impossible to ascertain exactly what the Negro is doing in any field, for the records are so poorly kept. This is particularly true in the case of the women of the race. During the past forty years there is no doubt that colored women in their poverty have contributed large sums of money to charitable and educational institutions as well as to the foreign and home missionary work. Within the twenty-five years in which the educational work of the African Methodist Episcopal Church has been systematized, the women of that organization have contributed at least five hundred thousand dollars to the cause of education. Dotted all over the country are charitable institutions for the aged, orphaned and poor which have been established by colored women. Just how many it is difficult to state, owing to the lack of statistics bearing on the progress, possessions and prowess of colored women.

Up to date, politics have been religiously eschewed by colored women, although questions affecting our legal status as a race are sometimes agitated by the most progressive class. In Louisiana and Tennessee colored women have several times petitioned the legislatures of their respective states to repel the obnoxious Jim-Crow laws. Against the convict-lease system, whose atrocities have been so frequently exposed of late, colored women here and there in the South are waging a ceaseless war. So long as hundreds of their brothers and sisters, many of whom have committed no crime or misdemeanor whatever, are thrown into cells whose cubic contents are less than those of a good size grave, to be overworked, underfed and only partially covered with vermin infested rags, and so long as children are born to the women in these camps who breathe the polluted atmosphere of these dens of horror and vice from the time they utter their first cry in the world till they are released from their suffering by death, colored women who are working for the emancipation and elevation of their race know where their duty lies. By constant agitation of this painful and hideous subject, they hope to touch the conscience of the country, so that this stain upon its escutcheon shall be forever wiped away.

Alarmed at the rapidity with which the Negro is losing ground in the world of trade, some of the farsighted women are trying to solve the labor question, so far as it concerns the women at least, by urging the establishment of schools of domestic science wherever means therefore can be secured. Those who are interested in this particular work hope and believe that if colored women and girls are thoroughly trained in domestic service, the boycott which has undoubtedly been placed upon them in many sections of the country will be removed. With so few vocations open to the Negro and with the labor organizations increasingly hostile to him, the future of the boys and girls of the race appears to some of our women very foreboding and dark.

The cause of temperance has been eloquently espoused by two women, each of whom has been appointed national superintendent of work among colored people by the Woman's Christian Temperance Union. In business, colored women have had signal success. There is in Alabama a large milling and cotton business belonging to and controlled by a colored woman, who has sometimes as many as seventy-five men in her employ. Until a few years ago the principal ice plant of Nova Scotia was owned and managed by a colored woman, who sold it for a large amount. In the professions there are dentists and doctors whose practice is lucrative and large. Ever since a book was published in 1773 entitled "Poems on Various Subjects, Religious and Moral by Phillis

Wheatley, Negro Servant of Mr. John Wheatley," of Boston, colored women have given abundant evidence of literary ability. In sculpture we were represented by a woman upon whose chisel Italy has set her seal of approval; in painting by one of Bouguereau's pupils and in music by young women holding diplomas from the best conservatories in the land. In short, to use a thought of the illustrious Frederick Douglass, if judged by the depths from which they have come, rather than by the heights to which those blessed with centuries of opportunities have attained, colored women need not hang their heads in shame. They are slowly but surely making their way up to the heights, wherever they can be scaled. In spite of handicaps and discouragements they are not losing heart. In a variety of ways they are rendering valiant service to their race. Lifting as they climb, onward and upward they go struggling and striving and hoping that the buds and blossoms of their desires may burst into glorious fruition ere long. Seeking no favors because of their color nor charity because of their needs they knock at the door of Justice and ask for an equal chance.

THE BURDEN OF THE EDUCATED
COLORED WOMAN

If the educated colored woman has a burden, and we believe she has—
what is that burden? How can it be lightened, how may it be lifted?
What it is can be readily seen perhaps better than told, for it constantly
annoys to irritation; it bulges out as did the load of Bunyan's Christian
ignorance with its inseparable companions, shame and crime and
prejudice. That our position may be more readily understood, let us refer
to the past. . .

During the days of training in our first mission school slavery
that which is the foundation of right training and good government,
the basic rock of all true culture the home, with its fire side training,
mother's molding, woman's care, was not only neglected but utterly
disregarded. There was no time in the institution for such teaching. We
know that there were, even in the first days of that school, isolated cases
of men and women of high moral character and great intellectual worth,
as Phillis Wheatley, Sojourner Truth, and John Chavers (Chavis?),
whose work and lives should have taught, or at least suggested to their
instructors, the capabilities and possibilities of their dusky slave pupils.

The progress and the struggles of these for noble things should have
led their instructors to see how the souls and minds of this people then
yearned for light the real life. But alas! these dull teachers, like many
modern pedagogues and school keepers, failed to know their pupils to
find out their real needs, and hence had no cause to study methods of
better and best development of the boys and girls under their care. What
other result could come from such training or want of training than a
conditioned race such as we now have? For two hundred and fifty years
they married, or were given in marriage. Oft times marriage ceremonies
were performed for them by the learned minister of the master's church;
more often there was simply a consorting by the master's consent, but
it was always understood that these unions for cause, or without cause,
might be more easily broken, than a divorce can be obtained in Indiana
or Dakota. Without going so long a distance as from New York to
Connecticut, the separated could take other companions for life, for a
long or short time; for during those two hundred and fifty years there
was not a single marriage legalized in a single southern state, where
dwelt the mass of this people. There was something of the philosopher

in the plantation preacher, who, at the close of the marriage ceremony, had the dusky couple join their right hands, and then called upon the assembled congregation to sing, as he lined it out, "Plunged in a gulf of dark despair," for well he knew the sequel of many such unions. If it so happened that a husband and wife were parted by those who owned them, such owners often consoled those thus parted with the fact that he could get another wife; she, another husband. Such was the sanctity of the marriage vow that was taught and held for over two hundred and fifty years.

Habit is indeed second nature. This is the race inheritance. I thank God not of all, for we know, each of us, of instances, of holding most sacred the plighted love and keeping faithfully and sacredly the marriage vows. We know of pure homes and of growing old together. Blessed heritage! If we only had the gold there might be many "Golden Weddings." Despair not; the crushing burden of immorality which has its root in the disregard of the marriage vow, can be lightened. It must be, and the educated colored woman can and will do her part in lifting this burden. In the old institution there was no attention given to homes and to home making. Homes were only places in which to sleep, father had neither responsibility nor authority; mother, neither cares nor duties. She wielded no gentle sway nor influence. The character of their children was a matter of no concern to them; surroundings were not considered. It is true, house cleaning was sometimes enforced as a protection to property, but this was done at stated times and when ordered. There is no greater enemy of the race than these untidy and filthy homes; they bring not only physical disease and death, but they are very incubators of sin; they bring intellectual and moral death.

The burden of giving knowledge and bringing about the practice of the laws of hygiene among a people ignorant of the laws of nature and common decency, is not a slight one. But this, too, the intelligent women can and must help to carry. The large number of young men in the state prison is by no means the least of the heavy burdens. It is true that many of these are unjustly sentenced; that longer terms of imprisonment are given Negroes than white persons for the same offences; it is true that white criminals by the help of attorneys, money, and influence, oftener escape the prison, thus keeping small the number of prisoners recorded, for figures never lie. It is true that many are tried and imprisoned for trivial causes, such as the following, clipped from the Tribune, of Elberton, Ga.: "Seven or eight Negroes were arrested and tried for stealing two fish hooks last week. When the time of our courts is wasted in such a manner as this, it is high time to stop and consider whither we are driving. Such picayunish cases reflect on the intelligence of a community.

It is fair to say the courts are not to blame in this matter." Commenting on this The South Daily says: "We are glad to note that the sentiment of the paper is against the injustice. Nevertheless these statistics will form the basis of some lecturer's discourse." This fact remains, that many of our youth are in prison, that large numbers of our young men are serving out long terms of imprisonment, and this is a very sore burden. Five years ago while attending a Teacher's Institute at Thomasville, Ga., I saw working on the streets in the chain gang, with rude men and ruder women, with ignorant, wicked, almost naked men, criminals, guilty of all the sins named in the decalogue, a large number of boys from ten to fifteen years of age, and two young girls between the ages of twelve and sixteen. It is not necessary that prison statistics be quoted, for we know too well the story, and we feel most sensibly this burden, the weight of which will sink us unless it is at once made lighter and finally lifted.

Last, but not least, is the burden of prejudice, heavier in that it is imposed by the strong, those from whom help, not hindrance, should come. They are making the already heavy burden of their victims heavier to bear, and yet they are commanded by One who is even the Master of all: "Bear ye one another's burdens, and thus fulfill the law." This is met with and must be borne everywhere. In the South, in public conveyances, and at all points of race contact; in the North, in hotels, at the baptismal pool, in cemeteries; everywhere, in some shape or form, it is to be borne. No one suffers under the weight of this burden as the educated Negro woman does; and she must help to lift it. Ignorance and immorality, if they are not the prime causes, have certainly intensified prejudice. The forces to lighten and finally to lift this and all of these burdens are true culture and character, linked with that most substantial coupler, cash. We said in the beginning that the past can serve no further purpose than to give us our present bearings. It is a condition that confronts us.

With this we must deal, it is this we must change. The physician of today inquires into the history of his patient, but he has to do especially with diagnosis and cure. We know the history; we think a correct diagnosis has often been made let us attempt a cure. We would prescribe: homes better homes, clean homes, pure homes; schools better schools; more culture; more thrift; and work in large doses; put the patient at once on this treatment and continue through life. Can woman do this work? She can; and she must do her part, and her part is by no means small. Nothing in the present century is more noticeable than the tendency of women to enter every hopeful field of wage earning and philanthropy, and attempt to reach a place in every intellectual arena.

Women are by nature fitted for teaching very young children; their maternal instinct makes them patient and sympathetic with their charges. Negro women of culture, as kindergartners and primary teachers have a rare opportunity to lend a hand to the lifting of these burdens, for here they may instill lessons of cleanliness, truthfulness, loving kindness, love for nature, and love for Nature's God. Here they may daily start aright hundreds of our children; here, too, they may save years of time in the education of the child; and may save many lives from shame and crime by applying the law of prevention. In the kindergarten and primary school is the salvation of the race. For children of both sexes from six to fifteen years of age, women are more successful as teachers than men. This fact is proven by their employment.

Two thirds of the teachers in the public schools of the United States are women. It is the glory of the United States that good order and peace are maintained not by a large, standing army of well trained soldiers, but by the sentiment of her citizens, sentiments implanted and nourished by her well trained army of four hundred thousand school teachers, two thirds of whom are women. The educated Negro woman, the woman of character and culture, is needed in the schoolroom not only in the kindergarten, and in the primary and the secondary school; but she is needed in high school, the academy, and the college. Only those of character and culture can do successful lifting, for she who would mould character must herself possess it. Not alone in the schoolroom can the intelligent woman lend a lifting hand, but as a public lecturer she may give advice, helpful suggestions, and important knowledge that will change a whole community and start its people on the upward way.

To be convinced of the good that can be done for humanity by this means one need only recall the names of Lucy Stone, Mary Livermore, Frances Harper, Frances Willard and Julie Ward Howe. The refined and noble Negro woman may lift much with this lever. Women may also be most helpful as teachers of sewing schools and cooking classes, not simply in the public schools and private institutions, but in classes formed in neighborhoods that sorely need this knowledge. Through these classes girls who are not in school may be reached; and through them something may be done to better their homes, and inculcate habits of neatness and thrift. To bring the influence of the schools to bear upon these homes is the most needful thing of the hour. Often teachers who have labored most arduously, conscientiously, and intelligently have become discouraged on seeing that society had not been benefited, but sometimes positively injured by the conduct of their pupils. The work of the classroom has been completely neutralized by the training of the home. Then we must have better homes, and better homes mean better mothers, better fathers, better born children.

Emerson says, "To the well born child all the virtues are natural, not painfully acquired." But "The temporal life which is not allowed to open into the eternal life becomes corrupt and feeble even in its temporalness." As a teacher in the Sabbath school, as a leader in young people's meetings and missionary societies, in women's societies and Bible classes our cultured women are needed to do a great and blessed work. Here they may cause many budding lives to open into eternal life. Froebel urged teachers and parents to see to the blending of the temporal and divine life when he said, "God created man in his own image; therefore man should create and bring forth like God." The young people are ready and anxiously await intelligent leadership in Christian work. The less fortunate women already assembled in churches, are ready for work. Work they do and work they will; that it may be effective work, they need the help and leadership of their more favored sisters.

A few weeks ago this country was startled by the following telegram of southern women of culture sent to Ex Governor Northern of Georgia, just before he made his Boston speech: "You are authorized to say in your address tonight that the women of Georgia, realizing the great importance to both races of early moral training of the Negro race, stand ready to undertake this work when means are supplied." But more startled was the world the next day, after cultured Boston had supplied a part of the means, $20,000, to read the glaring head lines of the southern press, "Who will Teach the Black Babies?" because some of the cultured women who had signed the telegram had declared when interviewed, that Negro women fitted for the work could not be found, and no self-respecting southern white woman would teach a colored kindergarten. Yet already in Atlanta, Georgia, and in Athens, Georgia, southern women are at work among Negroes. There is plenty of work for all who have the proper conception of the teacher's office, who know that all men are brothers, God being their common father. But the educated Negro woman must teach the "Black Babies;" she must come forward and inspire our men and boys to make a successful onslaught upon sin, shame, and crime.

Lynch Law in America

Our country's national crime is lynching. It is not the creature of an hour, the sudden outburst of uncontrolled fury, or the unspeakable brutality of an insane mob. It represents the cool, calculating deliberation of intelligent people who openly avow that there is an "unwritten law" that justifies them in putting human beings to death without complaint under oath, without trial by jury, without opportunity to make defense, and without right of appeal. The "unwritten law" first found excuse with the rough, rugged, and determined man who left the civilized centers of eastern States to seek for quick returns in the gold-fields of the far West. Following in uncertain pursuit of continually eluding fortune, they dared the savagery of the Indians, the hardships of mountain travel, and the constant terror of border State outlaws.

Naturally, they felt slight toleration for traitors in their own ranks. It was enough to fight the enemies from without; woe to the foe within! Far removed from and entirely without protection of the courts of civilized life, these fortune-seekers made laws to meet their varying emergencies. The thief who stole a horse, the bully who "jumped" a claim, was a common enemy. If caught he was promptly tried, and if found guilty was hanged to the tree under which the court convened.

Those were busy days of busy men. They had no time to give the prisoner a bill of exception or stay of execution. The only way a man had to secure a stay of execution was to behave himself. Judge Lynch was original in methods but exceedingly effective in procedure. He made the charge, impaneled the jurors, and directed the execution. When the court adjourned, the prisoner was dead. Thus lynch law held sway in the far West until civilization spread into the Territories and the orderly processes of law took its place. The emergency no longer existing, lynching gradually disappeared from the West.

But the spirit of mob procedure seemed to have fastened itself upon the lawless classes, and the grim process that at first was invoked to declare justice was made the excuse to wreak vengeance and cover crime. It next appeared in the South, where centuries of Anglo-Saxon civilization had made effective all the safeguards of court procedure. No emergency called for lynch law. It asserted its sway in defiance of law and in favor of anarchy. There it has flourished ever since, marking the thirty years of its existence with the inhuman butchery of more than ten thousand men, women, and children by shooting, drowning, hanging, and burning them alive. Not only this, but so potent is the force of example that the lynching mania has spread throughout the North and middle West. It is now no uncommon thing to read of lynchings north of Mason and Dixon's line, and those most responsible for this fashion gleefully point to these instances and assert that the North is no better than the South.

This is the work of the "unwritten law" about which so much is said, and in whose behest butchery is made a pastime and national savagery condoned. The first statute of this "unwritten law" was written in the blood of thousands of brave men who thought that a government that was good enough to create a citizenship was strong enough to protect it. Under the authority of a national law that gave every citizen the right to vote, the newly-made citizens chose to exercise their suffrage. But the reign of the national law was short-lived and illusionary. Hardly had the sentences dried upon the statute-books before one Southern State after another raised the cry against "negro domination" and proclaimed there was an "unwritten law" that justified any means to resist it.

The method then inaugurated was the outrages by the "red-shirt" bands of Louisiana, South Carolina, and other Southern States, which were succeeded by the Ku-Klux Klans. These advocates of the "unwritten law" boldly avowed their purpose to intimidate, suppress, and nullify the negro's right to vote. In support of its plans the Ku-Klux Klans, the "red-shirt" and similar organizations proceeded to beat, exile, and kill negroes until the purpose of their organization was accomplished and the supremacy of the "unwritten law" was effected. Thus lynchings began in the South, rapidly spreading into the various States until the national law was nullified and the reign of the "unwritten law" was supreme. Men were taken from their homes by "red-shirt" bands and stripped, beaten, and exiled; others were assassinated when their political prominence made them obnoxious to their political opponents; while the Ku-Klux barbarism of election days, reveling in the butchery of thousands of colored voters, furnished records in Congressional investigations that are a disgrace to civilization.

The alleged menace of universal suffrage having been avoided by the absolute suppression of the negro vote, the spirit of mob murder should have been satisfied and the butchery of negroes should have ceased. But men, women, and children were the victims of murder by individuals and murder by mobs, just as they had been when killed at the demands of the "unwritten law" to prevent "negro domination." Negroes were killed for disputing over terms of contracts with their employers. If a few barns were burned some colored man was killed to stop it. If a colored man resented the imposition of a white man and the two came to blows, the colored man had to die, either at the hands of the white man then and there or later at the hands of a mob that speedily gathered. If he showed a spirit of courageous manhood he was hanged for his pains, and the killing was justified by the declaration that he was a "saucy nigger." Colored women have been murdered because they refused to tell the mobs where relatives could be found for "lynching bees." Boys of fourteen years have been lynched by white representatives of American civilization. In fact, for all kinds of offenses—and, for no offenses—from murders to misdemeanors, men and women are put to death without judge or jury; so that, although the political excuse was no longer necessary, the wholesale murder of human beings went on just the same. A new name was given to the killings and a new excuse was invented for so doing.

Again the aid of the "unwritten law" is invoked, and again it comes to the rescue. During the last ten years a new statute has been added to the "unwritten law." This statute proclaims that for certain crimes or alleged crimes no negro shall be allowed a trial; that no white woman shall be compelled to charge an assault under oath or to submit any such charge to the investigation of a court of law. The result is that many men have been put to death whose innocence was afterward established; and today, under this reign of the "unwritten law," no colored man, no matter what his reputation, is safe from lynching if a white woman, no matter what her standing or motive, cares to charge him with insult or assault.

It is considered a sufficient excuse and reasonable justification to put a prisoner to death under this "unwritten law" for the frequently repeated charge that these lynching horrors are necessary to prevent crimes against women. The sentiment of the country has been appealed to, in describing the isolated condition of white families in thickly populated negro districts; and the charge is made that these homes are in as great danger as if they were surrounded by wild beasts. And the world has accepted this theory without let or hindrance. In many cases there has been open expression that the fate meted out to the victim was only what he deserved. In many other instances there has been a silence that says more forcibly than words can proclaim it that it is right and proper that a human being should be seized by a mob and burned to death upon the unsworn and the uncorroborated charge of his accuser. No matter that our laws presume every man innocent until he is proved guilty; no matter that it leaves a certain class of individuals completely at the mercy of another class; no matter that it encourages those criminally disposed to blacken their faces and commit any crime in the calendar so long as they can throw suspicion on some negro, as is frequently done, and then lead a mob to take his life; no matter that mobs make a farce of the law and a mockery of justice; no matter that hundreds of boys are being hardened in crime and schooled in vice by the repetition of such scenes before their eyes—if a white woman declares herself insulted or assaulted, some life must pay the penalty, with all the horrors of the Spanish Inquisition and all the barbarism of the Middle Ages. The world looks on and says it is well.

Not only are two hundred men and women put to death annually, on the average, in this country by mobs, but these lives are taken with the greatest publicity. In many instances the leading citizens aid and abet by their presence when they do not participate, and the leading journals inflame the public mind to the lynching point with scare-head articles and offers of rewards. Whenever a burning is advertised to take place, the railroads run excursions, photographs are taken, and the same jubilee is indulged in that characterized the public hangings of one hundred years ago. There is, however, this difference: in those old days the multitude that stood by was permitted only to guy or jeer. The nineteenth century lynching mob cuts off ears, toes, and fingers, strips off flesh, and distributes portions of the body as souvenirs among the crowd. If the leaders of the mob are so minded, coal-oil is poured over the body and the victim is then roasted to death. This has been done in Texarkana and Paris, Tex., in Bardswell, Ky., and in Newman, Ga. In Paris the officers of the law delivered the prisoner to the mob. The mayor gave the school children a holiday and the railroads ran excursion trains so that the people might see a human being burned to death. In Texarkana, the year before, men and boys amused themselves by cutting off strips of flesh and thrusting knives into their helpless victim. At Newman, Ga., of the present year, the mob tried every conceivable torture to compel the victim to cry out and confess, before they set fire to the faggots that burned him. But their trouble was all in vain—he never uttered a cry, and they could not make him confess.

This condition of affairs were brutal enough and horrible enough if it were true that lynchings occurred only because of the commission of crimes against women—as is constantly declared by ministers, editors, lawyers, teachers, statesmen, and even by women themselves. It has been to the interest of those who did the lynching to blacken the good name of the helpless and defenseless victims of their hate. For this reason they publish at every possible opportunity this excuse for lynching, hoping thereby not only to palliate their own crime but at the same time to prove the negro a moral monster and unworthy of the respect and sympathy of the civilized world. But this alleged reason adds to the deliberate injustice of the mob's work. Instead of lynchings being caused by assaults upon women, the statistics show that not one-third of the victims of lynchings are even charged with such crimes. The Chicago Tribune, which publishes annually lynching statistics, is authority for the following:

In 1892, when lynching reached high-water mark, there were 241 persons lynched. The entire number is divided among the following States:

Alabama	22	Montana	4
Arkansas	25	New York	1
California	3	North Carolina	5
Florida	11	North Dakota	1
Georgia	17	Ohio	3
Idaho	8	South Carolina	5
Illinois	1	Tennessee	28
Kansas	3	Texas	15
Kentucky	9	Virginia	7
Louisiana	29	West Virginia	5
Maryland	1	Wyoming	9
Arizona Ter	3	Missouri	6
Mississippi	16	Oklahoma	2

Of this number, 160 were of negro descent. Four of them were lynched in New York, Ohio, and Kansas; the remainder were murdered in the South. Five of this number were females. The charges for which they were lynched cover a wide range. They are as follows:

Rape	46	Attempted rape	11
Murder	58	Suspected robbery	4
Rioting	3	Larceny	1
Race Prejudice	6	Self-defense	1
No cause given	4	Insulting women	2

Incendiarism	6	Desperadoes	6
Robbery	6	Fraud	1
Assault and battery	1	Attempted murder	2
No offense stated, boy and girl			2

In the case of the boy and girl above referred to, their father, named Hastings, was accused of the murder of a white man. His fourteen-year-old daughter and sixteen-year-old son were hanged and their bodies filled with bullets; then the father was also lynched. This occurred in November, 1892, at Jonesville, La.

Indeed, the record for the last twenty years shows exactly the same or a smaller proportion who have been charged with this horrible crime. Quite a number of the one-third alleged cases of assault that have been personally investigated by the writer have shown that there was no foundation in fact for the charges; yet the claim is not made that there were no real culprits among them. The negro has been too long associated with the white man not to have copied his vices as well as his virtues. But the negro resents and utterly repudiates the efforts to blacken his good name by asserting that assaults upon women are peculiar to his race. The negro has suffered far more from the commission of this crime against the women of his race by white men than the white race has ever suffered through his crimes. Very scant notice is taken of the matter when this is the condition of affairs. What becomes a crime deserving capital punishment when the tables are turned is a matter of small moment when the negro woman is the accusing party.

But since the world has accepted this false and unjust statement, and the burden of proof has been placed upon the negro to vindicate his race, he is taking steps to do so. The Anti-Lynching Bureau of the National Afro-American Council is arranging to have every lynching investigated and publish the facts to the world, as has been done in the case of Sam Hose, who was burned alive last April at Newman, Ga. The detective's report showed that Hose killed Cranford, his employer, in self-defense, and that, while a mob was organizing to hunt Hose to punish him for killing a white man, not till twenty-four hours after the murder was the charge of rape, embellished with psychological and physical impossibilities, circulated. That gave an impetus to the hunt, and the Atlanta Constitution's reward of $500 keyed the mob to the necessary burning and roasting pitch. Of five hundred newspaper clippings of that horrible affair, nine-tenths of them assumed Hose's guilt—simply because his murderers said so, and because it is the fashion to believe the negro peculiarly addicted to this species of crime. All the negro asks is justice—a fair and impartial trial in the courts of the country. That given, he will abide the result.

But this question affects the entire American nation, and from several points of view: First, on the ground of consistency. Our watchword has been "the land of the free and the home of the brave." Brave men do not gather by thousands to torture and murder a single individual, so gagged and bound he cannot make even feeble resistance or defense. Neither do brave men or women stand by and see such things done without compunction of conscience, nor read of them without protest. Our nation has been active and outspoken in its endeavors to right the wrongs of the Armenian Christian, the Russian Jew, the Irish Home Ruler, the native women of India, the Siberian exile, and the Cuban patriot. Surely it should be the nation's duty to correct its own evils!

Second, on the ground of economy. To those who fail to be convinced from any other point of view touching this momentous question, a consideration of the economic phase might not be amiss. It is generally known that mobs in Louisiana, Colorado, Wyoming, and other States have lynched subjects of other countries. When their different governments demanded satisfaction, our country was forced to confess her inability to protect said subjects in the several States because of our State-rights doctrines, or in turn demand punishment of the lynchers. This confession, while humiliating in the extreme, was not satisfactory; and, while the United States cannot protect, she can pay. This she has done, and it is certain will have to do again in the case of the recent lynching of Italians in Louisiana. The United States already has paid in indemnities for lynching nearly a half million dollars, as follows:

Paid China for Rock Springs (Wyo.) massacre $147,748.74
Paid China for outrages on Pacific Coast 276,619.75
Paid Italy for massacre of Italian prisoners at
    New Orleans... 24,330.90
Paid Italy for lynchings at Walsenburg, Col................ 10,000.00
Paid Great Britain for outrages on James Bain
    and Frederick Dawson 2,800.00

Third, for the honor of Anglo-Saxon civilization. No scoffer at our boasted American civilization could say anything more harsh of it than does the American white man himself who says he is unable to protect the honor of his women without resort to such brutal, inhuman, and degrading exhibitions as characterize "lynching bees." The cannibals of the South Sea Islands roast human beings alive to satisfy hunger. The red Indian of the Western plains tied his prisoner to the stake, tortured him, and danced in fiendish glee while his victim writhed in the flames. His savage, untutored mind suggested no better way than that of wreaking vengeance upon those who had wronged him. These people knew nothing about Christianity and did not profess to follow its teachings; but such primary laws as they had they lived up to. No nation, savage or civilized, save only the United States of America, has confessed its inability to protect its women save by hanging, shooting, and burning alleged offenders.

Finally, for love of country. No American travels abroad without blushing for shame for his country on this subject. And whatever the excuse that passes current in the United States, it avails nothing abroad. With all the powers of government in control; with all laws made by white men, administered by white judges, jurors, prosecuting attorneys, and sheriffs; with every office of the executive department filled by white men—no excuse can be offered for exchanging the orderly administration of justice for barbarous lynchings and "unwritten laws." Our country should be placed speedily above the plane of confessing herself a failure at self-government. This cannot be until Americans of every section, of broadest patriotism and best and wisest citizenship, not only see the defect in our country's armor but take the necessary steps to remedy it. Although lynchings have steadily increased in number and barbarity during the last twenty years, there has been no single effort put forth by the many moral and philanthropic forces of the country to put a stop to this wholesale slaughter. Indeed, the silence and seeming condonation grow more marked as the years go by.

A few months ago the conscience of this country was shocked because, after a two-weeks trial, a French judicial tribunal pronounced Captain Dreyfus guilty. And yet, in our own land and under our own flag, the writer can give day and detail of one thousand men, women, and children who during the last six years were put to death without trial before any tribunal on earth. Humiliating indeed, but altogether unanswerable, was the reply of the French press to our protest: "Stop your lynchings at home before you send your protests abroad."

To the Nations of the World

In the metropolis of the modern world, in this the closing year of the nineteenth century, there has been assembled a congress of men and women of African blood, to deliberate solemnly upon the present situation and outlook of the darker races of mankind. The problem of the twentieth century is the problem of the color line, the question as to how far differences of race—which show themselves chiefly in the color of the skin and the texture of the hair—will hereafter be made the basis of denying to over half the world the right of sharing to utmost ability the opportunities and privileges of modern civilization.

To be sure, the darker races are today the least advanced in culture according to European standards. This has not, however, always been the case in the past. And certainly the world's history, both ancient and modern, has given many instances of no despicable ability and capacity among the blackest races of men. In any case, the modern world must remember that in this age when the ends of the world are being brought so near together the millions of black men in Africa, America and the Islands of the Sea, not to speak of the brown and yellow myriads elsewhere, are bound to have a great influence upon the world in the future, by reason of sheer numbers and physical contact.

If now the world of culture bends itself towards giving Negroes and other dark men the largest and broadest opportunity for education and self-development, then this contact and influence is bound to have a beneficial effect upon the world and hasten human progress. But if, by reason of carelessness, prejudice, greed and injustice, the black world is to be exploited and ravished and degraded, the results must be deplorable, if not fatal—not simply to them, but to the high ideals of justice, freedom and culture which a thousand years of Christian civilization have held before Europe.

And now, therefore, to these ideals of civilization, to the broader humanity of the followers of the Prince of Peace, we, the men and women of Africa in world congress assembled, do now solemnly appeal: Let the world take no backward step in that slow but sure progress which has successively refused to let the spirit of class, of caste, of privilege, or of birth, debar from life, liberty and the pursuit of happiness a striving human soul. Let no color or race be a feature of distinction between white and black men, regardless of worth or ability.

Let not the natives of Africa be sacrificed to the greed of gold, their liberties taken away, their family life debauched, their just aspirations repressed, and avenues of advancement and culture taken from them. Let not the cloak of Christian missionary enterprise be allowed in the future, as so often in the past, to hide the ruthless economic exploitation and political downfall of less developed nations, whose chief fault has been reliance on the plighted faith of the Christian church.

Let the British nation, the first modern champion of Negro freedom, hasten to crown the work of Wilberforce, and Clarkson, and Buxton, and Sharpe, Bishop Colenso, and Livingston, and give as soon as practicable, the rights of responsible government to the black colonies of Africa and the West Indies. Let not the spirit of Garrison, Phillips, and Douglass wholly die out in America; may the conscience of a great nation rise and rebuke all dishonesty and unrighteous oppression toward the American Negro, and grant to him the right of franchise, security of person and property, and generous recognition of the great work he has accomplished in a generation toward raising nine millions of human beings from slavery to manhood.

Let the German Empire, and the French Republic, true to their great past, remember that the true worth of colonies lies in their prosperity and progress, and that justice, impartial alike to black and white, is the first element of prosperity. Let the Congo Free State become a great central Negro state of the world, and let its prosperity be counted not simply in cash and commerce, but in the happiness and true advancement to its black people.

Let the nations of the world respect the integrity and independence of the free Negro states of Abyssinia, Liberia, Haiti, and the rest, and let the inhabitants of these states, the independent tribes of Africa, the Negroes of the West Indies and America, and the black subjects of all nations take courage, strive ceaselessly, and fight bravely, that they may prove to the world their incontestable right to be counted among the great brotherhood of mankind. Thus we appeal with boldness and confidence to the Great Powers of the civilized world, trusting in the wide spirit of humanity, and the deep sense of justice and of our age, for a generous recognition of the righteousness of our cause.

WHAT IT MEANS TO BE COLORED IN THE CAPITAL OF THE U.S.

Washington, D.C., has been called "The Colored Man's Paradise." Whether this sobriquet was given to the national capital in bitter irony by a member of the handicapped race, as he reviewed some of his own persecutions and rebuffs, or whether it was given immediately after the war by an ex-slaveholder who for the first time in his life saw colored people walking about like free men, minus the overseer and his whip, history saith not. It is certain that it would be difficult to find a worse misnomer for Washington than "The Colored Man's Paradise" if so prosaic a consideration as veracity is to determine the appropriateness of a name.

For fifteen years I have resided in Washington, and while it was far from being a paradise for colored people when I first touched these shores it has been doing its level best ever since to make conditions for us intolerable. As a colored woman I might enter Washington any night, a stranger in a strange land, and walk miles without finding a place to lay my head. Unless I happened to know colored people who live here or ran across a chance acquaintance who could recommend a colored boarding-house to me, I should be obliged to spend the entire night wandering about. Indians, Chinamen, Filipinos, Japanese and representatives of any other dark race can find hotel accommodations, if they can pay for them. The colored man alone is thrust out of the hotels of the national capital like a leper.

As a colored woman I may walk from the Capitol to the White House, ravenously hungry and abundantly supplied with money with which to purchase a meal, without finding a single restaurant in which I would be permitted to take a morsel of food, if it was patronized by white people, unless I were willing to sit behind a screen. As a colored woman I cannot visit the tomb of the Father of this country, which owes its very existence to the love of freedom in the human heart and which stands for equal opportunity to all, without being forced to sit in the Jim Crow section of an electric car which starts form the very heart of the city—midway between the Capital and the White House. If I refuse thus to be humiliated, I am cast into jail and forced to pay a fine for violating the Virginia laws. . .

As a colored woman I may enter more than one white church in Washington without receiving that welcome which as a human being I have the right to expect in the sanctuary of God. . . Unless I am willing to engage in a few menial occupations, in which the pay for my services would be very poor, there is no way for me to earn an honest living, if I am not a trained nurse or a dressmaker or can secure a position as teacher in the public schools, which is exceedingly difficult to do. It matters not what my intellectual attainments may be or how great is the need of the services of a competent person, if I try to enter many of the numerous vocations in which my white sisters are allowed to engage, the door is shut in my face.

From one Washington theater I am excluded altogether. In the remainder certain seats are set aside for colored people, and it is almost impossible to secure others. . . With the exception of the Catholic University, there is not a single white college in the national capitol to which colored people are admitted. . . A few years ago the Columbian Law School admitted colored students, but in deference to the Southern white students the authorities have decided to exclude them altogether.

Some time ago a young woman who had already attracted some attention in the literary world by her volume of short stories answered an advertisement which appeared in a Washington newspaper, which called for the services of a skilled stenographer and expert typewriter. . . The applicants were requested to send specimens of their work and answer certain questions concerning their experience and their speed before they called in person. In reply to her application the young colored woman. . . received a letter from the firm stating that her references and experience were the most satisfactory that had been sent and requesting her to call. When she presented herself there was some doubt in the mind of the man to whom she was directed concerning her racial pedigree, so he asked her point-blank whether she was colored or white. When she confessed the truth the merchant expressed. . . deep regret that he could not avail himself of the services of so competent a person, but frankly admitted that employing a colored woman in his establishment in any except a menial position was simply out of the question. . .

Not only can colored women secure no employment in the Washington stores, department and otherwise, except as menials, and such positions, of course, are few, but even as customers they are not infrequently treated with discourtesy both by the clerks and the proprietor himself. . . Although white and colored teachers are under the same Board of Education and the system for the children of both races is said to be uniform, prejudice against the colored teachers in the public schools is manifested in a variety of ways. From 1870 to 1900 there was a colored superintendent at the head of the colored schools. During all that time the directors of the cooking, sewing, physical culture, manual training, music and art departments were colored people. Six years ago a change was inaugurated. The colored superintendent was legislated out of office and the directorships, without a single exception, were taken from colored teachers and given to the whites. . .

Now, no matter how competent or superior the colored teachers in our public schools may be, they know that they can never rise to the height of a directorship, can never hope to be more than an assistant and receive the meager salary therefore, unless the present regime is radically changed. . .

Strenuous efforts are being made to run Jim Crow cars in the national capital. . . Representative Heflin, of Alabama, who introduced a bill providing for Jim Crow street cars in the District of Columbia last winter, has just received a letter from the president of the East Brookland Citizens' Association "indorsing the movement for separate street cars and sincerely hoping that you will be successful in getting this enacted into a law as soon as possible." Brookland is a suburb of Washington.

The colored laborer's path to a decent livelihood is by no means smooth. Into some of the trades unions here he is admitted, while from others he is excluded altogether. By the union men this is denied, although I am personally acquainted with skilled workmen who tell me they are not admitted into the unions because they are colored. But even when they are allowed to join the unions they frequently derive little benefit, owing to certain tricks of the trade. When the word passes round that help is needed and colored laborers apply, they are often told by the union officials that they have secured all the men they needed, because the places are reserved for white men, until they have been provided with jobs, and colored men must remain idle, unless the supply of white men is too small. . .

And so I might go on citing instance after instance to show the variety of ways in which our people are sacrificed on the altar of prejudice in the Capital of the United States and how almost insurmountable are the obstacles which block his path to success. . .

It is impossible for any white person in the United States, no matter how sympathetic and broad, to realize what life would mean to him if his incentive to effort were suddenly snatched away. To the lack of incentive to effort, which is the awful shadow under which we live, may be traced the wreck and ruin of score of colored youth. And surely nowhere in the world do oppression and persecution based solely on the color of the skin appear more hateful and hideous than in the capital of the United States, because the chasm between the principles upon which this Government was founded, in which it still professes to believe, and those which are daily practiced under the protection of the flag, yawn so wide and deep.

Lynching, Our National Crime

The lynching record for a quarter of a century merits the thoughtful study of the American people. It presents three salient facts: First, lynching is color-line murder. Second, crimes against women is the excuse, not the cause. Third, it is a national crime and requires a national remedy. Proof that lynching follows the color line is to be found in the statistics which have been kept for the past twenty-five years. During the few years preceding this period and while frontier law existed, the executions showed a majority of white victims. Later, however, as law courts and authorized judiciary extended into the far West, lynch law rapidly abated, and its white victims became few and far between. Just as the lynch-law regime came to a close in the West, a new mob movement started in the South.

This was wholly political, its purpose being to suppress the colored vote by intimidation and murder. Thousands of assassins banded together under the name of Ku Klux Klans, "Midnight Raiders," "Knights of the Golden Circle," et cetera, et cetera, spread a reign of terror, by beating, shooting and killing colored in a few years, the purpose was accomplished, and the black vote was supressed. But mob murder continued. From 1882, in which year fifty-two were lynched, down to the present, lynching has been along the color line. Mob murder increased yearly until in 1892 more than two hundred victims were lynched and statistics show tht 3,284 men, women and children have been put to death in this quarter of a century. During the last ten years from 1899 to 1908 inclusive the number lynched was 959. Of this number 102 were white, while the colored victims numbered 857. No other nation, civilized or savage, burns its criminals; only under that Stars and Stripes is the human holocaust possible. Twenty-eight human beings burned at the stake, one of them a woman and two of them children, is the awful indictment against American civilization— the gruesome tribute which the nation pays to the color line.

Why is mob murder permitted by a Christian nation? What is the cause of this awful slaughter? This question is answered almost daily—always the same shameless falsehood that "Negroes are lynched to protect womanhood." Standing before a Chautauqua assemblage, John Temple Graves, at once champion of lynching and apologist for lynchers, said: "The mob stands today as the most potential bulwark between the women of the South and such a carnival of crime as would infuriate the world and precipitate the annihilation of the Negro race." This is the never-varying answer of lynchers and their apologists. All know that it is untrue. The cowardly lyncher revels in murder, then seeks to shield himself from public execration by claiming devotion to woman. But truth is mighty and the lynching record discloses the hypocrisy of the lyncher as well as his crime.

The Springfield, Illinois, mob rioted for two days, the militia of the entire state was called out, two men were lynched, hundreds of people driven from their homes, all because a white woman said a Negro assaulted her. A mad mob went to the jail, tried to lynch the victim of her charge and, not being able to find him, proceeded to pillage and burn the town and to lynch two innocent men. Later, after the police had found that the woman's charge was false, she published a retraction, the indictment was dismissed and the intended victim discharged. But the lynched victims were dead. Hundreds were homeless and Illinois was disgraced.

As a final and complete refutation of the charge that lynching is occasioned by crimes against women, a partial record of lynchings is cited; 285 persons were lynched for causes as follows: Unknown cause, 92; no cause, 10; race prejudice, 49; miscegenation, 7; informing, 12; making threats, 11; keeping saloon, 3; practicing fraud, 5; practicing voodooism, 1; refusing evidence, 2; political causes, 5; disputing, 1; disobeying quarantine regulations, 2; slapping a child, 1; turning state's evidence, 3; protecting a Negro, 1; to prevent giving evidence, 1; knowledge of larceny, 1; writing letter to white woman, 1; asking white woman to marry, 1; jilting girl, 1; having smallpox, 1; concealing criminal, 2; threatening political exposure, 1; self-defense, 6; cruelty, 1; insulting language to woman, 5; quarreling with white man, 2; colonizing Negroes, 1; throwing stones, 1; quarreling, 1; gambling, 1.

Is there a remedy, or will the nation confess that it cannot protect its protectors at home as well as abroad? Various remedies have been suggested to abolish the lynching infamy, but year after year, the butchery of men, women and children continues in spite of plea and protest. Education is suggested as a preventive, but it is as grave a crime to murder an ignorant man as it is a scholar. True, few educated men have been lynched, but the hue and cry once started stops at no bounds, as was clearly shown by the lynchings in Atlanta, and in Springfield, Illinois.

Agitation, though helpful, will not alone stop the crime. Year after year statistics are published, meetings are held, resolutions are adopted and yet lynchings go on. Public sentiment does measurably decrease the sway of mob law, but the irresponsible bloodthirsty criminals who swept through the streets of Springfield, beating an inoffensive law-abiding citizen to death in one part of the town, and in another torturing and shooting to death a man who for threescore years had made a reputation for honesty; integrity and sobriety, had raised a family and had accumulated property; were not deterred from their heinous crimes by either education or agitation.

The only certain remedy is an appeal to law. Lawbreakers must be made to know that human life is sacred and that every citizen of this country is first a citizen of the United States and secondly a citizen of the state in which he belongs. This nation must assert itself and protect its federal citizenship at home as well as abroad. The strong arm of the government must reach across state lines whenever unbridled lawlessness defies state laws and must give to the individual under the Stars and Stripes the same measure of protection it gives to him when he travels in foreign lands.

Federal protection of American citizenship is the remedy for lynching. Foreigners are rarely lynched in America. If, by mistake, one is lynched, the national government quickly pays the damages. The recent agitation in California against the Japanese compelled this nation to recognize that federal power must yet assert itself to protect the nation from the treason of sovereign states. Thousands of American citizens have been put to death and no President has yet raised his hand in effective protest, but a simple insult to a native of Japan was quite sufficient to stir the government at Washington to prevent the threatened wrong. If the government has power to protect a foreigner from insult, certainly it has power to save a citizen's life.

The practical remedy has been more than once suggested in Congress. Senator Gallinger, of New Hampshire, in a resolution introduced in Congress called for an investigation "with the view of ascertaining whether there is a remedy for lynching which Congress may apply." The Senate Committee has under consideration a bill drawn by A. E. Pillsbury, formerly Attorney General of Massachusetts, providing for federal prosecution of lynchers in cases where the state fails to protect citizens or foreigners. Both of these resolutions indicate that the attention of the nation has been called to this phase of the lynching question.

As a final word, it would be a beginning in the right direction if this conference can see its way clear to establish a bureau for the investigation and publication of the details of every lynching, so that the public could know that an influential body of citizens has made it a duty to give the widest publicity to the facts in each case; that it will make an effort to secure expressions of opinion all over the country against lynching for the sake of the country's fair name; and lastly, but by no means least, to try to influence the daily papers of the country to refuse to become accessory to mobs either before or after the fact.

Several of the greatest riots and most brutal burnt offerings of the mobs have been suggested and incited by the daily papers of the offending community. If the newspaper which suggests lynching in its accounts of an alleged crime, could be held legally as well as morally responsible for reporting that "threats of lynching were heard"; or, "it is feared that if the guilty one is caught, he will be lynched"; or, "there were cries of 'lynch him,' and the only reason the threat was not carried out was because no leader appeared," a long step toward a remedy will have been taken.

In a multitude of counsel there is wisdom. Upon the grave question presented by the slaughter of innocent men, women and children there should be an honest, courageous conference of patriotic, law-abiding citizens anxious to punish crime promptly, impartially and by due process of law, also to make life, liberty and property secure against mob rule.

Time was when lynching appeared to be sectional, but now it is national—a blight upon our nation, mocking our laws and disgracing our Christianity. "With malice toward none but with charity for all" let us undertake the work of making the "law of the land" effective and supreme upon every foot of American soil—a shield to the innocent; and to the guilty, punishment swift and sure.

The Kind of Democracy of the Negro Expects

Democracy is the most used term in the world today. But some of its uses are abuses. Everybody says "Democracy"! But everybody has his own definition. By the extraordinary weight of the presidency of the United States many undemocratic people have had this word forced upon their lips but have not yet had the right ideal forced upon their hearts. I have heard of one woman who wondered with alarm whether "democracy" would mean that colored women would have the right to take any vacant seat or space on a street car, even if they had paid for it. That such a question should be asked, shows how many different meanings men may attach to the one word DEMOCRACY. This woman doubtless believes in a democracy of me-and-my-kind, which is no democracy. The most autocratic and the worst caste systems could call themselves democratic by that definition. Even the Prussian junker believes in that type of democracy; he has no doubt that he and the other junkers should be free and equal in rights and privileges. Many have accepted the word DEMOCRACY merely as the current password to respectability in political thinking. The spirit of the times is demanding democracy; it is the tune of the age; it is the song to sing. But some are like that man who belonged to one of the greatest political parties: after hearing convincing arguments by the stump-speaker of the opposite party, he exclaimed: "Wa-al, that fellow has convinced my judgment, but I'll be d—d if he can CHANGE MY VOTE!"

It is in order, therefore, for the Negro to state clearly what he means by democracy and what he is fighting for.

FIRST. Democracy in Education. This is fundamental. No other democracy is practicable unless all of the people have equal right and opportunity to develop according to their individual endowments. There can be no real democracy between two natural groups, if one represents the extreme of ignorance and the other the best of intelligence. The common public school and the state university should be the foundation stones of democracy. If men are artificially differentiated at the beginning, if we try to educate a "working class" and a "ruling class," forcing different race groups into different lines without regard to individual fitness, how can we ever hope for democracy in the other relations of these groups? Individuals will differ, but in democracy of education peoples living on the same soil should not be widely diverged in their training on mere racial lines. This would be illogical, since they are to be measured by the same standards of life. Of course, a group that is to live in Florida should be differently trained from a group that is to live in Alaska; but that is geography and general environment, and not color or caste.—The Negro believes in democracy of education as first and fundamental: that the distinction should be made between individual talents and not between color and castes.

SECOND. Democracy in Industry. The right to work in any line for which the individual is best prepared, and to be paid the standard wage. This is also fundamental. In the last analysis there could be very little democracy between multi-millionaires and the abject poor. There must be a more just and fair distribution of wealth in a democracy. And certainly this is not possible unless men work at the occupations for which they are endowed and best prepared. There should be no "colored" wages and no "white" wages; no "man's" wage and no "woman's" wage. Wages should be paid for the work done, measured as much as possible by its productiveness. No door of opportunity should be closed to a man on any other ground than that of his individual unfitness. The cruelest and most undemocratic thing in the world is to require of the individual man that his whole race be fit before he can be regarded as fit for a certain privilege or responsibility. That rule, strictly applied, would exclude and man of any race from any position. For every man to serve where he is most able to serve is public economy and is to the best interest of the state. This lamentable war that was forced upon us should make that plain to the dullest of us. Suppose that, when this war broke out, our whole country had been like Mississippi (and I refer to geography unividiously),—suppose our whole country had bee like Mississippi, where a caste system was holding the majority of the population in the triple chains of ignorance, semi-serfdom and poverty. Our nation would be now either the unwilling prey or the golden goose for the Prussian. The long-headed thing for any state is to let every man do his best all of the time. But some people are so short-sighted that they only see what is thrust against their noses. The Negro asks American labor in the name of democracy to get rid of its color caste and industrial junkerism.

THIRD. Democracy in State. A political democracy in which all are equal before the laws; where there is one standard of justice, written and unwritten; where all men and women may be citizens by the same qualifications, agreed upon and specified. We believe in this as much for South Africa as for South Carolina, and we hope that our American nation will not agree with any government, ally or envy, that is willing to make a peace that will bind the Africa Negro to political slavery and exploitation.

Many other evils grow out of political inequality. Discriminating laws are the mother of the mob spirit. The political philosopher in Washington, after publishing his opinion that a Negro by the fault of being a Negro is unfit to be a member of Congress, cannot expect an ignorant white man in Tennessee to believe that the same Negro is, nevertheless, fit to have a fair and impartial trial in a Tennessee court. Ignorance is too logical for that. I disagree with the premises but I agree with the reasoning of the Tennesseean: that if being a Negro unfits a man for holding a government office for which he is otherwise fit, it unfits the same man for claiming a "white man's" chance in the courts. The first move therefore against mob violence and injustice in the petty courts is to wipe out discriminating laws and practices in the higher circles of government. The ignorant man in Tennessee will not rise in ideal above the intelligent man in Washington.

FOURTH. Democracy without Sex-preferment. The Negro cannot consistently oppose color discrimination and support sex discrimination in democratic government. This happened to be the opinion also of the First Man of the Negro race in America,—Frederick Douglass. The handicap is nothing more nor less than a presumption in the mind of the physically dominant element of the universal inferiority of the weaker or subject element. It is so easy to prove that the man who is down and under, deserves to be down and under. In the first place, he is down there, isn't he? And that is three-fourths of the argument to the ordinary mind; for the ordinary mind does not seek ultimate causes. The argument against the participation of colored men and of women in self-government is practically one argument. Somebody spoke to the Creator about both of these classes and learned that they were "created" for inferior roles. Enfranchisement would spoil a good field-hand,—or a good cook. Black men were once ignorant,—women were once ignorant. Negroes had no political experience—women had no such experience. The argument forgets that people do not get experience on the outside. But the American Negro expects a democracy that will accord the right to vote to a sensible industrious woman rather than to a male tramp.

FIFTH. Democracy in Church. The preachings and the practices of Jesus of Nazareth are perhaps the greatest influence in the production of modern democratic ideas. The Christian church is, therefore, no place for the caste spirit or for snobs. And the colored races the world over will have even more doubt in the future than they have had in the past of the real Christianity of any church which hold out to them the prospect of being united in heaven after being separated on earth.

FINALLY. The great colored races will in the future not be kinder to a sham democracy than to a "scrap-of-paper" autocracy. The private home, private right and private opinion must remain inviolate; but the commonwealth, the public place and public property must not be appropriated to the better use of any group by "Jim-Crowing" and segregating any other group. By the endowments of God and nature there are individual "spheres"; but there are no such widely different racial "spheres." Jesus' estimate of the individual soul is the taproot of democracy, and any system which discourages the men of any race from individual achievement, is no democracy. To fix the status of a human soul on earth according to the physical group in which it was born, is the gang spirit of the savage which protects its own members and outlaws all others.

For real democracy the American Negro will live and die. His loyalty is always above suspicion, but his extraordinary spirit in the present war is born of his faith that on the side of his country and her allies is the best hope for such democracy. And he welcomes, too, the opportunity to lift the "Negro question" out of the narrow confines of the Southern United States and make it a world question. Like many other questions our domestic race question, instead of being settled by Mississippi and South Carolina, will now seek its settlement largely on the battlefields of Europe.

THE SHAME OF AMERICA, OR THE NEGRO'S CASE AGAINST THE REPUBLIC

The author of the Declaration of Independence said once that he trembled for his country when he remembered that God was just. And he did well to do so. But while he was about it he might have quaked a little for himself. For he was certainly guilty of the same crime against humanity, which had aroused in his philosophic and patriotic mind such lively sensations of anxiety and alarm in respect to the Nation. Said Jefferson on paper: "We hold these truths to be self evident, that all men are created equal; that they are endowed by their Creator with certain unalienable rights; that among these are life, liberty and the pursuit of happiness," while on his plantation he was holding some men as slaves, and continued to hold them as such for fifty years thereafter, and died at the end of a long and brilliant life, a Virginia slaveholder. And yet Thomas Jefferson was sincere, or fancied that he was, when he uttered those sublime sentiments about the rights of man, and when he declared that he trembled for his country when he remembered that God was just. This inconsistency between the man's magnificence in profession and his smallness in practice, between the grandeur of what he promised and the meanness of what he performed, taken in conjunction with his cool unconsciousness of the discrepancy, is essentially and emphatically an American trait, a national idiosyncrasy. For it has appeared during the last one hundred and forty four years with singular boldness and continuity in the social; political, and religious life of the American people and their leaders. I do not recall in all history such another example of a nation appearing so well in its written words regarding human rights, and so badly when it comes to translating those fine words into corresponding action, as this Republic has uniformly exhibited from its foundation, wherever the Negro has been concerned.

Look at its conduct in the War of the Revolution, which it began with the high sounding sentiments of the Declaration of Independence. The American colonists rose in arms because they were taxed by England without their consent, a species of tyranny which bore no sort of comparison to the slavery which they themselves were imposing on the Negro. But with such inconsistency of conduct the men of the Revolution bothered not their heads for a simple, and to them, a sufficient reason. They were white and the Negro was black and was their property. Since they were fighting for a political principle in order the better to protect their pockets, they were not disposed to give up their property rights in anything, not even in human beings. They were contending for the sacred right of loosening their own purse strings, not for the sacred privilege of loosening the bonds of their slaves. Not at all. Millions they were willing to spend in defense of the former, but not a cent to effect the latter, their loud talk in the Declaration of Independence to the contrary, notwithstanding.

Their subsequent conduct in respect to the Negro was of a piece with this characteristic beginning. First they accepted the services of the blacks, both bond and free, as soldiers, and then they debated the expediency and justice of their action, not from the point of view of the slaves but from that of the masters, and later decided upon a policy of exclusion of the slaves from the Continental army. With the adoption of such a policy the chattel rights of masters in those poor men would be better conserved. Hence the policy of exclusion. But when the British evinced a disposition to enlist the slaves as soldiers, a change passed quickly over the leaders of the Revolution, with Washington at their head. The danger to the master of a policy of inclusion was overridden readily enough in the greater danger to the cause of one of exclusion. Without a thought for the slave, he was put on the military chessboard, withdrawn, then put back in response to purely selfish considerations and needs.

Thus it happened that black men fought in that war shoulder to shoulder with white men for American Independence. In every colony from Massachusetts to Georgia, they were found faithful among the faithless, and brave as the bravest during those long and bitter years, fighting and dying with incomparable devotion and valor, by the side of Warren at Bunker Hill, and of Pulaski at Savannah.

The voluntary surrender of life for country has been justly held by all ages to be an act of supreme virtue. It is in the power of any man to give less; it is in the power of none, however exalted in station, to give more. For to lay down one's life at the call of Duty is to lay down one's all. And this all of the general weighs no more than the all of a common soldier. Weighed in the scales of truth this supreme gift of the beggar on foot balances exactly that of the prince on horseback. When prince or beggar, master or slave, has given his life to a cause, he has given his utmost. Beyond that absolute measure of devotion neither can add one jot or tittle to the value of his gift. Thank God there is no color line in acts of heroism and self-sacrifice, save the royal one of their blood tinted humanity. Such was the priceless contribution which the poor, oppressed Negro made to American Independence.

What was his guerdon? In the hour of their triumph did the patriot fathers call to mind such supreme service to reward it? In the freedom which they had won by the aid of their enslaved countrymen, did they bethink them of lightening the yoke of those miserable men? History answers, no! Truth answers, no! The descendants of those black heroes answer, no! What then? What did such bright, such blazing beacons of liberty, the Washingtons, Hamiltons, Madisons and Franklins, the Rufus Kings, Roger Shermans, and Robert Morrises? They founded the Republic on slavery, rested one end of its stately arch on the prostrate neck of the Negro. They constructed a national Constitution which safeguarded the property of man in man, introducing into it for that purpose its three fifths slave representation provision, its fugitive slave clause, and an agreement by which the African slave trade was legalized for nineteen years after the adoption of that instrument. That was the reward which the founders of the Republic meted out with one accord to a race which had shed freely its blood to make that Republic a reality among the nations of the earth. Instead of loosening and lifting his heavy yoke of oppression, they strengthened and tightened it afresh on the loyal and long suffering neck of the Negro. Notwithstanding this shameful fact, the founders of the Republic were either so coolly unconscious of its moral enormity or else so indifferent to the amazing contradiction between what they said and what they did, as to write over the gateway of the new Constitution this sonorous preamble: "We, the people of the United States, in order to form a more perfect union, establish justice, insure domestic tranquility, provide for the common defense, promote the general welfare, and secure the blessings of liberty to ourselves and our posterity, do ordain and establish this Constitution for the United States of America."

"We the people!" From the standpoint of the Negro, what grim irony; "establish justice"! What exquisitely cruel mockery; "to insure domestic tranquility"! What height and breadth and depth of political duplicity; "to provide for the common defense"! What cunning paltering with words in a double sense; "to promote the general welfare"! What studied ignoring of an ugly fact; "and secure the blessings of liberty to ourselves and posterity"! What masterly abuse of noble words to mask an equivocal meaning, to throw over a great national transgression an air of virtue, so subtle and illusive as to deceive the framers themselves into believing in their own sincerity. You may ransack the libraries of the world, and turn over all the documents of recorded time to match that Preamble of the Constitution as a piece of consummate political dissimulation and mental reservation, as an example of how men juggle deliberately and successfully with their moral sense, how they raise above themselves huge fabrics of falsehood, and go willingly to live and die in a make believe world of lies. The muse of history, dipping her iron pen in the generous blood of the Negro, has written large across the page of that Preamble, and the face of the Declaration of Independence, the words, "sham, hypocrisy."

It is the rage now to sing the praises of the fathers of the Republic as a generation of singularly liberty loving men. They were so, indeed, if judged by their fine words alone. But they were, in reality, by no means superior to their sons in this respect, if we judge them by their acts, which somehow speak loader, more convincingly to us than their words, albeit those words proceed out of the Declaration of Independence, and the Preamble of the Constitution. If the children's teeth today are set on edge on the Negro question, it is because the fathers ate the sour grapes of race wrong, ate those miserable grapes during their whole life, and, dying, transmitted their taste for oppression, as a bitter inheritance to their children, and children's children, for God knows how many black years to come.

Take the case of Washington as an example. He was rated an abolitionist by his contemporaries. And so he was if mere words could have made him one. On paper he was one person, but on his plantation quite another. And as far as I know his history, he never made any effectual attempt to bring this second self of his into actual accord with the first. In theory he favored emancipation, while in practice he was one of the biggest, if not the biggest slaveholder in the country, who enriched himself and his family out of the unpaid toil of more than two hundred slaves. The father of his country did not manumit them during his lifetime, or of that of his wife. Not until his death, not until the death of his widow, did he, as a matter of fact, release his hold upon the labor of those people, did they escape from his dead hands. As first President, moreover, he signed the first fugitive slave law and was not ashamed to avail himself of its hateful provisions for the reclamation of one of his runaway slave women. And yet Washington, and Jefferson also, are the two bright, particular stars of our American democracy. They had very fine words for liberty, no two men ever had finer, but when it came to translating them into action, into churning them into butter for the poor Negro's parsnips, no atom of butter did they yield, or will ever yield, churn them ever so long. Ex pede Herculem.

Naturally enough under the circumstances of its origin and antecedents, American democracy has never cared a fig in practice for the fine sentiments of its Declaration of Independence, or for the high sounding ones of the Preamble to its Constitution, wherever and whenever the Negro has been concerned. It used him to fight the battles for its independent political existence, and rewarded his blood and bravery with fresh stripes and heavier chains.

History repeats itself. In America, on the Negro question, it has been a series of shameful repetitions of itself. The Negro's history in the first war with England was repeated exactly in the second. In this conflict no more loyal and daring hearts bled and broke for the country than were those of its colored soldiers and sailors. On land and water in that war the Negro died as he fought, among the most faithful and heroic defenders of the American cause. But to praise him is to condemn the country, which in this instance I will leave to no less an American than General Jackson. Out of his mouth shall this condemnation be spoken. Said Jackson three weeks before the battle of New Orleans to the black soldiers who had rallied at his summons to repel a formidable invasion of our national domain by a powerful foreign enemy:

"From the shores of Mobile I called you to arms. I invited you to share in the perils and divide the glory of your white countrymen. I expected much from you, for I was not uninformed of those qualities which must render you so formidable to an invading foe. I knew you could endure hunger and thirst, and all the hardships of war. I knew that you loved the land of your nativity, and that, like ourselves, you had to defend all that is most dear to men. But you surpass my hopes. I have found in you, united to those qualities, that noble enthusiasm that impels to great deeds."

"Soldiers: The President of the United. States shall be informed of your conduct on the present occasion, and the voice of the representatives of the American nation shall applaud your valor, as your General now praises your ardor. The enemy is near. His sails cover the lakes, but the brave are united. and if he finds us contending among ourselves, it will be for the prize of valor, and fame its noblest reward."

Jackson's black troops proved themselves in the actions of Mobile Bay and New Orleans entitled to every mouthful of the ringing applause which Old Hickory gave them without stint. They got fair enough words as long as the enemy was in sight and his navy covered the waters of the country. But as soon as the peril had passed those fear words were succeeded by the foulest ingratitude. On every hand Colorphobia reared its cursed head, and struck its cruel fangs into those brave breasts which had just received the swords and the bullets of a foreign foe. They were legislated against everywhere, proscribed by atrocious laws everywhere. They had given the nation in its dire need, blood and life, and measureless love, and had received as reward black codes, an unrelenting race prejudice, and bondage bitterer than death.

Strange irony of fate which reserved to Andrew Jackson, whose mouth overflowed with praise in 1814 for his black soldiers and with fair promises of what he intended to do for them Strange irony of fate, I say, which reserved to that man, as President in 1836, the elevation of Roger B. Taney to the Chief Justiceship of the United States, of Taney, the infamous slave Judge who wrote the Dred Scott Decision, which argued that black men had no rights in America which white men were bound to respect. The downright brutality of that opinion was extremely shocking to some sensitive Americans, but it was no more so than was the downright brutality of the facts, which it reflected with brutal accuracy. The fell apparition of American inhumanity, which those words conjured up from the depths of an abominable past and from that of a no less abominable present, was indeed black, but it was no blacker than the truth. The dark soul of the nation was embodied in them, all of its savage selfishness, greed and iniquity. There they glared, large and lifelike, a devil's face among the nations, seamed and intersected with the sinister lines of a century of cruelty and race hatred and oppression. Of course the fair idealism of the Declaration of Independence was wanting in the photographic naturalism of the picture, and so was the fictive beauty of the Preamble of the Constitution, because they were wanting in the terrible original, in the malignant, merciless, and murderous spirit of a democracy which the dark words of the dark judge had limned to the life.

God has made iniquitous power ultimately self destructive. Into every combination of evil He puts the seed of division and strife. Without this effective check wickedness would conquer and permanently possess the earth. The law of the brute would rule it forever. Where today are the empires of might and wrong, which men reared in their pride and strength, on the Nile, the Tigris, and the Euphrates, on the Tiber, the Bosporus, and the Mediterranean? They flourished for a season and seasons, and spread themselves like green bay trees. But behold they are gone, perished, burnt up by the fires of evil passions, by the evil power which consumed them to ashes. Centuries have flown over their graves, and the places once cursed by their violence, and crushed by their oppressions, shall know them and their vulture laws and trampling armies no more forever.

So it happened in the case of the American people when in order "to form a more perfect union," they ordained and established their Constitution. Within the "more perfect union" was enfolded a fruitful germ of division and discord. No bigger at first than the smallest of seeds, the germ grew apace with the growth of the new nation, drawing abundant nourishment from the dark underworld of the slave. Slender sapling in 1815, it was a fast growing tree in 1820, bearing even then its bitter apples of Gomorrah. Where its bitter fruit fell, there fell also on the spirit of the people mutual distrust, and incipient sectional hate. And no wonder, for when the North clasped hands with her Southern sister in "a more perfect union," she did so the better to conserve a set of interests and institutions peculiar to herself and inherently hostile to those of the South, and vice versa with respect to the action of the latter in the premises. The "more perfect union" had, thank God, effected a conjunction, under a single political system, of two sets of mutually invasive and destructive social ideas and industrial forces. Differences presently sprang up between the partisans of each set, and discontent, and wide spreading fear and contention. National legislation which oxidized and enriched the blood of the North, not only impoverished but actually poisoned that of the South. And so it came to pass that the compromise Constitution which was designed "to form a more perfect union," failed of its purpose, because with human slavery at the core of it, it brought face to face two warring social systems, whose unappeasable strife it had not the secret or the strength to subdue.

As in Egypt more than three thousand years ago, the Eternal spoke to the master race at divers times and with divers signs, saying, "let my people go," so he spoke to the master race in this land through divers omens and events, saying likewise, "let my people go." Those with ears to hear might have heard that divine voice in the Hartford Convention and the causes which led to its call; in the successive sectional conflicts over Missouri, the Tariff, and Texas; in the storm winds of the Mexican war, as in the wild uproar which followed the annexation of new national territory at its close; in the political rage and explosions of 1850 and 1854, and in the fierce patter of blood drops over Kansas. They might have surely heard that commanding voice from the anointed lips of holy men and prophets, from the mouths of Garrison and Summer, and Phillips, and Douglass, from the sacred gallows where John Brown heard and repeated it while his soul went marching on from city to city, and State to State, over mountain and river, across a continent, and from the Lakes to the Gulf with rising accent saying, "let my people go." Alas! the nation hearkened not to the voice of justice, but continued to harden its heart, until thunder like that voice broke in the deep boom of Civil War.

When masters fall out a way oftentimes opens for the escape of their slaves. In the death grapple of the sections for political supremacy, the dead weight of two centuries of oppression lifted from the neck of the Negro. The people and their leaders of both sections despised him to such a degree that neither would in the beginning enlist his aid against the other. "We the people" of the glorious union of 1789 had quarreled like two bloody scoundrels over their ill gotten gains, and had come to murderous blows. Yet in spite of their deadly hatred of each other, they said in their mad race pride and prejudice, the North to the South, and the South to the North, "go to, shall we not settle our differences without the aid of him who is our slave? Shall not we white men fight our duel to a finish; shall either of us appeal for help to that miserable being who by our laws, written and unwritten, has never possessed any rights among us which we have ever respected?" They chose to forget how in two wars this faithful man had for their sakes, received into his sad but brave breast the swords and the bullets of a foreign enemy, and all unmindful of self had helped them to achieve and maintain their liberty and independence. And thus choosing to forget his past services and to remember only their bitter race prejudice against him, they fought on with deadly malice and violence, the one side against the other, rending their dear Union with fraternal strife, and drenching it with fraternal blood.

Perceiving the unlimited capacity of mankind for all sorts of folly, no wonder Puck exclaimed, "What fools these mortals be!" Yes, what fools, but of all the fools who have crawled to dusty death the most stupendous and bedeviled lot are those who strut their fools' feet and toss their fools' heads across their little stage of life, thanking their fools' selves that God made them different from other men superior to other men to rule over other men. Puffed up with their stupid race pride and prejudice, inflated to the bursting point with their high and mighty notions, and noli me tangere airs, the North and the South went on for nearly two years goring and tearing each other like two infuriated bulls of nearly equal strength, before either would call on the Negro for assistance. Not until bleeding at every pore, sickened at the loss of its sordid dollar, and in despair at the threatened destruction of that to which it ascribed, as to the Almighty, all of its sectional progress, prosperity and power, viz.: the dear Union, did the North turn for help to the Negro, whom it had despised and wronged, and whom it even then, in its heart of hearts, despised and intended, upon occasion, to wrong anew.

Think of the incredible folly and selfishness of a people fighting for existence and yet begrudging freedom to an enslaved race, whom it had called upon to help defend that existence; doling out to its faithful black allies, with miserly meanness, its blood money and its boasted democratic equality and fair play; denying to its colored soldiers equal pay and promotion with its white ones, albeit many of those white ones were mercenary aliens from Europe. Nevertheless, of such bottomless depths of folly and meanness was the National Government certainly guilty. The Fifty fourth and the Fifty fifth Massachusetts regiments enlisted to fight the battles of the country, with the understanding that there would be no discrimination against them on account of their color. Yet the government violated its understood pledge, and proceeded to pay, or tried to pay those men ten dollars a month where it was paying other men, because they were white, thirteen dollars a month for the same service. All honor to Massachusetts for objecting to this shameful act, and for offering to make up to her colored regiments the three dollars out of which the National government was endeavoring to cheat them. Three times three cheers for the brave and true men who had the sagacity and the courage, and the self respect, to resist the injustice of the government, and to refuse firmly to compromise by a cent their right to equality of pay in the army.

Take another instance of the meanness of the government's conduct toward its colored defenders. In January of 1864, Henry Wilson embodied, in a bill to promote enlistments, a clause which provided that when "any man or boy of African descent, in service or labor in any State under its laws, should be mustered into the military or naval service of the United States, he and his mother, wife and children, shall he forever free." Now will you believe that this just and moderate measure took thirteen long months before its friends could get Congress to enact it into laws? "Future generations," exclaimed Charles Summer in closing his remarks on the subject, "future generations will read with amazement, that a great people when national life was assailed, hesitated to exercise a power so simple and beneficent; and this amazement will know no bounds, as they learn that Congress higgled for months on a question, whether the wives and children of our colored soldiers should be admitted to freedom."

Need I repeat in this presence the old, grand story, how in numbers nearly two hundred thousand strong our colored boys in blue, left their blood and their bones in every State from Virginia to Louisiana? How, like heroes, they fought and died for the Union at Port Hudson, and Fort Wagner, and Petersburg, and Honey Hill, and Olustee, and Milliken's Bend? How in winter and summer, in cold and heat, in valley and on hilltop, on horse and on foot, over rivers and swamps, through woods and brakes, they rushed to meet the foe? How leaving behind them fields strown thick with their dead and wounded, they mounted the blazing sides of grim fortresses, climbing on great deeds and self-sacrifices through storms of shot and shell, to death and a place among the stars?

No, no, it is not required of me on this occasion to read afresh that glorious record. Sufficient then this: The Northern army, reinforced by the strength which it drew from that of the Negro, broke in time the back of the Rebellion, and saved the Union, so that in 1865 the flag of the nation floated again over an undivided country, and the Republic, strong and great beneath that flag, launched anew to meet the years, and to reach her fair ideals of liberty and equality which were flashing like beacon lights upon her way.

Amid widespread rejoicing on the return of peace and the restoration of the Union, the Negro rejoiced among the gladdest, for his slave fitters were broken, he was no longer a chattel. He imagined in his simple heart, in his ignorance and poverty, that he had not only won freedom, but the lasting affection and gratitude of the powerful people for whom he had entered hell to quench for them it's raging fires with his blood. Yes, although black and despised, he, the slave, the hated one, had risen above his centuries of wrongs, above their bitter memories and bitterer sufferings to the love of enemies, to the forgiveness of those who had despitefully used him, ay, to those moral heights where heroes are throned and martyrs crowned. Surely, surely, he, who had been so unmindful of self in the service of country, would not be left by that country at the mercy of those who hated him then with the most terrible hatred for that very cause. He who had been mighty to save others would surely, now in his need, be saved by those whom he had saved. "Oh! Justice, thou has fled to brutish beasts, and men have lost their gratitude."

I would gladly seal forever the dark chapter of our history, which followed the close of the war. Gladly would I forget that record of national shame and selfishness. But as it is better to turn on light than to shift it off, I will, with your forbearance, turn it on for our illumination and guidance, in the lowering present.

The chapter opened with an introduction of characteristic indifference on the part of the country in respect to the fate of the Negro. With his shackles lying close beside him, he was left in the hands of his old master who, seizing the opportunity, proceeded straightway to refit them on the disenthralled limbs of the former slave. State after State did so with such promptitude and to such effect that within a few months a formidable system of Negro serfdom had actually been constructed, and cunningly substituted in place of the system of Negro slavery, which the war had destroyed. An African serf power, Phoenix like, was rising out of the ashes of the old slave power into national politics. At sight of this truly appalling apparition, the apparition of a returning slave power in thin disguise, all the old sectional fear and hatred which had existed against it in the free States before the Rebellion, awoke suddenly and hotly in the breast of the North. Thinking mainly, if not wholly of its own safety in the emergency which confronted it, and how best to avert the fresh perils which impended in consequence over its ascendancy, the North prepared to make, and did in fact make, for the time being, short shrift of this boldly retroactive scheme of the South to recover within the Union all that it had lost by its defeated attempt to land itself outside of the Union.

Having tested to its entire satisfaction the Negro's value as a soldier in its war for the preservation of the Union, the North determined at this juncture to enlist his aid as a citizen in its further conflicts with the South, for the preservation or its sectional domination in the newly restored Union. To this end the Fourteenth and the Fifteenth Amendments to the Constitution were, in the progress of events, incorporated into that instrument. By these two great acts, the North had secured itself against the danger of an immediate return of the South to anything like political equality with it in the Republic. Between its supremacy and the attacks of its old rival, it had erected a solid wall of Negro votes. But immensely important as was the ballot to its black contingent, it was not enough to meet all of his tremendous needs. Nevertheless, as the North was considering mainly its own and not the Negro's necessities at this crisis, and as the elective franchise in his hands was deemed by it adequate to satisfy its own pressing floods, it gave the peculiar wants of the Negro beyond that of the ballot but scant attention.

Homeless, landless, illiterate, just emerging from the blackness of two centuries of slavery, this simple and faithful folk had surely other sacred claims on the North and the National Government than this right to the ballot. They had in truth a strong claim to unselfish friendship and statesmanship, to unfaltering care and guardianship, during the whole of their transition from slavery to citizenship. They needed the organized hands, the wise heads, the warm hearts, the piled up wealth, the sleepless eyes, the faith, hope, and charity of a Christian people and a Christian government to teach them to walk and to save them from industrial exploitation by their old masters, as well as to vote. Did they receive from the Republic what the Republic owed them by every consideration of justice, gratitude and humanity, as of enlightened self interest.? Alas? not a tithe of this immense debt has the Republic ever undertaken to pay to those who should have been, under all circumstances, its sacredly preferred creditors. On the contrary they were left to themselves by the government in the outer darkness of that social state which had been their sad lot for more than two centuries. They were left in that darkest night of moral and civil anarchy to fight not alone their own terrible battle with poverty, ignorance, and untutored appetites and passions, but also the unequal, the cruel battle for the preservation of Northern political domination in the Union. For ten awful years they fought that battle for the North, for the Republican party, in the face of persecutions and oppressions, terrors and atrocities, at the glare of which the country and the civilized world shrank aghast.

Aghast shrank the North, but not for the poor Negro, faithful unto death to it. For itself rather it shrank from the threatening shadows which such a carnival of horrors was casting athwart its vast and spreading network of trade and production. The clamor of all its million wheeled industry and prosperity was for peace. "Let us have peace," said Grant, and "let us have peace" blew forthwith and in deafening unison, all the big and little whistles of all the big and little factories and locomotives, and steamships from Maine to California. Every pen of merchant and editor scratched paper to the same mad tune. The pulpit and the platform of the land cooed their Cuckoo song in honor of those piping times of peace. The lone noise of chinking coin pouring into vaults like coal into bins, drowned the, agonized cry of the forgotten and long suffering Negro. Deserting him in 1876, the North, stretching across the bloody chasm its two greedy, commercial hands, grasped the ensanguined ones of the South, and repeated, "let us have peace." Little did the Northern people and the government reck then or now that at the bottom of that bloody chasm lay their faithful black friends. Little did they care that the blood on those Southern hands had been wrung drop by drop from tire loyal heart of the Negro. But enough.

Years of struggle and oppression follow and we come to another chapter of American history; namely, the Spanish American War. In the Spanish American War the Negro attracted the attention of the world by his clashing valor. He attracted the attention of his country also. His fighting quality was of the highest, unsurpassed, and perhaps unequalled in brilliancy by the rest of the American army that invaded Cuba. He elicited applause and grudging justice from his countrymen, clashed with envy and race prejudice. Still it seemed for a brief time that his conspicuous service had given his case against the Republic a little better standing in Court a little better chance for a fair hearing at the Bar of Public Opinion. But our characteristic national emotionalism was too shallow and insincere to last. In fact, it died aborning. The national habit of a century and a half reasserted itself. There was no attempt made to square national profession and national practice, national promise and national performance. The Negro again had given his all to his country and had got in return at the hands of that country wrong and injustice. Southern propaganda presently renewed all of its vicious and relentless activity against the Negro. He was different, he was alien, he was unassimilable, he was inferior, and he must be kept so, and in the scheme of things he must be made forever subordinate to the white race. In this scheme of things white domination could best be preserved by the establishment of a caste system based on race and color. And so following the Spanish American War the North and the South put their heads together to complete their caste system. Everywhere throughout the Republic race prejudice, color proscription grew apace. One by one rights and privileges which the Negroes had enjoyed for a brief space were withdrawn and the wall of caste rose higher and higher. 11e was slowly arid surely being shut out from all the things which white men enjoyed by virtue of their Citizenship, and stint. within limits of freedom. Everywhere within his prison house he read in large and sinister letters, "Thus far and no father." He was trapped, and about to be caged. In spit of the Emancipation Proclamation and the three War Amendments he found that white men were becoming bolder in ignoring or violating his freedom and citizenship under them. The walls of the new bondage were closing about his right to life, liberty and the pursuit of happiness in this boasted Land of the Free and Christian Home of Democratic Hypocrisy and Cruelty.

Then Mr. Taft appeared upon the scene and became famous or infamous as a builder on the walls of the Temple of the New American Jerusalem, where profession is High Priest to the God of Broken Promises. He proved himself a master workman in following the lines of caste, in putting into place a new stone in the edifice when he announced as his policy at the beginning of his administration that he would not appoint any colored man to office in the South where the whites objected. Caste had won and the Negro's status was fixed, as far as this bourgeois apostle of American Democracy was able to fix it. His adds but another illustrious name to the long list of those architects of national dishonor who sought to build the Temple of American Liberty upon a basis of caste.

Then in the fullness of time came Woodrow Wilson, the ripe consummate fruit of all this national contradiction between profession and practice, promise and performance. He can give Messrs. Washington, Jefferson, Jackson and Company odds and beat them in the subtle art of saying sonorously, grandiosely, what in action he does not hesitate to flout and spurn. When seeking the Negro's vote in 1912, he was the most profuse and generous in eloquent profession, in iridescent promises, but when he was elected he forgot straightway those fair professions and promises and began within a week after he entered the White House to put into office men filled with colorphobia, the better to finish the work of undoing in the government the citizenship of the Negro, to whom he had promised not grudging justice but the highly sympathetic article, heaping up and running over. Mr. Taft had established the principle that no Negro was to be appointed to office in the South where the whites objected—Mr. Wilson carried the principle logically one step farther, namely, no Negro was to be put to work in any department of the government with white men and women if these white men and women objected to his presence. Segregation along the color line in Federal employment became forthwith the fixed policy of the Wilson administration.

There sprang up under the malign influence of this false prophet of the New Freedom all sorts of movements in the District of Columbia and in the Federal Government hostile to the Negro—movements to exclude him from all positions under the Civil Service above that of laborer and messenger and charwoman, to jim-crow him on the street cars, to prohibit him from intermarrying with the whites, to establish for him a residential pale in the District; in short, to fix forever his status as a permanently inferior caste in the land for which he had toiled in peace and bled and died in war. The evil influence of this false apostle of freedom spread far and wide and spurred the enemies of the Negro to unwonted activity. The movement of residential segregation and for rural segregation grew in volume and momentum in widely separated parts of the country until it was finally checked by the decision of the Supreme Court in 1917.

The condition of the Negro was at its worst and his outlook in America at its darkest when the Government declared war against Germany. Then was revived the Republic's program of false promises and hypocritical professions in order to bring this black man with his brawn and brains, and with his horny hands and lion heart, with his unquenchable loyalty and enthusiasm to its aid. No class of its citizens surpassed him in the swiftness and self-forgetfulness of his response to the call of country. What he had to give he brought to the alter and laid it there—labor and wealth, wounds and death, with unsurpassed devotion and patriotism. But what he received in return was the same old treatment, evil for his good, ingratitude and treachery for his loyalty and service. He was discriminated against everywhere— was used and abused, shut out from equal recognition and promotion with white men and women. Then when he went overseas he found American colorphobia more deadly than the gun and poison gas of the Germans. In the American army there was operated a ceaseless propaganda of meanness and malice, of jealousy and detraction against him. If our Expeditionary Force had given itself with a tithe of the zeal and industry to fighting the Germans, which a large section of it devoted to fighting the black soldier, it would have come out of the war with more honor and credit, and left behind in France a keener sense of gratitude, and regard than exists for them in that country today. But, alas, thousands of them were more interested in watching the Negro and his reception by the French, in concocting villainous plots to degrade him in the eyes of that people, in segregating him from all social contact with them, and in keeping him in his place, within the hard and fast lines of caste which they had laid for him in America.

But the Negro went and saw—saw the incredible meanness and malice of his own country by the side of the immense genius for Liberty and Brotherhood of France. There he found himself a man and brother regardless of his race and color. But if he has seen these things in France he has also conquered certain other things in himself, and has come back not as he went but a New Negro. He has come back to challenge injustice in his own land and to fight wrong with a courage that will not fail him in the bitter and perhaps bloody years to come. For he knows now as he has never known before that he is an American citizen with the title deeds of his citizenship written in a century and a half of labor and suffering and blood. From his brave black lips I hear the ringing challenge, "This is my right and by the Eternal I have come back to claim all that belongs to me of industrial and political equality and liberty." And let us answer his high resolve with a courage and will to match his own, and so help to redeem our country for its shame of a century and a half of broken promises and dishonored ideals.

But be not deceived, friends. Let us, like brave men and women, face the stern reality of our situation. We are where we are. We are in the midst of a bitter and hitherto an invincible race prejudice, which beats down into the dust of all our rights, all of our attainments, all of our aspirations after freedom and excellence. The North and the South are in substantial accord in respect to us and in respect to the position which we are to occupy in this land. We are to be forever exploited, forever treated as an alien race, allowed to live here in strict subordination and subjection to the white race. We are to hew for it wood, draw for it water, till for it the earth, drive for it coaches, wait for it at tables, black for it boots, run for it errands, receive from it crumbs and kicks, to be for it, in short, social mudsills on which shall rest the foundations of the vast fabric of its industrial democracy and civilization.

No one can save us from such a fate but God, but ourselves. You think, I know, that the North is more friendly to you than the South, that the Republican party does more for the solution of this problem than the Democratic. Friends, you are mistaken. A white man is a white man on this question, whether he lives in the North or the South. Of course, there are splendid exceptions. Scratch the skin of Republican or Democrat, of Northern white men or southern white men, and you will find close to the surface race prejudice, American colorphobia. The difference, did you but know it, is not even epidermal, is not skin-deep. The hair is Democratic Esau's, and the voice is Republican Jacob's. That is all. Make no mistake here, for a true understanding of our actual position at this point is vital.

On Boston Commons stands a masterpiece in bronze, erected to commemorate the heroism and patriotism of Col. Robert Gould Shaw and his black regiment. There day and night, through summer and winter, storm and shine, are to march forever those brave men by the side of their valiant young leader. Into the unknown they are hurrying to front and to fight their enemies and the enemies of their country. They are not afraid. A high courage looks from their faces, lives in the martial motion of their bodies, flashes from the barrels of their guns. On and yet ever on they are marching, grim bolts of war, across the Commons, through State Street, past the old State House, over ground consecrated by the martyr's blood of Crispus Attucks, and the martyr's feet of William Lloyd Garrison. Farther and father they are pressing forward into the unknown, into the South, to Wagner and immortal deeds, to death and an immortal crown.

Friends, we too are marching through a living and lowering present into the unknown, through an enemy's land, at the summons of duty. We are to face great labors, great dangers, to fight like men our passions and American caste—prejudice and oppression, and God helping us, to conquer them.

OUR DEMOCRACY AND THE BALLOT

Ladies and Gentlemen: For some time since I have had growing apprehensions about any subject especially the subject of a speech that contained the word "democracy." The word "democracy" carries so many awe inspiring implications. As the key word of the subject of an address it may be the presage of an outpour of altitudinous and platitudinous expressions regarding "the most free and glorious government of the most free and glorious people that the world has ever seen." On the other hand, it may hold up its sleeve; if you will permit such a figure, a display of abstruse and recondite theorizations or hypotheses of democracy as a system of government. In choosing between either of these evils it is difficult to decide which is the lesser.

Indeed, the wording of my subject gave me somewhat more concern than the speech. I am not lure that it contains the slightest idea of what I shall attempt to say; but if the wording of my subject is loose it only places upon me greater reason for being more specific and definite in what I shall say. This I shall endeavor to do; at the same time, however, without being so, confident or so cocksure as an old preacher I used to listen to on Sundays when I taught school one summer down in the backwoods of Georgia, sometimes to my edification and often to my amazement.

On one particular Sunday, after taking a rather cryptic text, he took off his spectacles and laid them on the pulpit, closed the with a bang; and said, "Brothers and sisters, this morning I intend to explain the unexplainable, to find out the indefinable, to ponder over the imponderable, and to unscrew the inscrutable."

It is one of the commonplaces of American thought that we a democracy based upon the free will of the governed. The popular idea of the strength of this democracy is that it is founded upon the fact that every American citizen, through the ballot, is a ruler in his own right; that every citizen of age and outside of jail or the insane asylum has the undisputed right to determine through his vote by what laws he shall be governed and by whom these laws shall be enforced.

I could be cynical or flippant and illustrate in how many this popular idea is a fiction, but it is not my purpose to deal in cleverisms. I wish to bring to your attention seriously a situation, a condition, which not only runs counter to the popular conception of democracy in America but which runs counter to the fundamental law upon which that democracy rests and which, in addition, is a negation of our principles of government and a to our institutions.

Without any waste of words, I Come directly to a condition which exists in that section of our country which we call "the South," where millions of American citizens are denied both the right to vote and the privilege of qualifying themselves to vote. I refer to the wholesale disfranchisement of Negro citizens. There is no need at this time of going minutely into the methods employed to bring about this condition or into the reasons given as justification for those methods. Neither am I called upon to give proof of my general statement that millions of Negro citizens in the South are disfranchised. It is no secret. There are the published records of state constitutional conventions in which the whole subject is set forth with brutal frankness. The purpose of these state constitutional conventions is stated over and. over again, that purpose being to exclude from the right of franchise the Negro, however literate, and to include the white man, however illiterate.

The press of the South, public men in public utterances, and representatives of those states in Congress, have not only admitted these facts but have boasted of them. And so we have it as an admitted and undisputed fact that there are upwards of four million Negroes in the South who are denied the right to vote but who in any of the great northern, mid western or western states would be allowed to vote or world at least have the privilege of qualifying themselves to vote.

Now, nothing is further from me than the intention to discuss this question either from an anti-South point of view or from a pro-Negro point of view. It is my intention to put it before you purely as an American question, a question in which is involved the political life of the whole country.

Let us first consider this situation as a violation, not merely a violation but a defiance, of the Constitution of the United States. The Fourteenth and Fifteenth Amendments to the Constitution taken together express so plainly that a grammar school boy can understand it that the Negro is created a citizen of the United States and that as such he is entitled to all the rights of every other citizen and that those rights, specifically among them the right to vote, shall not be denied or abridged by the United States or by any state. This is the expressed meaning of these amendments in spite of all the sophistry and fallacious pretense which have been invoked by the courts to overcome it.

There are some, perhaps even here, who feel that serious a matter to violate or defy one amendment to the Constitution than another. Such persons will have in mind the Eighteenth Amendment. This is true in a strictly legal sense but any sort of analysis will show that violation of the two Civil War Amendments strikes deeper. As important as the Eighteenth Amendment may be, it is not fundamental; it contains no grant of rights to the citizen nor any requirement of service from him. It is rather a sort of welfare regulation for his personal conduct and for his general moral uplift.

But the two Civil War Amendments are grants of citizenship rights and a guarantee of protection in those rights, and therefore their observation is fundamental and vital not only to the citizen but to the integrity of the government.

We may next consider it as a question of political franchise equality between the states. We need not here go into a list of figures. A few examples will strike the difference:

In the elections of 1920 it took 82,492 votes in Mississippi to elect two senators and eight representatives. In Kansas it 570,220 votes to elect exactly the same representation. Another illustration from the statistics of the same election shows that vote in Louisiana has fifteen times the political power of one vote in Kansas.

In the Congressional elections of 1918 the total vote for the ten representatives from the State of Alabama was 62,345, while the total vote for ten representatives in Congress from Minnesota was 299,127, and the total vote in Iowa, which has ten representations was 316,377.

In the Presidential election of 1916 the states of Alabama, Arkansas, Georgia, Louisiana, Mississippi, North Carolina, South Carolina, Tennessee, Texas and Virginia cast a total vote for the Presidential candidates of 1,870,209. In Congress these states a total of 104 representatives and 126 votes in the electoral college. The State of New York alone cast a total vote for Presidential candidates of 1,706,354, a vote within 170,000 of all the votes cast by the above states, and yet New York has only 43 representatives and 45 votes in the electoral college.

What becomes of our democracy when such conditions of inequality as these can be brought about through chicanery, the open violation of the law and defiance of the Constitution?

But the question naturally arises, What if there is violation of certain clauses of the Constitution; what if there is an inequality of political power among the states? All this may be justified by necessity.

In fact, the justification is constantly offered. The justification goes back and makes a long story. It is grounded in memories of the Reconstruction period. Although most of those who were actors during that period have long since died, and although there is a new South and a new Negro, the argument is still made that the Negro is ignorant,. the Negro is illiterate, the Negro is venal, the Negro is inferior; and, therefore, for the preservation of civilized government in the South, he must be debarred from the polls. This argument does not take into account the fact that the restrictions are not against ignorance, illiteracy and venality, because by the very practices by which intelligent, decent Negroes are debarred, ignorant and illiterate white men are included.

Is this pronounced desire on the part of the South for an enlightened franchise sincere, and what has been the result of these practices during the past forty years? What has been the effect socially; intellectually and politically, on the South? In all three of these vital phases of life the South is, of all sections of the country, at the bottom. Socially, it is that section of the country where public opinion allows it to remain the only spot in the civilized world no, more than that, we may count in the blackest spots of Africa and the most unfrequented islands of the sea it is a section where public opinion allows it to remain the only spot on the earth where a human being may be publicly burned at the stake.

And what about its intellectual and political life? As to intellectual life I can do nothing better than quote from Mr. H. L. Mencken, himself a Southerner. In speaking of the intellectual life of the South, Mr. Mencken says:

"It is, indeed, amazing to contemplate so vast a vacuity. One thinks of the interstellar spaces, of the colossal reaches of the now mythical ether. One could throw into the South France, Germany and Italy, and still have room for the British Isles. And yet, for all its size and all its wealth and all the 'progress' it babbles of, it is almost as sterile, artistically, intellectually, culturally, as the Sahara Desert. . . If the whole of the late Confederacy were to be engulfed by a tidal wave tomorrow, the effect on the civilized minority of men in the world would be but little greater than that of a flood on the Yang tse kiang. It would be impossible in all history to match so complete a drying up of a civilization. In that section there is not a single poet, not a serious historian, a creditable composer, not a critic good or bad, not a dramatist dead or alive."

In a word, it may be said that this whole section where, at the cost of the defiance of the Constitution, the perversion of law, stultification of men's consciousness, injustice and violence upon a weaker group, the "purity" of the ballot has been preserved and the right to vote restricted to only lineal survivors of Lothrop Stoddard's mystical Nordic supermen that intellectually it is dead and politically it is rotten.

If this experiment in super democracy had resulted in one-hundredth of what was promised, there might be justification for it, but the result has been to make the South a section not only which Negroes are denied the right to vote, but one in which white men dare not express their honest political opinions. Talk about political corruption through the buying of votes, here is political corruption which makes a white man fear to express a divergent political opinion. The actual and total result of this practice has been not only the disfranchisement of the Negro but the disenfranchisement of the white man. The figures which I quoted a few moments ago prove that not only Negroes are denied the right vote but that white men fail to exercise it; and the latter condition is directly dependent upon the former.

The whole condition is intolerable and should be abolished. It has failed to justify itself even upon the grounds which it claimed made it necessary. Its results and its tendencies make it more dangerous and more damaging than anything which might result from an ignorant and illiterate electorate. How this iniquity might be abolished is, however, another story.

I said that I did not intend to present this subject either anti-South or pro-Negro, and I repeat that I have not wished to speak with anything that approached bitterness toward the South.

Indeed, I consider the condition of the South unfortunate, more than unfortunate. The South is in a state of superstition which makes it see ghosts and bogymen, ghosts which are the creation of its own mental processes.

With a free vote in the South the specter of Negro domination would vanish into thin air. There would naturally follow a breaking up of the South into two parties. There would be political light, political discussion, the right to differences of opinion, and the Negro vote would naturally divide itself. No other procedure would be probable. The idea of a solid party, a minority party at that, is inconceivable.

But perhaps the South will not see the light. Then, I believe, in the interest of the whole country, steps should be taken to compel compliance with the Constitution, and that should be done through the enforcement of the Fourteenth Amendment, which calls for a reduction in representation in proportion to the number of citizens in any state denied the right to vote.

And now I cannot sit down after all without saying one word for the group of which I am a member.

The Negro in the matter of the ballot demands only that he should be given the right as an American citizen to vote under the. identical qualifications required of other citizens. He cares not how high those qualifications are made whether they include the ability to read and write, or the possession of five hundred dollars, or a knowledge of the Einstein Theory just so long as these qualifications are impartially demanded of white men and black men.

In this controversy over which have been waged battles of words and battles of blood, where does the Negro himself stand?

The Negro in the matter of the ballot demands only that he be given his right as an American citizen. He is justified in making this demand because of his undoubted Americanism, an Americanism which began when he first set foot on the shores of this country more than three hundred years ago, antedating even the Pilgrim Fathers; an Americanism which has woven him into the woof and warp of the country and which has impelled him to play his part in every war in which the country has been engaged, from the Revolution down to the late World War.

Through his whole history in this country he has worked with patience; and in spite of discouragement he has never turned his back on the light. Whatever may be his shortcomings, however slow may have been his progress, however disappointing may have been his achievements, he has never consciously sought the backward path. He has always kept his face to the light and continued to struggle forward and upward in spite of obstacles, making his humble contributions to the common prosperity and glory of our land. And it is his land. With conscious pride the Negro say:

> *"This land is ours by right of birth,*
> *This land is ours by right of toil;*
> *We helped to turn its virgin earth,*
> *Our sweat is in its fruitful soil.*

> *"Where once the tangled forest stood,*
> *Where flourished once rank weed and thorn,*
> *Behold the path traced, peaceful wood,*
> *The cotton white, the yellow corn.*

"To gain these fruits that have been earned,
To hold these fields that have been won,
Our arms have strained, our backs have burned
Bent bare beneath a ruthless sun.

"That banner which is now the type
Of victory on field. and flood
Remember, its first crimson stripe
Was dyed by Attucks' willing blood.

"And never yet has come the cry
When that fair flag has been assailed
For men to do, for men to die,
That we have faltered or have failed."

The Negro stands as the supreme test of the civilization. Christianity and the common decency of the American people. It is upon the answer demanded of America today by the Negro that there depends the fulfillment or the failure of democracy in America. I believe that that answer will be the right and just answer. I believe that the spirit in which American democracy was founded; though often turned aside and often thwarted; can never be defeated or destroyed but that ultimately it will triumph.

If American democracy cannot stand the test of giving to any citizen who measures up to the qualifications required of others the full rights and privileges of American citizenship, then we had just as well abandon that democracy in name as in deed. If the Constitution of the United States cannot extend the arm of protection around the weakest and humblest of American citizens as around the strongest and proudest, then it is not worth the paper it is written on.

Whence and Whiter

I presume the reason I have been invited to come back to Paine College and talk to you today, after thirty years of fighting and climbing, until I have gained some laurels and reached the top of my calling, is that you may have the privilege of reading some pages out of my book of experience. As I stand here today in this beautiful chapel I can scarcely realize that more than three decades have passed since I walked, with others, from the old remodeled horse stables, which, in those days, served as dormitories and classrooms on this campus, down to old Trinity to the commencement exercise, and dreamed great dreams as I received my diploma from the hands of the lovable, lamented George Williams Walker. I little knew then to what I was going, when I stepped forth that day, eager, happy and hopeful, into the great world to make a name for myself. If I had known what awaited me perhaps I would have shrunk back aghast. However, I can say with all modesty, I have fought bravely, I have kept the faith fairly well, and I have weathered the many storms and fierce gales of spars and sails. And, today I have returned to the home port, like some grizzled and weather-beaten captain, to tell you something of the hardships and dangers of the voyage which you are about to begin. I warn you that this is truly the commencement of life for you. Those years you have spent here have been merely years of training for the real battles that are now before you. So I am asking you two vital questions, whence and whither? I myself shall try to answer my question whence? But I cannot answer the question whither? I can only give you some directions, which may help you on the way, while the passing years shall give answer to that question, whither?

Whence?

To every thoughtful and aspiring young Negro man and woman, whence are we as a race? Is an all-important question; for you must understand the whence of your race in order to know clearly whither you may carry it, as you journey onward.

In the beginning, let me emphasize the fact that there are many embarrassments and annoyances, but no disgrace in being a Negro. As Negroes, we may be as proud of our origin as any other race. For many years Africa, the country whence the Negro came, has been called the "dark continent," because the white world knew little or nothing of it. But it has been recently discovered that Africa is a land as rich n its ancient civilization and culture as it is in its present wealth of minerals, forests, and fertile fields. It is becoming well-known that Africa had evolved and developed a culture and civilization of its own which compares favorably with the famous civilizations of ancient Asia and Europe.

Professor George Reisner of Harvard University has been conducting researches in the Sudan. He states that his researches have established that the culture of Ethiopia stood as an outpost of Egyptian civilization in middle Africa, that in the art of the Ethiopian a Greek influence obtained, and, that the invention of a script of their own was evidence that the Ethiopians were a people of genius. The glory and grandeur that was Egypt's more than three thousand years ago was disclosed recently when the tomb of King Tut-Ankh-Amen was located and opened in the Valley of the Kings' Tombs.

Since the discoveries of the former greatness of the ancient Egyptians and Ethiopians, it has suddenly been discovered that they were not Negroes. The same professor Reisner says: "The Ethiopians are not and were not African Negroes." He describes them as "dark races in which brown prevailed." I fear the learned professor would have a hard time convincing his own people that the "dark, colored races in which brown prevails" in this country are not Negroes. Happily, you cannot sponge out ethnological facts with the bitter waters of race prejudice. The Negro has been called "Sons of Ham," "African," and "Ethiopian" in scornful derision for all these years, and now it is too late to try to make him something else when it is discovered that these designation link him with the greatest civilizations of the past. As Negroes, therefore, we claim kinship with the ancient Ethiopians and Egyptians, and all colored races, and share the greatness and glory of their achievements and history.

I was looking recently at some drawings of Egyptian kings and queens. Any unprejudiced observer would decide from those drawings that they were at least Negroid; for they have the lips, noses and hair which are characteristic of the Negro. The, King Tut-Ankh-Amen claimed Amenhotep III as his father. Dr. Alexander Francis Chamberlain of Clark University, Worcester, Massachusetts, show that this king had a strain of Negro blood. In his book, "The Contribution of the Negro to Human Civilization," we read: "The contributions of the Negro to human civilizations are innumerable and immemorial. Let us first get some glimpses of him, chiefly as an individual, in contact with the hosts of other cultures than his own. Ancient Egypt knew a few of the mighty Pharaohs. Nefertari, the famous queen of Aahmes, the King of Egypt, who drove the Hyksos from the land and founded the Eighteenth Dynasty (ca. 1700 B.C.), was a Negress of great beauty, strong personality and remarkable administrative ability. She was for years associated in the government with her son, Amenhotep I, who succeeded his father. Queen Nefertari was highly venerated, and many monuments were erected in her honor; she was venerated as 'ancestress and founder of the Eighteenth Dynasty' and styled 'the wife of God Ammon,' etc. Another strain of Negro blood came into the line of the Pharaohs with Mut-em-ua, wife of Thothmes IV, whose son, Amenhotep III, had a Negroid physiognomy." So the evidence is conclusive that we are kin to the planners and builders of the great palaces of Baalbec, Karnak, Luxor, ancient Memphis, the pyramids, and the Sphinx.

The question has often been asked why the Negro can so easily adapt himself to present day civilization, and can compete on terms of equality with other races in every walk of life. The answer is what scientists call atavism, which is defined as intermittent heredity, reversion to an ancestral type or trait. Atavism explains why the Negro race has produced a Coleridge-Taylor and a Harry Burleigh in music, a Pushkin, Dumas, Dunbar and DuBois in literature, a Frederick Douglass and Robert Brown Elliott in statescraft, a Booker T. Washington and Lucy Laney in education, a Price, Holsey and Turner in oratory, a Ned Gourdin, Harry West and Jack Johnson in athletics. It is a harking back of the race to the centuries of civilization and culture of its great ancestors. Atavism explains why the race in this country has made a progress which, as President Harding wrote a great convention of Negroes the other day: "has been one of the wonders of civilization's advance." It gives the reason why the Negro race has acquired, in the short space of the sixty years since its emancipation in this country, twenty-two millions of acres of land, six hundred thousand homes, forty-five thousand churches, and operates seventy-eight banks, a hundred insurance companies, besides seventy thousand other business enterprises, with a capital of one hundred and fifty million dollars.

This is the answer that history and learning give to the question of the whence? of the Negro race. We are justly proud.

But whither?

I say to you today that our past obligates us to high endeavor for the future. We, you and I, must "carry on" for the race, until we have shown to our critics we are worthy descendants of ancient great sires. Professor Kamerer, a Viennese biologist, makes the statement that "the skill, mental and physical, acquired by men and animals during their lives can be handed down to posterity." If this statement is true, and if the demonstration offered by this Austrian student is accepted by the scientists of Cambridge University, England, then we have as a heritage all the culture and skill and civilization of the past ages of our ancestors of Egypt and Ethiopia. This points us to the whither of the race. But I warn you that the race will go only so far as its individual members go. Therefore, the future of the race is in the keeping of such as you who hear me today.

Your coming in this institution, and spending years of toilsome study and privation preparing for your future activities, may be taken as indicative of your determination to help lift the race up to and beyond the heights which it once attained. I wish to mention a few of the qualities which are necessary for you in this great mission of racial renaissance.

First, you must have the God consciousness. I mean, you must realize that there is a God, and that he governs and guides you, directs, leads and protects you, in all of your ways. A constant study of the lives of men and women who have lived worthily, and have lifted the human race, convinces me that young men and women cannot accomplish much which will add to the sum total of human and racial betterment without a deep consciousness of the fact that God is with them. The stories of the lives of youthful Joseph in Egypt, and the early struggles of David, the poet-king of Israel, are gripping and instructive because of the constant emphasis laid upon the God consciousness. I cannot lay too much stress upon the thought that you cannot get along without God, and do anything of permanent value in the great world into which you are going.

I was reading recently a story of the life of Henry Ford, the automobile manufacturer, written by William L. Stidger, who knows him well. He tells of the simple faith of this great captain of industry. He believes in God and reads his Bible daily. Mr. Stidger says, when he asked Mr. Ford what part of the teachings of Jesus he liked best and thought most applicable to life, he replied, "The Sermon on the Mount." When he asked him, "Do you try to run your industry by the Sermon on the Mount?" he replied, "I do. It is our constitution. And it works." He was reminded during the interview, that Bishop Quayle had said of the late John Burroughs, the famous naturalist, and the intimate friend of Ford, "He knew the garden but never found the Gardener," he replied, "yes. That was too bad. It doesn't seem possible that one could fail to find the Gardener, with all of these beautiful things and all of these great things about us. It is too bad that Burroughs never found the Gardener."

In the beginning of your journey in search of the whither in the world, God's great garden, I pray you be sure to find the Gardener first. It will simplify greatly your search, and lighten the burdens of the way. Then, you must have thorough preparation.

You have finished a specified course of study here under the direction of teachers, but you have merely been learning how to make thorough preparation for real life. You have merely gotten the rudiments, but you have been trained to think clearly and systematically. If you are wise, you will be adding daily to your little store through all the coming years, by constant reading, and pondering, and storing the shelves of memory against the time of need. Do not get the idea that you are thoroughly prepared for the fierce conflicts which await you by what you have learned here. I recall this incident which happened some years ago at a General Conference of our church. During a sharp parliamentary battle over a question of procedure, a delegate was busily hunting up the mooted point in his parliamentary manual. The late Dr. Bonner laughingly said to him: "You haven't time to learn it now, son. You should have known it." That is the thought I am trying to impress. You must be thoroughly prepared when the time comes, by knowing the thing which you are called upon suddenly to say or do. Although I have been away from this institution more than thirty years, I read and study more now than I did while I was a student here. Unceasing acquisition of information and knowledge is the only sure path to the whither of wealth, or honor, or service. Do not be envious of those who excel you in ability or attainments or knowledge. Keep after them.

Also, you must have undaunted courage.

When I speak of courage I mean that "quality of mind which meets danger or opposition with intrepidity, calmness and firmness. Courage is of the intellect and will, and may be possessed in the highest degree by those who are constitutionally timid." Courage is stoutness of heart, self-reliance, red-bloodedness of spirit. As you go forward in life you will meet with ostracism on account of your race and color. You will encounter envy on account of your mental and material possessions. You will have to grapple with the green-eyed monster, jealousy, because of your achievements and popularity. You will meet ingratitude, that meanest of all sins, from those for whom you have done most and suffered most. You will be slandered by open and secret foes. There will be many hours of deep despondency, when you will debate whether it is worth while to continue to struggle and sacrifice for others. It is then you will need unfaltering courage to nerve your arm and strengthen your soul to march onward. But remember only those hearts of oak ever accomplish anything worth while. Some one has well said: "Everywhere and at all times, the men who have had definite convictions upon the great issues, and have courageously chosen righteousness, are the men who have directed the course of nations."

Also, you must have the ability to go the route morally.

When I say "the route," I am using a phrase used by baseball writers, meaning the ability to last through the entire game. One of the greatest assets which a young man or woman can possess on leaving school is a high moral standard—an acute sense of moral values. And this equipment must be able to stand the wear and tear of ever-changing circumstances and condition. You must not think that you can select the Commandments which you will keep and reject those which you do not like. The moral code of mankind, crystallized into the Ten Commandments by Moses, is the result of the reasoned experience of men who lived ages before Moses. Observation and experience convinced thoughtful men long ages ago that it is harmful to the individual, as well as to the community, to lie, to steal, to kill, and to commit adultery. I wish to emphasize that it is just as immoral to steal the good name of folks whom you do not like as it is to steal their goods. It is just as immoral to destroy the reputation and hinder the progress of those whom you envy as it is to take their lives.

I have in mind some brilliant men, whose great intellects gave promise, through their young manhood, of lives of usefulness and eminence, but they could not go the route morally, and today they are wrecks along the shore, and are but sad memories to their friends. Whatever the temptation to weaken morally as the years pass, and you reach places of authority and power, resolve to play the game through without faltering. My observation is that an immoral man or woman in a position of responsibility and power and, perhaps, possessed of wealth, and the influence which wealth carries with it, is a curse to every young person with whom they come in contact. Such persons contaminate the moral atmosphere and lower the moral temperature wherever they go.

Take along with you also as you go from here a great loyalty to some high vision and for some true friendship. You go out to a race poor, despised and ostracized. Get the vision of service. Resolve to live for them, not for yourself. "In a very deep and true sense it is wheat a man sees that either makes or unmakes him. The effect of vision upon character and service is transforming. It elevates or debases, according to its qualities. Whether a man grovels or soars, whether he remains in the realm of animalism or rises into the spiritual, and lives in the high places of the Sons of God, is determined by his seeing." The red-haired, dreamy-eyed shepherd boy, David, because Israel's hero-king because he was possessed of such a loyalty to his vision and friendship. One can not read of the bonds which bound him to his royal-souled friend, Jonathan, and of his sublime loyalty to his vision of service to his race, without being mightily impressed with the beauty of such a nature. You can do nothing worth while in this great world unless you are a dreamer of great dreams. You will never amount to much unless you are loyal to your dreams. When I speak of loyalty to friends I do not mean partners in crime, nor associates in questionable transaction, I mean loyalty to some true, high-thinking person whom you have discovered during your school days here. You will not mean much to aspiring young men and women as you rise in the world unless they find you loyal to your friends. The man or woman who uses friends as stepping stones on which to rise, or as tools with which to attain some purpose or desired end, and then throws them aside like a worn-out garment after the thing sought has been obtained, will reap an abundant harvest of hate and contempt as people learn of the baseness of their natures, and will die with none so poor to do them reverence.

Take with you reverence for law and authority.

Do not get the idea that you are above all authority and may break laws or disobey rules and regulations, however high you may climb in the world. Remember the man in authority who advises others to break laws or to disrespect others in authority is undermining his own authority. Only those who reverence law and authority have any business ruling over others. Only such persons can successfully rule men and women. People may fear the lawless, but will never love nor respect them. It matters not what you may think of the law or what may be your estimate of those placed over you, I counsel you to revere the law and bow to authority.

Further, let me urge you to be economical and thrifty. Do not spend every cent you lay your hands upon. If you know you are loose-fingered, tie your hands or tie your money in some way. Edison, the great electric wizard, had to do that. Recently, he told the story of taking a perfected carbon transmitter to Philadelphia in the hope of selling it for $5,000, which would just about pay his debts. The directors asked him if $100,000 would buy the transmitter. He was so astonished that he remained silent for a moment, and they inquired if they had offered enough. "The price is all right," said Edison, "yes, that's all right. But on condition that you pay me it at the rate of $7,500 a year. If you paid it to me all at once I'd probably put it into some fool invention and lose every cent of it." Store some of your wages or salary where you can not squander them. Savings banks or real estate are safe places for money.

And now a last word about race prejudice. You will meet it at every turn and everywhere you go. Sad to say, it is growing steadily. Your color will be against you in almost every field of activity. Do not deceive yourselves into believing that anywhere in this country you will escape this curse of the age. Often it will be veiled and stealthy. Frequently, it will walk openly and unafraid, but it will be the same illogical and unreasoning thing. Learn to expect it, and face it, and conquer it. You may console yourselves, however, with the fact that the Negro race is not the only race which suffers from race prejudice. Deport yourselves in such a gentle and quiet and confident and unassuming manner that you will make those ashamed who practice it. Wherever you go, let people learn that a colored skin can cover just as much culture and refinement and decency as any other kind of skin. Also, I exhort you, try to make friends with and command the respect of those with whom you live. Do not depend upon friends who are far away. Whatever the color of the people with whom you deal daily, they will respect refinement, modesty, integrity, scrupulous honesty, industry, and money.

If you equip yourselves with the qualities which I have outlined in this talk, you will surely reach the whither you seek in the great world into which you are going and you will take the race with you. Some of you will aspire to climb the mountain of fame and honor and responsibility, you may succeed in doing so. Listen to the expression of the thoughts of one who has climbed to the top of that mountain, Lloyd George, perhaps the most noted Englishman of today. Speaking in the Methodist church of his boyhood home, he said: "Mr. Davies has told you that I have climbed the mountain of fame, responsibility, and honor, and in a sense that is true; but, dear friends, let me assure you that the mountain is not an ideal place for any of us. There isn't much peace there, no real rest and comfort. The higher you climb, the colder it becomes. How exposed and bleak it is! You are at the mercy of the storm and tempest. The wind makes sport of you. On the mountain a man feels lonely. Often thick mists envelop him, and he misses his way: he can hardly see a yard ahead. What is the good of a telescope in the mist? When a person thinks he is on the right path, suddenly he comes to a part where he can go no farther, and a deep chasm opens before him. He retraces his steps and makes an effort to regain the path from which he strayed. Yes, that is the lot of the man who attempts to climb the mountain."

His experience is the experience of all of us who have climbed the mountain. Still youth will aspire to climb the mountain, and it is well that it should be thus. Else what would mankind do for leaders? Whether you are to essay climbing the mountain, or plan to serve the race in the quiet paths which lie at the base of the mountain, always bear in mind:

> "Wherever's a will there's a way, my lad,
>   If the will have the strength to serve;
> But the goal is not reached in a day, my lad,
>   And the winning takes patience and nerve.
> It's a long, long way and a hard, hard road,
>   And a lifetime is hardly enough;
>   But you'll win if you stick
>   To the roadway you pick
> And your heart is the right kind of stuff.
>
> "Oh, a bit of a song will help, my lad,
>   And a grin will ease many a pain.
> The coward goes down with a yelp, my lad,
>   Get up and go at them again.
> It's a long, long way and a hard, hard road
> To the thing that you're longing to do,
>   And the key to the game
>   Is to stick to your aim,
> And the courage will carry you through.
>
> "Aye, many a path leads out, my lad,
>   From the road to the thing you want,
> And they're pleasant to travel, no doubt, my lad,
>   And it's hard to know that you can't.
> It's a long, long way and a hard, hard road
>   And you haven't the time to rest,
>   So pick up your load
>   And stick to your road;
> You will win, if you give it your best."

PROFILE OF THE SPEAKERS

Jupiter Hammon
Poet and Preacher
(1711–1806)

Born into slavery at Lloyd Manor on Long Island, New York, Hammon was educated by the Anglican Church and developed a talent for reading and writing at a young age. In 1761, his poem "An Evening Thought: Salvation by Christ, with Penitential Cries" was published as a broadside, making Hammon the first Black published author in American history. During the Revolutionary War, he composed "An Address to Miss Phillis Wheatley," which appeared in print eighteen years after his debut. In 1786, at the inaugural assembly of the African Society in New York City, Hammon delivered a speech titled "Address to the Negroes in the State of New York." At 76 years old, still enslaved by the Lloyd family, he affirmed his faith in heavenly salvation and stated his hope for the freedom of future generations. He lived an astounding life, inspiring many and defying his captivity in subtle acts of resistance. Although his work is limited—four poems and four prose pieces—Hammon displayed a mastery of Christian theology and poetic form while pursuing a message of racial uplift and moral righteousness. Buried in an unmarked grave, enslaved for the entirety of his life on earth, Jupiter Hammon remains an insurmountable force in American history and a pioneer of African American literature.

Maria W. Stewart
Teacher, Journalist, Abolitionist, and Women's Rights Activist
(1803–1879)

Born Maria Miller to free African American parents in Hartford, Connecticut, she was orphaned at the age of three and sent to live with a local minister as an indentured servant. She was educated at Sabbath School and married James W. Stewart, a merchant, in 1826. Following his death in 1829, she was excluded from his will and left to fend for herself. Around this time, she began lecturing to audiences of men and women of all races. She was the first known African American woman to lecture publicly on women's rights, religion, and abolition, publishing some of her speeches and meditations in pamphlets with the help of William Lloyd Garrison's *The Liberator.* After a poorly-received speech at Boston's African Masonic Lodge, Stewart abandoned lecturing to move to New York City and later Washington, D.C., where she found work as a schoolteacher and head matron of Freedmen's Hospital.

Theodore S. Wright
Minister and Abolitionist
(1797–1847)

Born in Providence, Rhode Island, he moved with his family to New York as a boy. First educated at the African Free School, Wright gained admittance to the American Institute at age 28, only the second Black man to do so. He graduated from the seminary and was appointed minister of New York's First Colored Presbyterian Church around 1833. He founded the American Anti-Slavery Society and the American and Foreign Anti-Slavery Society, spoke at the national Colored Convention in 1837, and conducted a stop along the Underground Railroad at his home on West Broadway. By the end of his life, he supported Henry Highland Garnet's proposal for a violent uprising of slaves in the South, facing opposition by Frederick Douglass and others at the 1843 National Negro convention in Buffalo. In "Prejudice Against the Colored Man," a speech he gave at the 1837 New York Anti-Slavery Society in Utica, Wright addresses the scourge of racism faced by free Blacks living in the North.

Samuel H. Davis
Educator, Pastor, and, Civil Rights Leader
(1810–?)

Born in Temple Mills, Maine, Davis studied at Oberlin College in Ohio and lived briefly in Windsor, Canada. Returning to the United States, he settled in Buffalo, where he taught at a school for African Americans and served as pastor of the Michigan Street Baptist Church. The church, which Davis largely built himself, was a stop along the Underground Railroad. From August 15th to 19th, 1843, Davis chaired the National Convention of Colored Citizens of America, which featured speeches from Reverend Henry Garnet, Frederick Douglass, and Davis himself. His speech, titled "We Must Assert Our Rightful Claims and Plead Our Own Cause" encouraged African Americans to "make known (their) wrongs to the world and to (their) oppressors."

Henry Highland Garnet
Minister, Orator, and Abolitionist
(1815–1882)

Born into slavery, Garnet escaped with his family to Wilmington, Delaware in 1824 and were led north by Underground Railroad stationmaster Thomas Garrett. From 1826 to 1833, Garnet studied at the African Free School in New York City, where he first became an abolitionist. He cofounded the Garrison Literary and Benevolent Association with classmates William H. Day and David Ruggles in 1834 before moving to Troy and completing his education at the Oneida Institute. Garnet married Julia Williams in 1841 and became pastor of the Liberty Street Presbyterian Church the following year. In Troy, he published a prominent abolitionist newspaper and supported the growing temperance movement, gaining a reputation as a leading African American political activist. In 1843, he delivered his speech "Call to Rebellion," in which he stated his support for armed insurrection among the enslaved population in the American south. Deemed too radical by such figures as William Lloyd Garrison and Frederick Douglass, Garnet eventually founded the African Civilization Society and encouraged African Americans to emigrate from the United States and adopt the principles of Black nationalism. This movement ended with the Civil War, during which Garnet worked to recruit for the United States Colored Troops and became the first black minister to preach at the Capitol. He spent his final years in Pittsburgh and New York before moving to Liberia for the last months of his life. There, he received a state funeral as U. S. Ambassador and was buried in the capital of Monrovia.

Frederick Douglass
Abolitionist, Writer, Statesman, and Social Reformer
(1818–1895)

Born in Maryland, he escaped slavery at the age of twenty with the help of his future wife Anna Murray Douglass, a free Black woman from Baltimore. He made his way through Delaware, Philadelphia, and New York City—where he married Murray—before settling in New Bedford, Massachusetts. In New England, he connected with the influential abolitionist community and joined the African Methodist Episcopal Zion Church, a historically Black denomination which counted Sojourner Truth and Harriet Tubman among its members. In 1839, Douglass became a preacher and began his career as a captivating orator on religious, social, and political matters. He met William Lloyd Garrison, publisher of anti-slavery newspaper *The Liberator*, in 1841, and was deeply moved by his passionate abolitionism. As Douglass' reputation and influence grew, he traveled across the country and eventually to Ireland and Great Britain to advocate on behalf of the American abolitionist movement, winning countless people over to the leading moral cause of the nineteenth century. He was often accosted during his speeches and was badly beaten at least once by a violent mob. His autobiography, *Narrative of the Life of Frederick Douglass, an American Slave* (1845) was an immediate bestseller that detailed Douglass' life in and escape from slavery, providing readers a firsthand description of the cruelties of the southern plantation system. Towards the end of his life, he became a fierce advocate for women's rights and was the first Black man to be nominated for Vice President on the Equal Rights Party ticket, alongside Presidential candidate Victoria Woodhull. Arguably one of the most influential Americans of all time, Douglass led a life dedicated to democracy and racial equality.

Lucy Stanton
Abolitionist and Feminist
(1831–1910)

Born free, Stanton was raised by her mother, Margaret, and stepfather, an Ohio abolitionist named John Brown. In 1846, Stanton enrolled at Oberlin College, where she graduated with a degree in literature in 1849. Her graduation speech, "A Plea for the Oppressed," is a powerful call for abolition written in response to the impending passage of the 1850 Fugitive Slave Act. In 1852, Stanton married Oberlin graduate William H. Day, whom she would assist as editor of Cleveland's pioneering Black newspaper *The Aliened American*. In 1858, shortly after their daughter's birth, Day abandoned his family for England, forcing Stanton to raise Florence alone. While working as a seamstress, Stanton—who divorced Day in 1872—continued her activism and traveled to Georgia and Mississippi on behalf of the Freedmen's Aid Society to teach newly freed slaves. She married Levi Sessions in 1878 and moved with him to Tennessee, where she was active as a member of the Women's Relief Corps, the Women's Christian Temperance Union, and the African Methodist Episcopal Church. In 1904, having moved to Los Angeles, Stanton founded the Sojourner Truth Industrial Club and fought for the rights of working Black women arriving in the American West.

Jermain Wesley Loguen
Abolitionist and Bishop
(1813–1872)

Born into slavery in Davidson County, Tennessee, he escaped with his mother at 21 years old along the Underground Railroad to Canada. Loguen studied at the Oneida Institute and opened schools for Black students in Utica and Syracuse. At his home in Syracuse, Loguen and his wife Caroline housed fugitive slaves in a specially built chamber, feeding and clothing them while working to find employment for those who chose to settle nearby. In 1851, Loguen was involved in the high-profile rescue of William Henry, a former slave and cooper imprisoned under the Fugitive Slave Act in Syracuse. Accused of assaulting a federal marshal, Loguen briefly fled to Canada before ensuring that he would be safe upon his return home. A man of faith, Loguen was appointed bishop of the African Methodist Episcopal Zion Church in 1868. His speech "I Won't Obey the Fugitive Slave Law" was given on October 4, 1850 during a demonstration at Syracuse's city hall.

Sojourner Truth
Abolitionist, Feminist and Orator
(1797–1883)

Born into slavery in Swartekill, New York, her given name was Isabella Baumfree. Raised alongside twelve children, her first language was Dutch. She was sold several times until ending up at the West Park home of John Dumont, who beat and raped her frequently. Although New York began abolishing slavery in 1799, the process was drawn out until at least 1827. A year prior, Truth, now married with five children, escaped with her infant Sophia, making the impossible decision to leave the rest of her family behind. She found safety with the Van Wagenen family in New Paltz, who helped her file suit against Dumont for illegally selling her five-year-old, Peter, to a man in Alabama. She was reunited her son in 1828, making her one of the first Black women to win a court case against a white man. While living with the Van Wagenen's, she had a profound religious experience, and in 1843 converted to Methodism and took the name Sojourner Truth. While living in Florence, Massachusetts, Truth met William Lloyd Garrison, Frederick Douglass, and David Ruggles, who encouraged her to give her first anti-slavery speech in 1844. In 1850, Garrison published her memoir *The Narrative of Sojourner Truth: A Northern Slave*. The following year, at the Ohio Women's Rights Convention in Akron, Ohio, Truth gave her legendary "Ain't I a Woman?" speech, a fiery oration uniting the causes of abolition, labor, and women's rights. Over the next several decades, she gave countless speeches, recruited Black troops for the Union Army, and attempted to gain land grants for formerly enslaved people around the country.

Frances Ellen Watkins Harper
Abolitionist, Suffragist, Poet, and Novelist
(1825–1911)

Born free in Baltimore, Maryland, Harper became one of the first
women of color to publish a work of literature in the United States
when her debut poetry collection *Forest Leaves* appeared in 1845. In
1850, she began to teach sewing at Union Seminary in Columbus, Ohio.
The following year, alongside chairman of the Pennsylvania Abolition
Society William Still, she began working as an abolitionist in earnest,
helping slaves escape to Canada along the Underground Railroad. In
1854, having established herself as a prominent public speaker and
political activist, Harper published *Poems on Miscellaneous Subjects*, a
resounding critical and commercial success. Over the course of her life,
Harper founded and participated in several progressive organizations,
including the Women's Christian Temperance Union and the National
Association of Colored Women. At the age of sixty-seven, Harper
published *Iola Leroy, or Shadows Uplifted*, becoming one of the first
African American women to publish a novel.

Henry McNeal Turner
Minister, Bishop and Politician
(1834–1915)

Born into a free family in Newberry, South Carolina, Turner learned to read and write as a boy before receiving his preacher's license from the Methodist Church at 19 years old. After working as a traveling evangelist for several years, he moved with his wife Eliza and their young children to St. Louis, Missouri. He was ordained a minister of the African Methodist Episcopal Church, America's first independent Black denomination. During the Civil War, Turner organized Company B of the First United States Colored Troops and served as a chaplain. Towards the end of the war, during which his unit saw intense combat, Turner resigned from the army to devote himself to politics and evangelism. Heavily involved with Republican politics during Reconstruction, he was appointed postmaster of Macon by the Freedmen's Bureau in 1869. For just two months, beginning in July 1868, Turner served as an elected representative of the state of Georgia before the newly Democratic legislature expelled all Black members. His speech "I Claim the Rights of a Man" was given on September 3, 1868 in response to the expulsion on the floor of the legislature. As he witnessed the resurgence of disenfranchisement and violence throughout the South, Turner became an outspoken advocate for Black nationalism and the migration of Black Americans to Africa.

Ferdinand L. Barnett
Journalist, Activist and Lawyer
(1852–1936)

Born in Nashville, he fled with his mother and father to Windsor, Ontario in 1859. Although his father, a blacksmith, had legally purchased his family's freedom the year of Ferdinand's birth, he feared they would be captured under the Fugitive Slave Act, which allowed slave catchers to kidnap Black people with impunity, regardless of legal status. In 1869, they settled in Chicago, where Ferdinand graduated from Union College of Law and was admitted to the Illinois bar in 1878. That same year, the first edition of the *Conservator*, a radical Black newspaper cofounded by Barnett, appeared in print. As a delegate to the 1879 National Conference of Colored Men in his hometown of Nashville, he gave a highly regarded speech on equality in education, earning a national reputation as a leading African American political figure. In 1893, he took on anti-lynching activist Ida B. Wells' libel case against the *Memphis Commercial*. Although it was eventually dropped, Wells and Barnett—a widower—married two years later. They raised four children together in Chicago, where Barnett would be appointed the first Black assistant state's attorney in 1896. He remained active in Republican politics throughout his life and was nominated for a judgeship in 1906, losing the election by just over 300 votes.

Lucy E. Parsons
Labor Organizer, Anarcho-Communist, and Radical Socialist
(1851–1942)

Born into slavery in West Virginia, Parsons and her family were taken to Texas by their master in 1863. There, she worked as a seamstress and cook, briefly married a former slave, and lost a child during birth. Lucy married Albert Parsons, a former Confederate cavalryman, in 1871 before being forced to flee to Chicago on account of their interracial relationship. In Illinois, Lucy and Albert became high profile anarchist organizers and activists who used revolutionary tactics and journalism to fight for the rights of women, people of color, prisoners, and the poor. Lucy wrote for *The Socialist* and *The Alarm*, the latter being the journal of the International Working People's Association she founded with her husband in 1883. In 1886, Albert, accused of conspiring in the Haymarket Riot, was arrested, tried, and executed for his participation in the campaign for an eight-hour workday. Despite this tragic loss, Parsons continued to write and speak publicly, finding publication in *Les Temps Nouveaux* and participating in events with such figures as William Morris and Peter Kropotkin. In 1905, Parsons helped found the Industrial Workers of the World and became editor of the *Liberator* in Chicago. In her later years, Parsons became more active in communist-led organizations, including the International Labor Defense, and may have joined the Communist Party herself in 1939. She continued to speak publicly into her eighties.

Ida B. Wells
Investigative Journalist and Civil Rights Activist
(1862–1931)

Born into slavery in Holly Springs, Mississippi, Wells was freed with her family following the Emancipation Proclamation of 1863. Having lost both parents to the 1878 yellow fever epidemic, she moved with her siblings to Memphis, Tennessee to work as a teacher. As co-owner of the *Memphis Free Speech and Headlight*, Wells gained a reputation for her powerful reports on lynching and racial segregation. In 1892, a white mob attacked the newspaper's office, destroying the building and everything inside. Undeterred, she continued documenting the widespread practice of lynching in the American South, publishing her pamphlet *Southern Horrors* later that same year. In 1895, Wells published *The Red Record*, a more extensive account of the history of lynching and the lives of Black Americans in the South in the years following emancipation. Wells married attorney Ferdinand L. Barrett in Chicago in June 1895, having worked alongside him for several years as editor of pioneering Black newspaper *The Chicago Conservator*. Together, they raised two children from Barnett's previous marriage and four children of their own, adding motherhood to Wells' extensive responsibilities. This inspired her to establish Chicago's first kindergarten for Black children at the Bethel AME Church. She worked tirelessly as an organizer and activist throughout her life, often disagreeing with such figures as W. E. B. Du Bois, who initially excluded her from the list of the NAACP's founders.

Anna J. Cooper
Speaker, Activist, Scholar, Author and Educator
(1858–1964)

Born into slavery in Raleigh, North Carolina, Cooper received a scholarship in 1868 to attend Saint Augustine's Normal School and Collegiate Institute, where she excelled in liberal arts and the sciences alike. After her husband's death, Cooper graduated from Oberlin College with her B.A. and later her M.A. in Mathematics. In 1892, then living in Washington, D.C., Cooper cofounded the Colored Women's League with Ida B. Wells, Charlotte Forten Grimké, Helen Appo Cook, Mary Jane Peterson, Evelyn Shaw, and Mary Church Terrell. Together, they advocated for progress and unity in the African American community. While working as principal of M Street High School, she published her Black feminist book *A Voice from the South* (1892) and delivered a series of stirring speeches on the rights of African American women. At the age of 65, she completed her Ph.D. in history at the Sorbonne in Paris, making her just the fourth African American woman to do so. Considered the "Mother of Black Feminism," she resided in Washington, D.C. until her death at the age of 105.

Josephine St. Pierre Ruffin
Publisher, Journalist, Suffragist, and Civil Rights Leader
(1842–1924)

Born in Boston, her father was a prominent businessman and a founder of the Boston Zion Church. She was educated at public schools in Massachusetts and later at private school in New York City before completing her studies at the Bowdoin School. At 16, she married George Lewis Ruffin, the first African American to graduate from Harvard Law School. Together, they fought for the abolition of slavery and were active recruiters of Black soldiers for the 54th and 55th Massachusetts regiments during the Civil War. In 1869, Ruffin cofounded the American Woman Suffrage Association with Julia Ward Howe and Lucy Stone. In 1886, following her husband's death, Ruffin started the *Woman's Era*, the nation's first newspaper for African American women. In 1896, her National Federation of Afro-American Women merged with the Colored Women's League to form the National Association of Colored Women's Clubs, for which she was elected vice president under the leadership of Mary Church Terrell. Ruffin was a lifelong advocate for the rights of African American women and a charter member of the NAACP, founded in 1910.

Booker T. Washington
Orator, Author, Educator and Political Activist
(1856–1915)

Born into slavery in Virginia, his mother moved the family to West Virginia after emancipation in order to reunite with her husband. As a young man, Washington attended Hampton Norman and Agricultural Institute and Wayland Seminary before being named the leader of the groundbreaking Tuskegee Institute in Alabama. In 1895, he gained a national audience with his Atlanta Address, a speech in which he discussed his famous agreement with Southern white leaders on matters of civil rights. Although this moment later faced opposition from such leaders as W. E. B. Du Bois, it made Washington a powerful spokesman for African Americans of all walks of life and gained him access to some of the highest social and political circles in the nation. Throughout his career, he wrote over a dozen books, including his popular autobiography *Up from Slavery* (1901). In his time, he was unmatched in his ability to unite individuals and organizations across race and class divisions with the purpose of uplifting the Black community. While his work remained controversial through much of the twentieth century for its presumed assimilationism and conservativism, he has more recently been regarded as an important early figure in the movement for African American civil rights.

Mary Church Terrell
Educator and Activist
(1863–1954)

Born free to former slaves in Memphis, Tennessee, she was a member of the city's Black elite in the aftermath of the Civil War. Her father, a businessman, would eventually become the first African American millionaire in the South, while her mother was one of the first African American women to own and operate a hair salon. Mary studied Classics at Oberlin College, where she was nominated as class poet and served as editor of *The Oberlin Review*. She graduated alongside Anna Julia Cooper and Ida Gibbs Hunt as some of the first Black women in America to earn their bachelor's degrees. Terrell stayed at Oberlin until 1888, when she obtained her MA at the same time as Cooper. During this period, she began teaching modern languages at Wilberforce University, a historically Black college in Ohio. Upon graduating, she moved to Washington, D.C. to teach as a member of the Latin Department at the M Street School, where she met and married Robert Heberton Terrell. After two years in Europe, where she became fluent in French, German, and Italian, Terrell returned to the United States to focus on activism. She was a founding member of the Colored Women's League alongside Ida B. Wells-Barnett, Anna Julie Cooper, and others, as well as the Federation of Afro-American Women and later the National Association of Colored Women, for which she would serve as first president in 1896. Terrell was a nationally recognized speaker and activist for the cause of Black women's suffrage. Her 1898 speech "The Progress of Colored Women" was a powerful address to the biennial session of the National American Woman Suffrage Association in Washington. Other speeches, including "What it Means to be Colored in the Capital of the U.S." and "In Union There is Strength" characterize her commitment to racial equality and worker's rights.

Alexander Crummell
Minister, Academic and African Nationalist
(1819–1898)

Born in 1819, Crummell was born to a free woman of color named Charity Hicks and a former enslaved man named Boston Crummell. Passionate abolitionists, Crummell grew up instilled with a strong sense of African unity and even as a young child, worked for the American Anti-Slavery Society. His home was even the base for the first African American newspaper, *Freedom's Journal*. During his late teenage years, Crummell decided to become an Episcopal Priest but continued to find barriers to his profession as very few people were welcoming to the idea of a Black priest. Not to be deterred by rejection, in 1847 he traveled to England in order to raise money for his congregation and found success in these efforts by speaking on the plight of the enslaved in the United States and pursuing advanced education. A strong proponent of Pan-Africanism, he eventually moved to Africa with the goal of spreading his message of racial unity among Africans in Africa, America and the West Indies for the purpose of dismantling slavery, discrimination and racism among Black people worldwide. Eventually returning to the United States, he founded the first independent Black Episcopal church in D.C. and between 1895 and 1897 taught at Howard University. In spite of the obstacles, Crummell worked tirelessly as an advocate for racial unity up until the point of his death in 1898.

Francis J. Grimké
Minister and Political Activist
(1850–1937)

Born into slavery in South Carolina, Grimké was the son of Nancy
Weston and her white owner Henry Grimké. In 1852, Henry moved
with Weston and their children to a plantation near Charleston, where
he attempted to protect them from the rest of his family. Upon his death,
they were passed to his son and heir Montague, whose mistreatment
left Francis no choice but to run away during the Civil War. After the
war, he attended freedmen's schools and later Lincoln University with
his brother Archibald. When his paternal aunts Sarah and Angelina,
abolitionists who had left the South before Francis was born, learned of
his success as a student at Lincoln University in Pennsylvania, they paid
for him and his brother Archibald to continue their studies at Howard
University and Harvard University, respectively. After marrying
abolitionist Charlotte Forten in 1878, Grimké settled in Washington,
D.C. to lead the congregation at the 15th Street Presbyterian Church
in Logan Circle. Alongside his brother Archibald, he was an active
member of the Niagara Movement and a cofounder of the NAACP.

Lucy Craft Laney
Educator
(1854–1933)

Born free in Macon, Georgia, her parents were former slaves who bought their way to freedom and instilled in their ten children the values of charity and education. Although it was illegal for Black people to read, Laney earned at the age of four and went on to study at Lewis High School. In 1869, she enrolled as a member of Atlanta University's first incoming class, graduating in 1873 with a degree in teaching. A decade later, having taught at several schools across Georgia, she founded the Haines Normal and Industrial Institute, the first school for Black children in Augusta. By 1928, the school spanned a whole city block and was attended by over 800 students. During her time in Augusta, Laney was a member of the Niagara Movement and founded a local chapter of the NAACP in 1918. Her speech "The Burden of the Educated Colored Woman," which addressed the need for Black women as educators throughout the country, was given at the Hampton Negro Conference in July 1899. Alongside Reverend Henry McNeal Turner and Reverend Dr. Martin Luther King Jr., Laney was honored by Georgia Governor Jimmy Carter with the hanging of her portrait in the state capitol.

W. E. B. Du Bois
Sociologist, Historian, Civil Rights Activist, and Socialist
(1868–1963)

Born in Massachusetts, he was raised in Great Barrington, an integrated community. He studied at the University of Berlin and at Harvard, where he became the first African American scholar to earn a doctorate. He worked as a professor at Atlanta University, a historically Black institution, and was one of the leaders of the Niagara Movement, which advocated for equal rights and opposed Booker T. Washington's Atlanta compromise. In 1909, he cofounded the NAACP and served for years as the editor of its official magazine *The Crisis*. In addition to his activism against lynching, Jim Crow laws, and other forms of discrimination and segregation, Du Bois authored such influential works as *The Souls of Black Folk* (1903) and *Black Reconstruction in America* (1935). A lifelong opponent of racism and a committed pacifist, Du Bois advocated for socialism as a means of replacing racial capitalism in America and around the world. In the 1920s, he used his role at *The Crisis* to support the artists of the Harlem Renaissance and sought to emphasize the role of African Americans in shaping American society in his book *The Gift of Black Folk* (1924).

William Pickens
Orator, Teacher, Essayist and Journalist
(1881–1954)

Born to former slaves in South Carolina, he was raised in Arkansas. Pickens graduated with bachelor's degrees from Talladega College and Yale University before earning his master's degree from Fisk University and a Litt. D. from Selma University, which he completed in 1915. Fluent in Latin, Greek, German, and Esperanto, he taught sociology at Morgan State College, where he also served as dean. Pickens was a prominent member of the NAACP and was named assistant field secretary in 1920. In addition to two autobiographies—*The Heir of Slaves* (1911) and *Bursting Bonds* (1923)—Pickens published several essay collections on the "New Negro" and biographies of such figures as Abraham Lincoln and Frederick Douglass. He was also a gifted, award winning orator. "The Kind of Democracy a Negro Expects," a speech he gave several times, addresses the need for the United States to honor its commitment to international democracy by extending equal rights to its African American citizens.

Archibald Grimké
Lawyer, Diplomat, Journal, and Public Intellectual
(1849–1930)

Born into slavery in South Carolina, Grimké was the son of Nancy Weston and her white owner Henry Grimké. In 1852, Henry moved with Weston and their children to a plantation near Charleston, where he attempted to protect them from the rest of his family. Upon his death, they were passed to his son and heir Montague, whose mistreatment led to Archibald running away during the American Civil War. When his paternal aunts Sarah and Angelina, abolitionists who had left the South before Archibald was born, learned of his success as a student at Lincoln University in Pennsylvania, they paid for him and his brother Francis to continue their studies at Harvard and Howard University, respectively. Archibald settled in Boston, where he established his law practice and married Sarah Stanley, a white Midwesterner. Grimké attained a platform as a journalist and lecturer on African American rights and women's suffrage, eventually finding himself allied with Booker T. Washington. Throughout his life, he was a president of the Massachusetts Woman Suffrage Association, a member of the Niagara Movement, and a president of the American Negro Academy. During the First World War, while serving as vice-president of the NAACP, he led a protest in Washington, D.C. against segregation in the federal branch of the government.

James Weldon Johnson
Writer and Civil Rights Activist
(1871–1938)

Born in Jacksonville, Florida, he obtained an education from a young age, first by his mother, a musician and teacher, and then at the Edwin M. Stanton School. In 1894, he graduated from Atlanta University, a historically Black college known for its rigorous classical curriculum. With his brother Rosamond, he moved to New York City, where they excelled as songwriters for Broadway. His poem "Lift Ev'ry Voice and Sing" (1899), set to music by Rosamond, eventually became known as the "Negro National Anthem." Over the next several decades, he dedicated himself to education, activism, and diplomacy. From 1906 to 1913, he worked as a United States Consul, first in Puerto Cabello, Venezuela, and then in Nicaragua. He married Grace Nail, an activist and artist, in 1910, and would return to New York with her following the end of his diplomatic career. While in Nicaragua, he wrote and anonymously published *The Autobiography of an Ex-Colored Man* (1912), a novel exploring the phenomenon of racial passing. In 1917, Johnson began his work with the NAACP, eventually rising to the role of executive secretary. He became known as a towering figure of the Harlem Renaissance, writing poems and novels as well as compiling such anthologies as *The Book of American Negro Poetry* (1922). For his contributions to African American culture as an artist and patron, his activism against lynching, and his pioneering work as the first African American professor at New York University, Johnson is considered one of twentieth century America's leading cultural figures.

Randall Albert Carter
Methodist Episcopal Bishop
(1867–1954)

Born in Fort Valley, Georgia, he studied at Allen University and Paine College before becoming a pastor. Although little is known about his life, he was an influential political and religious figure in the nineteenth and early twentieth centuries. Carter was elected Bishop in St. Louis in 1914 and in 1923 read a powerful commencement address at his alma mater, Paine College. The speech, titled "Whence and Whither," reflects on African American history and offers an uplifting vision of the future to the students gathered before him.

A Note About the Book

The Voice of a People: Speeches from Black America is a collection of historical speeches by some of the nation's leading Black intellectuals, activists, artists, and organizers. Featuring such orators as Booker T. Washington, Frederick Douglass, Ida B. Wells, Sojourner Truth, and W. E. B. Du Bois, the collection reflects their leadership on issues ranging from abolition to lynching, women's suffrage, Black nationalism, and labor organizing. In transmitting the public medium of speech to the page, *The Voice of a People: Speeches from Black America* endeavors to provide proper historical context and relevant biographical information for each orator and their work. By keeping their words alive, we not only honor the sacrifices of leaders who paved the way for African Americans today, but ensure their work will continue to contribute towards a better future for all.

A Note from the Publisher

Spanning many genres, from non-fiction essays to literature classics to children's books and lyric poetry, Mint Edition books showcase the master works of our time in a modern new package. The text is freshly typeset, is clean and easy to read, and features a new note about the author in each volume. Many books also include exclusive new introductory material. Every book boasts a striking new cover, which makes it as appropriate for collecting as it is for gift giving. Mint Edition books are only printed when a reader orders them, so natural resources are not wasted. We're proud that our books are never manufactured in excess and exist only in the exact quantity they need to be read and enjoyed. To learn more and view our library, go to minteditionbooks.com

bookfinity & MINT EDITIONS

Enjoy more of your favorite classics with Bookfinity,
a new search and discovery experience for readers.
With Bookfinity, you can discover more vintage
literature for your collection, find your Reader Type,
track books you've read or want to read,
and add reviews to your favorite books.
Visit www.bookfinity.com, and click on
Take the Quiz to get started.

Don't forget to follow us
@bookfinityofficial and @mint_editions

9 781513 297033